THE

GALE

FAMILY RECORDS

IN

ENGLAND AND THE UNITED STATES;

TO WHICH ARE ADDED, THE

TOTTINGHAM FAMILY OF NEW EN-GLAND,

AND SOME ACCOUNT OF THE

BOGARDUS, WALDRON AND YOUNG FAMILIES

OF

NEW YORK.

BY GEORGE GALE, LL. D.,

GALESVILLE, WISCONSIN.
LEITH & GALE, PRINTERS.
1866.

Eng.^d by A.H. Ritchie

George Gale

PREFACE.

The writer of the following pages has devoted a portion of his time for the last four years in collecting and preparing for publication the records of the Gale Families in the United States and England.

In accomplishing this work, he sent circulars and letters to all the persons that he could hear of by this name, both in England and the United States, soliciting communications and family records. He also made one visit to Boston where he spent nearly three weeks in copying the military records of Massachusetts.

The writer, however, has to regret that the enterprise has not met with that favor which he thinks its importance demanded, as nearly one half of those who have received his circular, have failed to respond to its reasonable requests. In some instances, town and county officers have neglected to answer letters, even containing money, and stamps for return postage, while others have promptly, not only answered letters, but several have declined receiving any compensation for the information furnished. While many of the Gales have neglected to answer letters and circulars, others have taken hold of the enterprise with zeal and furnished all the information within their reach.

Of the Gale Families in England, we have obtained the most of our information from "Burke's Dictionary of the Lineage of the Landed Gentry of England."

The writer has, First, given the descendents of Richard Gale of Watertown, Massachusetts, who settled there about 1640;

Second, the genealogy of his mother's family; Tottingham;

Third, that of his wife, Young; and

Fourth, another family of Gales whom the writer believes were nephews to Richard Gale.

Of these families the writer has given all the information he has been able to collect, without personally visiting the different towns of their residences, which he had not the time to do. In many instances this information is very meagre, but he can only answer that it is all obtained.

The Author, however, hopes that this publication will so far attract the attention of the Gales, as to arouse some enterprising one, at some future time, to revise the work and make it more complete.

GALESVILLE, WIS., March, 1866.

THE AUTHOR.

ABBREVIATIONS.

To all towns in Massachusetts the name of the State has not been added ; but otherwise in other States ; b. born—m. married—unm. unmarried—d. deceased—dau. daughter—s. p. without issue. For abbreviations in Heraldry, see Webster's Dictionary

INTRODUCTION TO THE

GALE FAMILIES.

Gaoll in the Gaelic language means a stranger, *Gaoill* strangers and Gaolldoch, the country of the Scotts who speak English. According to Buchanan the ancient Scotts divided all the nations of Britain into Gaol and Galle, which he translates by the Latin Galli and Gallaeci.

When Julius Cæsar entered France, he found the nations including England, calling themselves "Celtae" or Celts, but remarked that in the Roman language they were called "Galli," but no where informs us of the origin of the name given them by the Romans.

As barbarians are generally known by some nickname given them by the persons first visiting them, it has been supposed that the early Romans named them with the word the Celts first used on meeting the Roman strangers, viz : *Gaoill*, or strangers, from which was first derived Gallie and Gael

In Lower's "Dictionary of Family Names of the United Kingdom ; London 1860"; the following remarks are made of the origin of the family name :

"Gale, A Scottish Highlander. Gale, Hundred Rolls, 1273. Two Saints, Galle, occur in the Roman Calendar, one of whom was a Scotch Abbot."

"Gael. The Gaels of Charlton Kings, Co., Gloucester, have written themselves at various periods, Galle, Gale.

Gael and originally De Galles. If this be correct, the family may have been of Welch origin in Anglo-Norman times when that country was known as Galles or Gales."

The English writers, however, quite generally derive the family name from some Scotch Highlander who settled in England and was called by the neighbors, *Gael,* or in English orthography *Gale.*

This might have been correct if the name is of late origin, but if ancient, the country people were too lately descended from the Gaels, and mixed with them too often to have such a neighbor attract any attention so as to give him the family name of his country. May we not with much greater probability, infer that the stranger was a Roman or Phinician and received the same name from the Celts, which for many years the Celts had applied to them. It is a fact in history, not now seriously doubted that the Ancient Greeks, Phinicians and Romans were accustomed to trade with the Britains, long before the invasion by Julius Cæsar.

But these speculations to establish a Roman ancestry are quite unnecessary as Geoffrey ap Arthur, the Bishop of St. Asaph, in the twelfth century, proved quite conclusively, in the opinion of Edward I, that Britain was first settled by a Trojan colony under Brutus, a grand-son of Æneas, from whose name the Greeks and Romans derived Britania. This theory was first promulgated by the Welch priest Tysilio, who flourished in the Seventh Century. The Romans with not much greater probability claim that Rome was first settled by a similar Trojan colony under Æneas himself. As the writer thinks it does not make much difference whether he descended from the Father or Grandson he will leave these speculations to those who may desire to pursue them further.

When Homer wrote of the brave Hector and the lovely Andromache he could not have anticipated that in a few centuries nearly all Europe would ignore the brave Achilles and claim to have descended from the defeated chivalry of Troy. But whatever might have been his origin, the head of the Gale family was evidently a stranger domiciled in England and as the name was not numerous in 1273 there may have been originally but one family who kept up the ancestral name, but since the introduction of surnames, commenced in 1066 and "settled among the common people fully, in1307." the name has increased rapidly until the present time, and has become numerous in both England and America.

In the "Domesday Book" which was compiled in 1085 by William the Conqueror and contained a list of most of the landed estates in England at that time with the names of the occupants for purposes of taxation, the name of Gale does not occur, from which we infer that the Gales, were not among the adventurers of that monarch from Normandy; for if they had been they would, like others have had some of the confiscated landed estates assigned to them; but the local names of the estates, which are nearly all English names, clearly indicate that before the Conquest the Gales belonged to the landed gentry of England, and probably lost their estates by confiscation for their loyalty to Harold, the defeated and slain sovereign of England, at the memorable battle of Hastings.

Upon this battlefield was erected the *l'Abbaye de la Bataille* which was dedicated to St. Martin the patron saint of the expedition and "endowed with the property of the English who had died in the battle." Indeed, so completely were the English despoiled "that,"in the language of Holinshed, "there was neither governor, bishop, nor abbot remaining therein of the English nation."

Thus we find in the Domesday Books the following landed estates : "Gal," in Schropshire in the possession of Count Rogers ; "Galeshore," in Devonshire Tavitone, in the possession of Count Moviton ; "Galtone," in Dorsetshire, in the possession of the "King's Servants" and some others which evidently derived their names from the Gales.

Having thus lost their estates, the Gales do not appear again among the landed gentry of England until the "Hundred Rolls of 1273."

The orthography of the name has been variously written. Gall, Galle, Gail, Gael and Gale, and in French De Galles, all pronounced nearly alike, but during the last 100 years nearly all the families in England and America have settled down on the simple English orthography, "Gale" which is probably correct according to the modern rules.

To enable our American Cousins to learn something of their English ancestors and cousins the writer makes the following extracts from Burke's Dictionary of the Lineage of the Landed Gentry of England and will commence with the old family of Yorkshire :

"The family of Gale, now merged in that of Coore, was of importance in the North and East Ridings of Yorkshire, early in the sixteenth century.

. James Gale, the first named in the pedigree was seated at Thirntoft, near Scruton, in the hundred of East Gilling and North Riding anno 1523. His son and heir, Oliver Gale of Thirntoft, m. Ellen Marshall, of Richmond and had. with another son, James, who m. and resided sometime in Spain, [James subsequently settled in Ireland, whence his descendents during the rebellion there, transplanted themselves to Whitehaven, Cumberland County. From this branch descended the present Lieut. Col. Gale Braddyll, of Cornish Priory.] George Gale Esq., Lord Mayor of York, in 1534 and 1546, who d. July 2, 1557, leaving, by Mary, his wife, dau. of Robert Lord, of Kendal, two sons, Robert or Francis Gale, Esq. of Akeham Grange, Co. York, in 1590, m. Anne, dau. of William Clapham, Esq. of Bramsley, and widow of Mr. Thwaite, of Marston, by whom (who m. 2 ndly., John Inglesby, Esq., brother of Sir William Inglesby, of Reply) he left at his decease, two sons, Robert, of Akeham Grange; and John of Scruton ; and a dau. Mary, wife of Thomas Meynell, Esq., of North Kilvington. The second son, John Gale, Esq., of Scruton, m. Jane, eldest dau. of John Frank, Esq. of Pontefract, and by her, who d. in 1624, had (with two daus., Margaret and Dorothy, three sons.) 1. Christopher, his heir ; 2. Ralph, citizen of London, who left two daus. ; 3. John, b. in 1601, who was in the Low Country wars, under Count Mansfield, in the time of James I. and resided many years at Farnley Hall. He m. Joanna, dau. of Miles Dodson, Esq., of Kirkby Overblows, and had three sons, Miles, Henry and Francis.

John Gale d. in 1624 and was succeeded by his eldest son Christopher Gale Esq. of Scruton, b. in 1597, who m. Frances, dau. of Conyers, of Holtby, and by her who d. in 1656, left at his decease an only surviving child. The Rev. Thomas Gale D. D., divine, critic and antiquary of distinguished erudition, b. at Scruton, in 1636.

He married Barbara, dau. of Thomas Pepys, Esq. of Inpington Co. Cambridge and by her, who d. in 1689, had with a dau. Elizabeth (m. to Rev William Stukely, the celebrated antiquary) four sons viz : 1. Roger his heir; 2. Charles, Rector of Scruton ; 3. Samuel b. in 1682, one of the land surveyors of the Customs, a reviser of the society of Antiquaries, in 1717, and its first treasurer ; and

4. Thomas, who d. s. p. Dr. Gale. whom Drake. no liberal panegyrist, styles "the good Dean" d. 28 April 1702, and was succeeded by his eldest son Roger Gale, Esq. of Scruton, M. P., for Northallerton, b. in 1672, the known author of the "Registrum Honoris de Richmond," the first Vice-President of the society of Antiquaries, and treasurer of the Royal Society. He m. Henrietta, dau. of Henry Raper, Esq. of Cowling Hall, Co. York, and by her who d. 29. Sept. 1720, he left at his decease, 25. June 1744, an only son and heir, Roger Henry Gale Esq. of Scruton, b. in 1710, who m. in 1740, Catharine, dau, of Christopher Crowe, Esq. of Kiplin, in Yorkshire, and dying in 1768,left with two daus. (Harriet m. to Capt. John Atkinson Blanshard ; and Catherine) four sons of whom the eldest, Henry Gale Esq., of Scruton, b. in 1744, m., 1779, Mary, only dau. of Francis Dalton, Esq. of Hawkeswell, and had issue to survive youth,three daus. Harriett his heiress, Catharine and Anne. Mr. Gale d. in 1821, and was succeeded by his eldest dau. Harriet Gale, of Scruton Hall, who m. in 1816 Lieut. Col. Foster Lechmere Coore. [This gentleman who is eldest son of John Coore, Esq., and Ann Lechmere, his wife, succeeded, in 1821, his uncle, Col. Thomas Coore, whose father, Foster, son of Alderman Thomas Coore of Liverpool, m. in 1736, Eleanor, only dau. of John Heaton,Esq., of Firby.] of Firby, in the North Riding of the same Shire, and dying 15. Dec., 1839, left with four daus. Mary, Sophia, Augusta and Charlotte, one son, the present Henry Coore, Esq., of Scruton."

From Burke's Dictionary, p. 456, is taken the following:

"GAEL OF CHARLTON KINGS.

Samuel Higgs Gael, Esq.,of Charlton Kings Co. Gloucester, b. Aug. 1808 ; m. in Nov. 1837, Annie, youngest dau. of George Hassard, Esq. of Skea, Co. Farmanagh, and has issue, one son, Charles Edward, and two daus. Elizabeth Ann and Jane.

Mr. Gale is magistrate for Co. Gloucester."

"The name of this family has been variously written, (Galle, Gale, Gael and originally De Gales) and the crest 'a cock gu.' is probably an illusive device.

John Gael Esq., son of Edmond Gael of Alstonfield, near Cheltenham, Co. Gloucester, first settled at Charlton Kings. He was father of Edward Gale Esq., of Charlton Kings, who m. Sarah Tuckevill and had four sons, all of whom d. issueless except John Gale, Esq. of Charlton Kings, who had by Anna, his wife, three sons, John his heir; Edward, Capt. in the Maryland Artillery, d. unm. in New Jersey, about the year 1785; and Henry, who d. s. p.

The eldest son, John Gale, Esq., of Charlton Kings m. in 1805, Susanna, youngest dau. and now only surviving child of Charles Higgs, Esq., of Charlton Kings, and Deerhurst Wa'ton, Co. Gloucester, by Susanna Cooke, his wife, heiress of the families of Cooke, Sloper, Cooper, Wager and Deighton, of Charlton Kings, and had two sons, John, who d. unm. at Milan, in 1829; and Samuel Higgs, now of Charlton Kings."

As a part of the further history of this family the writer will give the following:

Letter from Samuel Higgs Gael Esq.

LINCOLN'S INN, LONDON,
20. June 1864.

DEAR SIR:—I have received your letter addressed to me at Charlton Kings making inquiries about the Gale family.

It would have afforded me pleasure had it been in my

power, to have given you useful information on the subject. As it is, I will put you in possession of what I have
learned in looking over my old Registers and Papers
bearing on the questions which you put.

I should observe that the original name of my branch
of the family is Gaell, but it has been very variously spelt
and I now spell it Gael. In whatever form used,it means
I take it, a native of Wales domiciled in England.

In later times the man would be called and written
Welch, who at the earliest period of writing surnames,
would have written himself Gaell,or Gale or Gales. It by no
means follows, therefore, that all who bear the name came
from one stock or stem, an inference from names which,
indeed, can never be pretended of any name whatever.
But there are well known branches of families in Yorkshire, Devonshire, Gloucestershire, London and other
places, of Gales. I only speak of mine, which has been
in Gloucestershire for some centuries and has been so
much mixed up with what I believe is another family
named Gale, whose principal place was in Worcestershire
but occasionally lived at Charlton, in Gloucestershire, as
to create confusion in searching public Registers and Records, between the families. This principally occurs in
the junior members of families. Their successive heads
can be pretty well traced by the descent of property. When
then the junior members of a family severed off and settled in London, the plantations abroad or elsewhere, from
home, they were lost to the parent stock after the lapse of
a few generations. Thus for instance, I see by Letters
and Papers which have escaped the ravages of time, and I
learn by tradition, that in some of the more recent generations, the younger members did so migrate, that one
was a brewer in London, another a Captain of Artillery
in Maryland in the American Revolutionary wars, (an

adventure in which a great many young Englishmen of a free turn of politics sought their fortune in, and some perhaps found it,but which only produced disappointment and an early grave from the flux, to my unfortunate relatiye) and so on. These members when lost sight of would appear to have dropped off and to have left no descendents, which simply means none that the family remaining at the old spot know of.

Of the christian names you mention, I find John, Richard and Edmond, about the time named. Edmond I can account for, but not John and Richard. Hugh I have met with, later, but Ambrose or Bartholomew, never. If you had such names as Gratian, Alice, Isabella and Edith I could have better identified them.

But I will copy the names in the Generation, in the beginning of the seventeenth century :

In 1594 Andrew Gaell or Gale married Lucie Clarke, whence John, bap. 1606—no further trace of him—Edmond, bap. 1608 . d. at Cheltenham 1692. Will in the prerogative court of Canterbury.

In 1598, John Gaell, probably a brother of Andrew married Edith Machin, whence John Gaell or Gale, bap. 1613, of whom no further trace is found.

The latest Richard Galle about that time was of 1596.

The Rev. Theopilus Gale was the author of a book called the "Court of the Gentiles," I rather think there is something about him or his family in some old number of the Gentleman's Magazine. His will would probably mention the names of his relatives.

From Coats of Arms I do not think much information can be gleaned. A branch of the Galles obtained, a Grant in the Common Wealth's time, of a Coat which *resembles the Yorkshire Gales, to which family belonged*

Dr. Thomas Gale of St. Paul's School temp. c. 2. who wrote the anti-papal inscription on London Monument, which Pope says "like a tall bully lifts its head and lies." Roger Gale and Samuel Gale the Antiquarians, were of this family.

St. Katharine's near the Tower of London was a hospital. It was removed to the Regent's Park, London in the reign of George the 4th and the site devoted to the St. Katharine's Docks. The R'd Gale mentioned as there baptized could be none of mine, I think.

I have not seen any of the recent editions of 'Burke's Gentry.' Having no time now for such pursuits, the labors of the legal profession(which you, it would appear, have relinquished) engrossing it all. I have sent this through Messrs Trubner & Co. who also wrote to me, with a copy of your letter to them, that they may add by supplement, any further information they can furnish, and with every good wish for the prosperity of the American Gales, I remain.   Dear sir, your obed't Serv't,

George Gale Esq.   SAM'L H. GAEL."

The Rev. Theophilus Gale mentioned in the letter of Mr. Samuel H. Gael, was born at "Kings Trighton, in Devonshire in 1628 and d. in London 1678. He was a distinguished nonconformist minister, wrote many religious works and at his death bequeathed his very large Library to Harvard College, near Boston Mass. The College record says that this Library was larger than all the Libraries that were then in the College.

Our English cousins across the water have often joked us of America, with having no ancestors, but the two following letters will show that we might often return the compliment:

SHOTTER HILL
June 12, '64.

DEAR SIR:

Your favor with copy of letter from Dr. Gale, of America inclosed, has been forwarded me here, where I am ruralizing for a short time.

I should have been most happy if in my power, to have furnished any information on the subject of the letter, but unfortunately, I am not Genealogically learned.

Still, if the one important item which Dr. Gale lacks, is the names of Richard Gale's brothers and father, could probably be ascertained: and if, when I return to town I should be able to meet with this information, I will at once forward it to him.

There is a barrister of the name of Gale at Portsmouth or Southampton, who presides at some court, and in the local papers, (Hampshire Advertiser) is called "Judge Gale" who might perhaps be able to give information to Dr. Gale. His name would be found in the Law Dict.

For my part as I said before, I know not my genealogy but, I have always considered, the name should be spelt "Gael".

I conclude our ancestors came over to England long before the conqueror, and even before Julius Cæsar.

I am, Dear Sir,
Yours faithfully,
Josiah Child Esq.   WM. GALE.

FROM JUDGE GALE.

KITNOCKS, Southampton,
June 19, 1864.

GENTLEMEN:

I am sorry it is not in my power to forward the views of your correspondent, by giving him information of any early

members of a family bearing the same name as myself.
I cannot trace back my ancestors for any length of time.
The same I believe is very common in his country, and
in the south of England generally.

I remain,

Your obedient serv't

C. I. GALE.

Wm. Gale, Esq., of London having returned home,
wrote again as follows :

"LANGHAM CHAMBERS,
PORTLAND PLACE, LONDON W.
July 25, 1864.

DEAR SIR :—A friend of mine connected with the
house of Messrs Trubner & Co. forwarded me, a few
weeks since, a copy of your letter to them making inquiries respecting the Gale family, especially in reference to a
Richard Gale who left London in 1635.   It happens unfortunately, that I am no antiquarian, but on receiving the
letter I determined for the *name-o-sake* to make the re-
research you suggested, in the record of St. Katharine's
Church.

The first thing I discovered was that the site, where
once stood St. Katharine's church near the Tower is now
occupied by St. Katharine's Docks, and that the church
was rebuilt in Regent's Park.   On application there, I obtained permission to search the old Register and, I am
sorry to say, with little success.   According to the date
you give, Richard Gale in 1619.   Strangely enough the
Register for the years 1619 and 1620 are wanting ! and
for some years before until January 1635 the name of
Gale does not occur either in the register of births, deaths
or marriages ; we then meet with this notice : January
23d 1635, Ann, dau. of Nicholas Gale : (baptized, and

A 1

again in 1637 Nov. 20th, there is Margrett the dau. of Nicholas Gale, (baptized.)

I much fear the information will be of little service, but shall be happy to make any further research you might suggest, unless indeed you have met with some other correspondent here who has been or may be able to do you more service than I can.

You mention the priests of St. Katharine's. It seems there were always three "brothers," as they are called in the records. Two of them at the date mentioned (1635) were Walter Gray and Samuel Slater. The other is not mentioned. Is it one of these two named, who certified to the good standing of Richard Gale? It has occurred to me as very probable that although certified to by the priest of St. Katharine's, Richard Gale might never have belonged to to the Parish, but perhaps have merely had introductions or recommendations to the Priest from some distant part of the country. He coming to London to embark for America. Is this probable?

I am, Dear Sir, Your faithful and ob't Serv't,
To Dr. George Gale, &c.   WM. GALE."

Heraldry was an important institution in England after the conquest in 1066, by William of Normandy. It mainly originated in the holy wars, although in the Æneid it is said of the tomb of the Trojan Hector :

"On it Æneas piously heaped
A mighty mound, Sepulchral. The oar the trumpet,
Arms of the man, the airy Summit crowned."

During the reign of Henry III. heraldry became a science.

Arms were conferred on the Knights by which they were distinguished from each other, when clad in a coat of mail, and by the king for some important military ser-

vice. Arms were also obtained by petition to the Earl
Marshall. Thus, they were conferred on Sir Robert Lawrence, in 1191 by Richard I. for his bravery in scaling the
walls of Acre.

Coats of Arms were long regarded 'as an indispensable
appendage of a gentleman, but on the decline of the Feu-
dal System in 1688, and the rise of the Reformation, they
were treated, in a measure, as idle trappings of aristocracy
and lost the prestige originally attributed to them. [In
America,they have only been regarded as a family relic of
former family vanity. In England, in latter years, since
1688, they were not subject to any "visitation" or examination, and were assumed by any one at pleasure.

The Gales of England have adopted the following
"Coats of Arms" as appears in "Burke's Encyclopædia of
Heraldry ; 1849 :

"Gale, (Scruton Co. York) Az. on a fesse betw. three
Saltires arg. as many lions' heads erased of the field, lan-
gued gu. *Crest*, out of a ducal coronet or. a unicorn's head
paly of six az. and or. armed of the last." "*Motto*—Qui
semina vertu raccoglia fama."

"Gale or Gall, (Cornwall, Dartmouth and Crediton, Co.
Devon ; and Weveston, Co. Suffolk,) Az. a fesse ar. fretty
of the field. *Crest.*—A shankbone and palm branch in
saltire ppr."

"Gale, Whitehaven, Co. Cumberland,) Ar. on a fesse
betw. three Saltires az. an anchor betw. two lions'
heads erased or. *Crest.*—A unicorn's head az. charged
with an anchor or. betw. two palets ar."

"Gale, (Devonshire) Az. on a fesse ar. three saltires of
the field, (Another gu.")

"Gale, (Stalbridge, Dorsetshire) sa. a fesse ar. fretty
engr. of the first betw. three grayhounds sejant of the

second, collared gu.   *Crest.*—A horse's head, bendy wavy
of six ar. and sa."

"Gale.   Sa. a fesse ar. fretty of the field betw. three
grayhounds sejant of the second.   *Crest.*—A horse's head
barry wavy of six ar. and sa."

"Gale. Gu. a griffin sergeant or. within a bordure gobon-
ated ar. and vert.   *Crest.*—A unicorn's head, paly of six
az. and or. the horns twisted, of the second and first."

"Gale.   Az. a fesse ar. betw. three Saltires or."

"Gale.   (Ashfield Hall, Queens Co. now represented
by Peter Gale Esq. of Ashfield.)   As Gale of Yorkshire.

"Gale.   (as borne by John Gale, Co. Cornwall, Esq.)
Az. a fesse ar. fretty of the field.   *Crest.*—A horse's head
erased bendy wavy of six or. and sa."

There has been found but one coat of arms among the
Gales of America to the writer's knowledge, and that came
down to the present generation from Capt. Joseph Gale
of Connecticut.   At the bottom of the picture is the following: "He   beareth   SABLE   within a Bordure
Checkey Or. and Azure a Griffin Rampant of the second by the name of Gale."   This is all that is known of
its history.

In the early emigration to America shipping records
were kept, at the different ports in England, in which
were entered the name, age and destination of emigrants
and the fact that some priest giving his name and residence, had certified that the persons "conformed to the order and discipline of the Church of England."

This information enables the posterity to look up the
ancestors in England of these emigrants, but after about
1635 all *these* entries were not made but only the facts that

such a vessel sailed at such a day with so many emigrants for such a place.

The only Gale mentioned on the shipping records was Richard Gale certified to by the minister of St. Katharine's near the tower of London. He was only 16 years of age and sailed April 24, 1635 for Barbadoes and St. Christopers and embarked in the "Ann and Elizabeth" Capt. Brookehaven. There is no evidence that he ever came to Mass. although it was not uncommon for emigrants to other colonies to change to Mass. and *vice versa*.

Therefore in examining for the ancestry of the Gales in America, as yet, we have no evidence except what may have been preserved in England by the relatives of the emigrants. This evidence must be looked up hereafter by some enterprising member of the family who may visit England, and will probably be found, if at all, in the records of Wills and the settlement of Estates, and in the family records. Parish records will give names but other records will be necessary to show the emigration.

The following names of Gales have been discovered on the records in America :

John, in Boston Mass., admitted to the church in 1634 then in the employ of John Button ; d. soon after.

Edmond, Cambridge, Mass.. d. July 29, 1642, in Boston.

Hugh, of Kittery or Yorke Mass., admitted a freeman in 1652.

Richard, of Watertowne, Mass., purchased land in 1640.

Edmond, of Salesbury, probably of Marblehead, Mass., admitted a freeman 1660.

Bartholomew, of Salem, Mass., m. Martha dau. of Robert Lemon, 1662.

Ambrose, of Salem, Mass., May 17, 1663.

Thomas, of New Haven Conn., had dau. born May 6, 1655.

Edward, March 16, 1687 received 10 pounds for piloting His Majesty's Frigate King Fisher from Cape Ann to Nantucket Road and the attendance of his "Ketch" to assist Frigate.

Abel, Jamaica, Long Island N. Y. had lot granted to him 18, Oct. 1665 in Jamaica L. I.

Christopher, son of Miles and grand son of John, of Scruton, (b. 1601) was Att'y General and Chief Justice of N. Carolina about 1700, and m. *Sarah*, relict of Gov. Harvey and had son, Miles, and dau. Elizabeth.

Rasin, was an early settler in Kent Co. Maryland, whose grand son Thomas, now (1864) lives in Baltimore and is 73 years of age.

Barnard, of Boston Mass., 21 years of age, said to be a native of Old England served in Capt. Joseph Billings Co., in 1758, in the Expedition against Canada. Returned and discharged Oct. 16, 1758.

Francis, of Lignanea, Island of Jamaica, m. and had only dau. Susannah Hyde Gale who m. Alan, Lord Gardner, the celebrated Admiral. There was a Col. Gale of Jamaica, said to be descended from Yorkshire Gales whose dau. m. Wm. Foster a native of that Island.

These are all the early Gales I have collected, the most of whom were emigrants from England, and should our English Cousins ever collect the genealogies of the Families in England, they will doubtless all be identified with their ancestors.

I have thus given what information I can collect, of the English Ancestors and Cousins, for the information of the Cousins in America, hoping that at no distant day,

some one of our race will take hold of the subject in good
earnest, examine thoroughly the records of England, and
publish the genealogy of the entire race.

Nearly all the Gale families, in New York and New
England, have traditions that their ancestors were brothers
who came from England and landed at Boston Mass., in
early times, from whence they scattered to different locali-
ties, and these traditions are corroborated by the strong family likenesses which exist among the present generations,
but if these traditions are not strickly true, still the family
likeness indicates a common family origin.

THE FAMILY RECORD OF RICHARD GALE

AND HIS DESCENDENTS.

1. RICHARD GALE, the ancestor of the following Family in the United States, first appears, as the purchaser of a "homestall" of six acres in Watertowne, Mass. in 1640, it being a part of a lot of 9 acres, in the town plot granted to Elder Richard Browne. The balance of the lot of 3 acres, was purchased by Samuel Freeman, one of the first proprietors, who was said to be of Devonshire, England, and it became a part of his "homestall."

From whence came Richard Gale we find no positive record, but as the name and Colony where purely English, we infer, as beyond a reasonable doubt, that he was an emigrant from England, but the fact cannot at this day be proven by any evidence yet obtained, although the author has instituted investigations in England which he hopes will in time settle the question.

We also infer that Richard was a communicant of the Church of England. This inference rests on the fact that no person could emigrate from England to the Colonies until he had first procured a certificate from his parish priest, that, in his religion he was "conformable to the order and discipline of the Church of England," coupled with the following statement in his Will:

"I give my spirit unto the hands of God that gave it and my body to the earth from whence it was taken ; hoping through the meedeation of Jesus Christ to have it raised again at the great day."

While this evidence established his original religious position in the the Church of England, it does not negative the fact that, like most of the other emigrants, he might have united with the Watertown Congregational Church; but, in referring to those records, we neither find his name, or the baptism of his children. Besides this, he was never admitted a freeman, never voted, or held office ; the prerequisite of all of which was, membership in the Watertown Church.

Why he never united with the Watertown Church, can only be answered by the inference, that he might have been a "High Churchman" and unwilling to become a "Nonconformist." He might, however, have early been prejudiced against the Congregational Churches for their politico-ecclesiastical organization, and in the language of Sir Richard Saltonstall to the ministers of Boston, about this time, on account of their "tyranny and oppression,— fining, whipping und imprisoning men for their consciences." This Jesuitical intolerance, first manifested itself in the Plymouth Colony, by their banishing Mr. John Oldham from that Colony for his love of Episcopacy, in 1624, but four years after the "Pilgrims landed on Plymouth Rock. Thus the pious Pilgrims retaliated on the Church of England. About 1644 Gov Dudley, of Massachusetts Bay, in a letter to Sir Richard Saltonstall, then in England, refused the admission of Anabaptists, Seekers, Antinomians and other Independents, as Colonists. The poor Quakers were the especial objects of their hatred and the *General Court*, in 1657, passed a law fining anyone £100, who should "bring or cause to be brought" into the country, "any of that cursed sect of the Quakers" or other blasphemous heretics," and also fining any one "forty shillings for every hour's entertainment" of them.

The 2d, of Dec. 1661, Richard Gale purchased of Richard Dummer, the north east half of the "Oldham Farm," containing 250 acres, on which a part of the village of Waltham now stands. This was one of the most level and fine tracts of land in old Watertown, and was occupied by Richard until his death and his posterity after him, until about 1854, when it was sold by minor heirs and passed into the hands of Governor Banks, the Maj. Gen. commanding the Dept. of the S. W. in 1864, and is retained as his homestead.

However modest Richard might have been in everything else, we observe, that he was not particularly so in the size of his farm, which he evidently loved, or he would not have been so careful in his Will to preserve it for his posterity.

Whether Richard could read and write cannot be determined at this late day, but the fact, that he signed his Will with a mark, might lead one to believe that he could not write. This, however, does not necessary follow, for even at the present day, the Author knows from professional experience, that many men, who were good writers at a previous day, from their weakness, prefer to sign their Wills with a mark. As he never conveyed any land, held town office, had church membership, nor carried on any trade, the question, probably, can never be solved.

But if we conclude, that he could not, either read or write, it was not at that day considered any particular discredit, for the majority of our New England ancestors were suffering under the same misfortune. Indeed, so little did the people of Watertown regard education as necessary to the farmers, that they never erected the first school house until twenty years after the first settlement of the town, although Harvard College was founded for the education of ministers and others, the sons of the aristocracy, in the adjoining town as early as 1638. twelve years before the school house. But this school house, and the only one for fifty years, was but 22 feet long and 14 feet wide, and as it was robbed by an Indian of seventeen Greek and Latin books in 1664, it was probably monopolized by those only preparing for College.

Richard was probably married in England before he emigrated, and that his wife's name was "Mary," we only learn from the following record of Boston. "Sarah, dr. of Richard and Mary Gale b. 8 : 7 : 1641, of Watertown." They were probably stopping with relatives at Boston, at this critical period of married life,—to receive the first born,—the consumation of human happiness.

We have no record of the physical size or shape of Richard, but if we are allowed to judge of him by the average of his posterity, we may safely make him five feet and eleven inches in statue, strong and muscular, black eyes, black hair, rather long favored, and dark complexion, modest in his demeanor, of few words among strangers, social, domestic and temperate in his habits, fond of a good joke, liberal in his benevolence, firm in his will, and as a christian never bigoted.

As a race, the Gales have been more distinguished for their athletic powers than for the culture of their minds, but the late generations are fast changing in this particular, and the learned professions have a fair proportion of the present generation.

They have ever been reasonably jealous of their rights, *but strong friends* to a well-ordered government; and in

our Revolutionary struggle, they were an unit in taking
up arms and marching to the fields of strife, from which
several of them never returned alive. They were nearly
as unanimous in the support of the war of 1812.

In the war of the Great Rebellion, prosecuted to restore
the Union as established by our Fathers of the Revolution, we can only point to the long list of those named in
nearly every family, who have both perilled and sacrificed their lives for their flag and the Constitution.

It is a very common remark that the whole race never
produced a criminal, but the Author can only say that he
has never yet found one, unless Abraham and Henry, who
took part as captains in the Shays rebellion are to be considered as such.

WILL OF RICHARD GALE.

"I Richard Gael of Watertowne in the county of Middlesex in New England, yeoman: being under the afflict-
ing hand of the infinitely wise God: as to a bodily dis-
temper, yet through the goodness of God am sound in my
memory and understanding do declare this to be my last
will and testament as followeth:

I give my spirit unto the hands of God that gave it and
my body to the earth from whence it was taken: hoping
through the meedeation of Jesus Christ to have raised
again at the great day.

My will is that, except what of my estate just debts shall
call for: my well beloved wife shall enjoy my whole estate both houses and lands and cattle of all sorts and all
my household good for her comfort and maintenance during her natural life: my loving wife being dead: I give
unto my son Abraham the dwelling house he now lives
in with seven acres of upland adjoining to it which I gave
him at his marriage: so long as my son Abraham lives

and to his wife if she should out live him so long as she lives a widdow : and if their death : or my said sons death and his wife's marriage my will is the said house and seven acres of land shall be as an inheritance to my said sons two eldest sons namely Abraham Gall and Richard Gall :

I give and bequeath unto my son Abraham one fourth part of my orchard as long as he lives : and his wife as long as she lives or continues a widow : and it is to return to the two eldest sons of Abraham my son as they are above at prest : also my will is the two eldest of my son Abraham aforesaid should enjoy two fourths of my said orchard : and to be improved for their benefit until they come of age : and my will is that my son John Gall should enjoy one forth part of my orchard so long as he lives and at his death the said forth part is to return to my son Abraham and his heirs ; I give unto my daughter Sarah Garfield ten pound to be paid within seven years after my wives decease to be paid in country pay at an indefrant rate : and in case my said daughter shall die before the said seven years be expired then my will is the said ten pound should be paid to my said daughters children eequally among them : I give unto my daughter Mary Flag ten pound to be paid her in all respects as is said to my daughter Garfield and her children : allso my will is that my two sons Abraham Gall and John Gall should enjoy my whole farme containirg two hundred and fifty acres : save only the seven acres before given to my son Abraham : and it is my will that my son John Gall aforesaid should enjoy his half of my farme aforesaid no longer than the time of his natural life and at his decease my will is : my whole farm containing 250 Acres as aforesaid should return to my son Abraham and his heirs forever: Allso my will is that if God should give unto my son John Gall aforesaid a male heir that then my son Abraham shall when the said male heir atains to the age of one and twenty yeers a paid unto him twenty pound in country paie at an indeeferant rate and in case my son John aforesaid should depart this life without a male heir then my will is that the said twenty pound be paid to those children or child my said son John shall leave when he dies : to be paid divided equally among them either at their marriage or when they attain eighteen years of age.

And I doe nominate and appoint my well beloved son Abraham Gall to be sole executor to this my will and as a confirmation to this my last will and testament I have hereunto set my hand this five and twenteth of ffebruary sixteen hundred and seventy eight.

In the presence of us

Richard Gall, –!– his mark.

Joseph Taynter
William Bond

Endorsed by Judge :

1 : 2 : 79 : sworn by Joseph Taynter
& William Bond as attest.

J : R : C :

The foregoing Will is in the hand writing of the witness, Joseph Taynter. It is copied literally except the u. and v. are given according to modern style of writing. The Inventory is in the same hand writing. Joseph Taynter, aged 25 embarked at Southampton Apr. 24, 16-38 for New England, as the servant of Nicholas Guy, whose daughter he afterwards married, and was one of the select men of Watertown many times between 1657 and 1680.

INVENTORY OF THE ESTATE OF RICHARD GALE.

"This is an Inventory of the whole estate sometimes in ye possession of Richard Gall of Watertone who deceased the 22 of March 167⅞ taken and appraised the 29 of March 1679 by us who are ye subscribers as followeth:

A dwelling house and barne with about 250 Acres of Land adjoining to it whereof: 12 Acres is broke up: and aboute: 12 Acres is meadow and an Acre of it in an orchard: £ 150—00

Six Acres of upland upon the great
plaine joyning to ye farme   003—00

Seven Acres of remote meadow neer
ye pond at Mr. Samuells farme   007—00

Three Acres of meadow lieing upon
stonie brooke   006—00

Two Oxen five cows two heifers of
a year and vantage   025—00

One horse fifteen sheep and swine   005—06

His wearing cloths both woolin
and linin   1— 5

A fether bed a fether bollster:
2 fether pillows one rugg, one blanket.
paire of sheets with the bedstead a
trundle bed stove   3—02

A peuter plater a peuter bason
a peuter quart 6 spoons   000—06

2 iron kettles one iron pot a
pair of pot hooks a trarnell   001—01

Ten wooden milk vessells 2 pails:
2 keelers 5 barrels   001—00

A small table: 2 forms: one
chaire: 2 chests a little cubbard   001—00

About: 12 yards of woellin home

made clooth	1—04
An old spinning wheel a small parcel of Woollin yarn a paire of cards	000—07
About : 12 bushels of barlie and : 12 bushels of wheat	003—12
About 7 bushels of peese and 30 bus :hels of Indian corne	004—00
about : 8 bushels of rye a small parcel of salt meat in ye tub :	002—04
a firelock musket a spit a smoothing iron :: a firieng pan	000—16
utencells for husbandry a cart a pair of wheels anshod with irons belonging to them : 2 old chains	002—02
4 axes a beetle 4 wedges an irou pitch an old plow	001—04
a dung forke 2 pitch forks an old fann : an iron gripe for a plow	000—04
a barking iron a cross cut saw 4 old hows 2 old sickles other old iron	000—14
a small quantity of butter and cheese an old half bushel	000—08

The above particulars ware
Apprised the day and year as above said by us

Joseph Taynter
John Loarren
William Bond

and there is due from the estate which doe alreadie appear to be due to several persons £72

Endorsed :

"1 : 2 : 79 : Sworn to in court by ye executer as above.

J. R. C."

These endorsments on the Will and Inventory by the Judge, shows that they were proved April 1., 1679, O.S. or April 12, 1679 new style and that the Inventory was taken before the Will was proved up before the Court of Probate.

The Inventory illustrates in a high degree the simplicity of the original pioneers of New England.

According to Bond's Genealogies of Watertown, (page 229) Richard's wife was named Mary, and they had the following children :

2. 1. *Sarah*, b. Sept. 8, 1641 ; m. Joseph Garfield.

3. 2. *Abraham*, b. 1643 and m. Sarah Fiske.

4. 3. *Mary*, m. March 30, 1670, John Flagg.

5. 4. *John.* m. Elizabeth Spring.

6. 5. *Ephraim*, May, 1673, a vagrant, "distempered in his mind," according to the court files, and probably died before his father, unm. The only record of the birth of any of the children, is the following on the record of Boston : "Sarah, dr. of Richard and Mary Gale, born 8 : 7: 1641, of, Watertown." The names of Sarah, Abraham, Mary and John are the only names of children mentioned in the Will.

The quaint style of matchmaking of our old ancestors is well illustrated in the marriage of John, as appears in the testimony in a suit in 1679. One witness testified that "John Gale, son of Richard, in 1677, was a goodwiler to ye daughter of Henry Spring." Henry Spring, sen., and Mehitable his wife testified that "goodman Richard Gale came to our house to ask our goodwill to make a match between our daughter Elizabeth and his son John. *He promised to give* his son John half his farm" &c.

(2) II. JOSEPH GARFIELD, of Watertown b.
Sept. 11. 1637, m. SARAH GALE, April 3, 1663, admitted a freeman April 16, 1690 : and d. Aug. 14, 1691.—
His father was Edward Garfield Jr. who was adm. a
freeman May 6, 1635, Selectman of Watertown 1638,
'55, and '62, and one of the earliest proprietors of the
town. . SARAH d. sometime after her husband. They
had children :

7. 1. *Edward*, b. June 22, 1664.
8. 2. *Abigail*, b.—;m. Dec. 22, 1686, Joseph Gleason.
9. 3. *Benjamin*, b. Nov. 18, 1669.
10. 4. *Jonathan*, b. Feb. 17, 1671–2, a weaver of Sud.
11. 5. *Sarah*, b. Feb 18, 1673,4– unm. 1699.
12. 6. *Jerusha*, b. June 6, 1677 ; m. Jan. 12,1695,John
Bigelow,
13. 7. *John*, b. June 8, 1680.
14. 8 *Rebecca*, b. Sept. 24, 1683 ; m. Feb. 26, 1711–12,
Daniel Warren.
15. 9. *Grace*, b. July 6. 1688.

(3) II. ABRAHAM GALE, of Watertown m. Sept.
3, 1673, SARAH, dr. of Nathan Fiske of Watertown :—was
adm. freeman Oct. 11, 1682, and a selectman of Watertown, 1706 and 1718, and died Sept. 15, 1718, in the
occupancy of the homestead. His wife SARAH, d. May
14,1728,aged about 72 years. He left the following Will :

WILL OF ABRAHAM GALE.

"In the name of God, amen, the third day of September 1718, I, Abraham Gael, of Watertown, in the county
of middx, within his magesties Province of the Massachu-
sets Bay in New England yeo ;   Being very sick and
weak in body, But of perfect mind and memory, thanks
be given unto God : Therefore calling unto mind the

ol

mortality of my body, and knowing that it is appointed for all men once to Dye,. Do make & ordain this my last will & testament, That is to say, Principally, and first of all, I give & Recommend my soul into the hands of God that gave it: and my body I recomend to the earth, to be Decently buried in Christian burial at the Discretion of my executor : Nothing doubting but at the Genl. Resurection I shall receive the same againe by the mighty Power of God, and as touching such worldly estate wherewith it hath Pleased God, to Bless me in this life, I give & bequeath the same in the following manner and form : Imp.—I give and bequeath to Sarah, my well beloved wife, all my Personal estate within doors for her comfort & support during the time she Remains my widow; and further my will is that my wife shall have a comfortable Room in my mansion house, and to be constantly Provided with sufficient fier wood laid at the door fit for fire, and also to have Ten pounds annually pd. her in corn & meat & other Provisions by my two youngest sons, namely John & Joshua Gael. But in case my wife shall see cause to marry againe, my will is she shall be pd. the sum of Twenty pounds by my two above sons out of my Personal estate and no more, and the annual Rent to sese."

"Item : I give and bequeath unto my son Abraham Gael & to his heirs & assigns forever the land on which his mansion house now stands with all the land adjoining that I formerly staked out & designed for him, being about sixty or seventy acres by estimation but not measured to know the certainty. Provided my said son pay ten pounds in money, of the debts I now owe either into the Public Bank of the Province, or to Paul Dudly Esq. of Boston, an in case he shall Refuse to pay ten pounds as aforsaid, then my will is that he shall injoy Ten acres

short of the land before given, sd. ten acres to be taken
off conveniently together to be disposed of as I shall declare. I also give unto my said Son and his heirs aforesaid, one piece of meadow lying upon Charles River containing by estimation four acres, called Beaver hoel meadow. Further I give unto my sd. son as aforesd., one piece
of woodland, containing by estimation five acres lying on
the westerly side of the piece I formerly staked out to him,
upon condition he gives a Deed of Releas to my other sons
of one quarter of an acre of orchard and his Right to ye
land about my mansion-house by virtue of his grand fathers will and in case my said son shall Refuse to so do, then
my will is the aforesd. five acres of woodland to be disposed of as I shall hereafter declare, and this to be in full ·
of what I intend him for his portion out of my estate.

Item :—I give and bequeath to my son Richard Gael &
to his heirs and assigns for ever, the sum of thirty Pounds
to be pd. by my two youngest sons, viz: John & Joshua
equally within two years after my deces, upon condition
that he gives to my two youngest sons afore named a Deed
of quit-claim of some small Right he hath by virtue of his
Grand-fathers will to a Quarter of an acre of orchard &
his claim to the land about my mansion-house. But in
case he shall Refuse so to do, then my will is that my sd.
son Richard shall have only twenty shilliugs to be paid in
time and manner as aforesd., and that with what I have
already given him to be in full of his portion out of my
estate.

Item :—I give and bequeath to my son Ebenezer Gael
& to his heirs & assigns for ever, Two acres of Land joyning to what I have formerly given to him a Deed of lying
on the easterly side of the same, and this with what I have
already given him to be in full of what I intend him for
his portion out of my estate.

Item :—I give and bequeath to my Daughter Sarah Pratt and to her heirs and assigns for ever the sum of five pounds to be paid by my two youngest sons afore named in equal manner within three years after my deces, and that with what she hath alredy had to be in full of her Portion of my estate.

Item.—I give and bequeath to my Daughter Mercy Sanderson & to her heirs & assigns for ever the sum of five pounds to be paid by my two youngest sons above named within four years after my Deces. and that with what I have alredy given her to be her full portion of what I intend out of my estate.

Item :—I give and bequeath unto my Daughter Mary Gael and to her heirs & assigns for ever the sum of twelve pounds to be pd. by my two youngest sons named John & Joshua in equal halves within two years after my Deces, or at her day of marriage which may first happen, and that to be in full of her portion of what I intend out of my estate.

Item :—I give and bequeath to my Daughter Lydia Gael and to her heirs & assigns for ever, the sum of twelve pounds to be paid by my two youngest sons afore named, in equal halves within two years after my Deces. or her day of marriage if that be before two years are expired, and to be in full of her portion out of my estate.

Item :—I give and bequeath to my daughter Abigail Gael & to her heirs & assigns for ever the sum of Twelve pounds to be pd. by my two youngest sons afore mentioned within two years after my Deces. or the day of her marriage, if that first be, in equal halves and that to be her full portion of what I intend her out of my estate.

Item :—I give and bequeath unto my two youngest sons namely : John and Joshua Gael and to their heirs and assigns for ever, all my Real and Personal estate of what kind or Denominations soever not before given away in this my last will & Testament to be equally Divi- between them, they taking care of their antious and ten der mother and providing for & paying to her annually what I have assigned to her in this my last will, as also all my just Debts of all kinds, except the ten pounds I have ordered my son Abraham to pay in case he shall comply with it, and in case he doeth Refuse to pay the sd. ten pounds, then my will is that my two sons aforesd pay the same and they to injoy the ten acres of land con. ditionally given to my son Abraham as also the five acres of woodland in case he refuses to give a quit claim as be- fore expressed, and I do nominate appoint constitute and orda'n my wife Sarah Gael and my two youngest sons John Gael and Joshua Gael my executors to see this my last will and testament performed and I do hereby utterly disallow and Revoke all and ever other former Testament and executors in any before this time by me named, Rat- ifing & confirming this and no other to be my last will & testament.

In witness whereof I have hereunto set my hard and seal the day and year above written.

ABRAHAM GAEL.

Signed Sealed Published Pronounced and Declared by the
said Abraham Gael as his last
will and Testament in the pres-
of us the Subscribers

> JONAS BOND
> SAMUEL HARRINGTON
> MUNNING SAWIN."

The foregoing will of Abraham Gale was presented and *proved by the witnesess* thereof Sept. 22, 1718, and Sarah,

John and Joshua "Gael" appointed executors. All of them signed their executors bond by marks.

Abraham, by his faithful wife, Sarah, had the following children :

16. 1. *Abraham*, b. 1674 ; m. Rachel Parkhurst.
17. 2. *Sarah*, b. Feb. 15, 1674–5 ; d. young.
18. 3. *Richard*, b. Sept. 25, 1677 ; m. Sarah Knight.
19. 4. *Hopestell*, b. and d. Dec. 1678.
20. 5. *Mary*, b. March 27, 1680 ; d. young.
21. 6. *Abigail*, b. March 12, 1681–2 ; d. Nov. 21, 1696.
22. 7. *Mercy*, b. Sept. 16, 1683 ; m. April 13, 1708, Samuel Sanderson.
23. 8. *Ebenezer*, b. April 30, 1686 : m. Elizabeth Green.
24. 9. *John*, b. April 23, 1688 ; m. Lydia—.
25. 10. *Mary*, bapt. April 1689 ; m m Michael Pratt.
26. 11. *Sarah*, b. Aug. 29, 1694 ; m. —Pratt.
27 12. *Jonas*, bapt. Nov. 14, 1697 ; d. March 17, 1718.
28. 13. *Joshua*, b. Feb. 22, 1696–7 ; He died Sept. 15, 1719, intestate, and his property was divided by mutual agreement between his brothers, Abraham, Ebenezer and John, and sisters, Mercy, Abigail, Mary and Lydia. In this division part of the heirs first spelt the name "Gale."
29. 14. *Elizabeth*, ⎫
30. 15. *Lydia*, ⎬ b. July 9, 1699—twins.
31. 16. *Abigail*, b.—;m. Edward Jackson, Jr. of Newton ; son of Edward and Mary, and grandson of Sebas : had 11 chidren.–see Jackson Genealogy.

4. 11. JOHN FLAGG, of Watertown, who, March 30, 1670, married MARY GALE, was b. June 14, 1643, *adm.* freeman Oct. 11, 1682, Constable and Collector of *Watertown* 1685, and d. Feb. 6, 1696–7. He was son of

Thomas Flagg, who settled in Watertown as early as 1648 and was Select-man in 1671, '74, '75, '76 and '78.

John Flagg, by his wife, Mary, had children :

32. *Mary*, b.—; m. Ebenezer Pratt, of Sherburne.

33. *Sarah*, b. June 5 ; d. Dec. 2, 1675.

34. *John*, b. Nov. 6, 1677.

5. 11. JOHN GALE, of Framingham, m. Sept. 27, 1677, ELIZABETH, dau. of Henry Spring, of Watertown, who was *prizer*, or the one appointed to fix the value at which personal property should be received for taxes and debts, from 1680 to 1695 ; and the grand son of John Spring, one of the first proprietors of the town in 1636. Elizabeth was b. Oct. 13, 1659, and after the death of her husband m. 2d. John Mellon, of Framingham.— John Gale removed to Framingham after the birth of his youngest child and died previous to 1694. They had children : (*See Barry's Hist. Fram.*)

35. 1. *Elizabeth*, b. June 1, 1678 ; m, Feb. 21, 1700, John Nurse, of Fram.

36. 2. *John*, b. April 5, 1680 ; d. 1698.

37. 3. *Sarah*, b. Dec. 12, 1681 ; m. about 1700, Jonathan Pratt, of Fram.

38 4. *Abigail*, bap. June 19, 1687 ; m. in Fram., Jan. 10, 1716–17, Jonathan Cutler.

39. 5. *Anna*, bap. June 19, 1687 ; m. Apr. 22, 1714, Jabez Pratt, of Fram.

40. 6. *Abia*, bap. July 14, 1689; m. June 18, 1719, Joseph Trumball, of Fram.

(16) III. ABRAHAM GALE, Jr. of Watertown,
m. Dec. 6, 1699, RACHEL, dau. of John and Abigail (Gar,
field) Parkhurst, of Watertown, and grand dau. of George-
Parkhurst, a native of England and early settler in
Watertown. SARAH was b. Dec. 20, 1678, and d. Jan.
30, 1767. Abraham Gale, Jr., was an extensive farmer
on the old homestead, and Selectman in 1718. The 10,
of March 1726–7 he sold his homestead to his son Samuel
and took back a mortgage conditioned for the support of
himself and wife during their natural lives. They were
both alive when Samuel made his will, Jan. 3, 1749–50,
as he provided for the continued maintainance of "Hon.
Father and Mother." No record has been preserved of
his death. But few parents ever raised a more important
family of sons. Nearly all became well off in the world;
part served in the French, Indian and Revolutionary wars
and each became the head of a very extensive generation.
—:children :

41. 1. *Abraham*, b. Nov. 28, 1700 ; m. Esther Cun-
        ningham.
42. 2. *Rachel*, b. Dec. 14, 1702; m. Gershom Bigelow.
43. 3. *Samuel*, b. Jan. 31, 1704–5 ; m. Rebecca.——.
44. 4. *Isaac*, b. Jan. 15, 1708 ; m. Judith Sawyer.
45. 5. *Enos*, b. July 30, 1711 ; m. Benjamin Allen.
46. 6. *Abigail*, b. Aug. 15, 1714 ; m. Samuel Phil-
        lips.
47. 7. *Daniel*, bap. April 7, 1717 ; No further notice ;
        brobably died young.
48. 8. *Josiah*, b. April 8, 1722, bap. 1733 ; m. Eliza-
        beth—.

(18) III. RICHARD GALE, m. SARAH KNIGHT,
        Jan. 7, 1705–6.
This Richard and family appear to have left Watertown
soon after the birth of the last child named, and we have

no positive account of the place at which he settled, but from the facts here given we think it very probable that he removed to Canterbury, Connecticut. The records of deeds in Middlesex Co., Mass., have the copy of a deed dated 1723; signed by "Richard Gael, of Canterbury, Conn.," and conveying land in Watertown to John and Joshua Gael of Watertown.

We also find the following in Caulkin's Hist. of Norwich, Conn :

"A very sad accident happened in the year 1728. The Inhabitants were engaged in raising a cart bridge 20 feet high and 250 feet long over Showtucket river, near three miles from the town and had nearly completed the frame, when on the 28th of June, as they were putting together the upper work a principal piece of timber which lay on the foundation of this upper work being spliced, gave way at the joint, and falling tripped up the dependent frame, which, with its own weight, careened and overset—100 feet of the bridge fell with 40 men on it, and th people were precipitated upon the rocks in all directions.—20 were severely wounded, and two killed instantly. These two were Jonathan Gale of Canterbury, 19 years of age, the only son of a widowed mother, a very hopeful youth, the darling of the family ; and Mr. Daniel Tracy," &c.

As the writers letter to the town clerk of Canterbury remains unanswerd he can get no further information, positive, of the family. The marriages of these of the daughters, as given by "Bond's Genealogies of Watertown," are of doubtful identity, and we give them with a mark of doubt.

Children born at Watertown :

49. 1. *Sarah*, b. Nov. 30, 1706; m. March 14 1744, Josiah Pierce.

50. 2. *Jonathan*, b. Nov. 26, 1708 ; supposed to have

been killed by the fall of a bridge in Norwich, Con., June 28 , 1728.

51. 3. *Mercy*, b. Dec. 4, 1710; m. (?) Dec. 26, 1749, Abraham Jones, of Weston,

52. 4. *Thankful*, b. and d. Dec, 1714.

53. 5. *Thankful*, b. Feb. 24, 1715–6.

54. 6. *Lydia*, b. Aug. 11, 1717; m. (?) April 28, 1736, John Sadler.

(22) III. SAMUEL SANDERSON, m. April 13, 1708, MERCY GALE, and was killed by lightning, July 8, 1722. Mercy died May 8, 1776. Samuel was b. May 28 1681, at Cambridge, and d. at Watertown. He was the Son of Dea. Jonathan Sanderson, of Cambridge ;— children :

55. 1. *Samuel*, b. Dec. 29, 1708 ; d. July 21, 1744.

56. 2. *Abraham*, b. March 28, 1711 ; m. Dec. 6, 1733, at Wat. Patience Smith.

57. 3. *Jonathan*, b. Feb. 24, 1714 ; d. March 31, 1780.

58. 4. *Mercy*, b. Nov. 26, 1718.

59. 5. *Moses*, b. Feb. 22, 1722 ; m. Jan. 1, 1750–1, Mary Flagg,, who d. and he m. (2d) Elizabeth Goddard, Feb. 7, 1766, and in Apr. removed from Waltham to Littleton.

(23) III. EBENEZER GALE, m. Dec. 27, 1709, ELIZABETH GREEN. He delt some in real estate, in Watertown, and finally deeded what he had left to Samuel Gale, of Watertown, May 21, 1726, and soon after removed to Oxford, and was mentioned in the Will of Mrs. Elizabeth Miller,as residing there, Feb. 12, 1736–7. His son Ebenezer Jr., married and had a family in Oxford.— The records of Oxford, however do not mention the name of any Gale, except Ebenezer, Jr., at least, so says the town clerk, although the war records show that Abijah *Gale, served* from Oxford in the wars of 1755 and 1776.

They had the following children :

60. 1. *Elizabeth*, bap. May 25, 1712 ; m. Feb. 3, 1729
    30, Isaac Whitney, and had *Elizabeth* bap. July
    19, 1741.

61. 2. *Grace*, b. Dec. 12, 1713.

62. 3. *Hannah*, bap. Oct. 9, 1715 ; m. Eleazer Good-
    ale, of Sutton, Sept. 7, 1738.

63. 4. *Prudence*, bap. Aug. 18, 1717 ; m. Jonathan
    Kenney, of Sutton, March 3, 1735.

64. 5. *Jonas*, b. July 8, 1719.

65. 6. *Ebenezer*, bap. Feb. 24, 1724 ; m. Elizabeth
    Kenney.

66. 7. *Lydia*, b. June 11, 1727 ; m. David Bates.

67. 8. *Abijah*, b. about 1727 ; m. Mary Gregory.

68. 9. *Abigail*, bap. May 10, 1730.

69. 10. *David*, bap. Sept. 23, 1733 ; m. Elizabeth Ken-
    ney.

(24) III. JOHN GALE, m, April 23, 1787, Lydia-and
d. Feb. 15, 1734-5, intestate at Watertown, leaving an
estate returned by the appraisers as valued at £823 9s 5d.
The Real estate was set over to son *Joshua,* who paid each
child £45 11s. 4½d., and the widow Lydia £275 for his re-
lease of dower;—children :

70. 1. *Joshua*, b. Oct. 17, 1721 ; d. unm. Oct. 1747.—
    By his will dated April 22, 1746, at Waltham,
    which was proved before the court Oct. 26, 1747
    he gave his sister *Sarah*, wife of Josiah Pierce,
    Waltham, £60 ; and the same to his "sister
    Lydia Gale, Spinster." "To half sister Hannah,
    Sadler, the daughter of Mr. John Sadler, of Upton,
    30 pounds, all in bills of said Province of ye old
    Tenor,"and "to my 2 brothers John and Jonus Gale
    all the rest and residue of my estate." His will

was signed "Joshua Gale," but a receipt given
in 1742 he signed Joshua "Gael." This half
sister "Hannah" must have been the daughter of
his mother by a second marriage, after the death
of his father.

71. 2. *John*, b. Jan. 23, 1722–3. He entered the military service in the French war and was probably
killed.

72. 3. *Jonas*, b. Sept. 23, 1724 ; m. March 10, 1747,
Mary Benjamin.

73. 4. *Sarah*, b. 1726 ; m. Josiah Pierce.

74. 5. *Lydia*, b. Nov. 15, 1728 ; m. Nov. 16, 1749,
John Chaddick, of Worcester.

On May 10, 1736, Daniel Benjamin was appo'nted the
Guardian of the children, and their ages were Severally
ment on.d.

By the Will of Joshua, the chidren severally received
the following sums:

John Gale,	£291 8s. 8d.
Jonas Gale,	291 8. 8.
Josiah Pierce, for Sarah,	63 12. 0.
Lylia Gale,	67 4. 0.

This Daniel Benjamin was a trader in Waltham in
17 9, Representative chosen in 1738, Selectman in 1738,
'39, '40, '4', and Assessor many times from 1738 to 1752.
Jonas married his daughter, Mary, and removed to Worcester, and afterwards to Holden, where he died. He
was a "Jeweller."

(35) III. JOHN NURSE, of Framingham, m. Feb.
2¹, 1 90, O. S. Elizabeth, dau. of John Gale, late of
Watertown, and d. at Framingham at an "advanced age."
There has no record been found of the d. of Elizabeth.
Children :

75. 1. *John,* b. Aug. 27, 1701 : d. at Waterford, Me.
76. 2. *Joseph,* b. Oct. 7, 1703 ; d. at Fitzwilliam, N. H.
77. 3. *Sarah,* b. May 2, 1705 ; m. William Weston, or
Wessen, and d. at Hopkinton.
78. 4. *Elizabeth,* b. Nov. 26, 1708 ; m. Thomas Bigelow and removed to Marlboro.
79. 5. *Mehetable,* b. April 12, 1712 ; m. John Belknap,
and removed to and d. at Westboro, before 1747.
80. 6. *Samuel,* b. Feb. 18, 1713–4.
81. 7. *Thamesin,* b. Aug. 21, 1716 ; m. Abner .Bixby
in 1734, lived a while with his father-in-law and
then removed to Hopkinton.

(38) III. JONATHAN CUTLER, of Framingham,
m. Jan. 10, 1716–7, ABAGAIL, dau. of John Gale.
Children :
82. 1. *Jonathan,* b. March 26, 1719.
83. 2. *David,* b. Oct. 7, 1721.

(39) III. JABEZ PRATT, m. HANNAH or ANNA
GALE, April 22, 1714, and removed to Hopkinton.
Children :
84. 1. *Abiel,* b. Feb. 24, 1716.
85. 2. *Jabez,* b. July 7, 1718.
86. 3. *Benoni,* b. April 3, 1720 ; m. Hannah Parmenter, of Sudbury, and had ten children ; lived at
Framingham.

(40) III. JOSEPH TRUMBULL, m. June 18, 1719,
ABIA or ABIEL, dau. of John Gale, and lived, at
least, a few years in Framingham.
Children :
87. 1. *Abigail,* bapt. Aug. 28, 1720.
88. 2. *John,* bapt. Sept. 29, 1723.

(41.) (IV.) ABRAHAM GALE, of Weston, who m. ESTHER CUNNINGHAM about 1720, was a blacksmith at Weston, wrote a good hand and a man of note in his town. Abraham d. Sept. 30, 1779 and his wife Esther, July 16, 1782. His sons all served with credit in the French and Indian wars :—children

89.   1. *Daniel*, b. June 17, 1721; m. Sept. 8, 1743, Sarah Lamson.

90.   2. *Henry*, b. March 2, 1722—3 ; m. Abigail Smith.

91.   3. *Thaddeus*, b. Sept. 26, 1724 ; m. Lydia Amsden.

92.   4. *Abijah*, b. March 8, 1725—6 ; d. Apl. 28.

93.   5. *Abijah* b. July 5, 1727 ; m. Abigail Amsden.

94.   6. *Jonathan*, b. Mar. 18, 1728–9 ; m. Abigail Beal.

95.   7. *Esther*, b. July 28, 1731.

96.   8. *Abraham*, b. Aug. 18, 1734. He was an ensign under Capt. John Taplin, in the Reg. of Col. Jonathan Bagley, in the "French and Indian war," was at the battle of Port Wm. Henry in Aug. 1756, when the French army was defeated and Baron Dieskau, its commander, mortally wounded and taken prisoner ; and in Aug. 1757, was at Fort Wm. Henry when it was captured by the French, under Gen. Montcalm, but escaped with part of his company, so that they were not included in the capitulation, and thereby escaped the Indian massacre. The 17th, of Nov. 1757, he returned home, was discharged from service and died during the following winter, probably from the effects of wounds. His father was appointed the administrator of his estate April 17, 1758. There is no evidence of his

having been married, as stated in Bond's Genealogies of Watertown, nor is any wife or children
spoken of in the settlement of the estate.

97.   9.   *Elisha*, b. Jan. 1, 1735–6 ; m. 1762 Sarah
Jones.

(42.)   IV.   GERSHAM BIGELOW, who m. 1724
RACHEL GALE ; was b. Sept 1701 at Watertown and was
the son of Joshua Bigelow of Watertown, who was wounded in the "King Phillip's war," for which he received a
grant of land in Worcester, and removed to Westminister
1742, when he d. 1745, aged 90.   Gershom removed to
Sutton, to which church his wife Sarah, was dismissed
from the Watertown church Oct. 5, 1733.   She died in
Ward, 1800.   They had the following children in Watertown before their removal :

98.   1.   *Susanna*, b. Oct. 24, 1724.

99.   2.   *Jabez*, b. Oct. 4, 1726.

100.   3.   *Joshua*, b. Dec. 19, 1728.

101.   4.   *Eunice*, b. Feb, 9, 1730–1.

(43.)   (IV.)   SAMUEL GALE, of Waltham, m.
REBECCA———, and lived on the old homestead at
Waltham, received a deed of the farm and gave back a
mortgage, dated March 10, 1726–27, conditioned for the
support of his father and mother during their natural
lives   By his will, dated Jan. 3, 1749–50, in the "23d.
year of his majisty George 3d.," he gave his dau. "Re-
bekah Gale £500,—bills old Tenor or an equivalent of
New Tenor to be paid by my son Samuel Gale after decease of Hon. Father & Mother—viz :   Abraham and
Rachel Gale of Waltham," to his dau., Rachel Lackey,
£100, to be paid in three years, to his dau. Esther Gale,
£300, in three years, and to his son, Samuel, he gave all the
balance of his estate, conditioned on his paying the legacies and supporting his father and mother.   He says

nothing in his will of a wife,or other children,which were probably dead. Will was proved and Samuel appointed executor Feb. 5, 1749–50. Children :

102. 1. *Rebecca*, b. May 24, 1725 ; m.Edward Holman, of Oxford, May 7, 1754 and had *Lucy*, b. Feb. 3, 1761.

103 2. *Samuel*, b. May 6, 1726 ; m. Ann Fiske.

104. 3. *Rachel*, b. Nov. 6, 1729 ; m. William Lackey.

105. 4. *Esther*, b. Dec. 21, 1730.

106. 5. *Abraham*, b. Sept. 23, 1733.

107. 6. *Lois*, bap. Dec. 1, 1734 ; d. young.

108. 7. *Lois*, bap. July 11, 1736.

109. 8. *Richard*, b. July 9, 1733.

(44.) (IV.) Capt. ISAAC GALE, of Sutton, m. about 1731, Judith Sawyer, of Framingham, to which place he removed, where his first child, Isaac, was b. in 1732, and the following year, he removed to that part of Sutton afterwards set into a new town called Millbury, where he spent a long and useful life and died about Oct 1793.— But few items of his history can be gathered at this late date, but the Muster Rolls of the old "French and Indian war," show that as Lieutenant, he made a campaign in Aug. 1757 for the relief of Fort William Henry,but when they reached Sheffield, the news reached them of the surrender of that Fort the 9th of Aug., when they were ordered back. They marched the distance of 113 miles and were absent 17 days. He received as wages of Lieut., £3 4s. 5l. His brother Josiah, son Nehemiah and nephew Daniel were in the same company from Sutton, and his son served through most of the same war after that date. Lieut. Isaac Gale held his post in the Military Company of Sutton, until March 1, 1763, when he was appointed by the Governor of Mass., Captain of the *the same Company*, which office he held with honor until he resigned, in Sept. 1769, and was succeeded by Capt. Elisha Goddard. In those days of French wars and Indian raids the Captain of the Militia was regarded as the most important office in town. He gave his sword to his son, Isaac, with instructions, as tradition says, to have it preserved by his descendants of that name, and in 1864 it was in the hands of Isaac Gale, of Royalston, who presented it to Galesville University, Wis., for preservation as a family relic ; his own son, Isaac, who would have been entitled to the sword, having died in 1854.

On the first day of October, 1776, Capt. Gale sold his farm and most of his property, that he had not previously given to his other children, to his son Nehemiah and received back a mortgage conditioned for the life support of himself and wife.

By an assessment, of Sutton, in 1778, for taxes, this homestead property was rated as follows :

Two houses and out-buildings,	Val. £110.	
Eighteen acres plowing,	"	180.
Ten acres meadow,	"	74.
Twelve acres pasture,	"	84.
One hundred and ninety acres of woodland,	"	550.
Two horses,	"	50.
Two oxen over 4 years old,	"	30.
Eight cows,	"	80.
Eight steers,	"	30.
Twenty-eight sheep,	"	24. 10s.
Grain,	"	10. 10s.
Four carriages,		
Ten tons English hay,		

D1

Ten do. meadow,
130 bushels of corn,
Twenty barrels of "cyder"
other produce   "   8s.

In addition to this there were assessed to his son Nehe
miah, £100, money at interest.

By his Will, dated April 17, 1792, in which he is called "Gentleman," his few items of property left in his
hands he gave to his children and grand children as follows :

The best suit of clothes to the children of son Isaac,
deceased.

The balance of his clothes to sons Jonas, Nehemiah
and Elisha.

All "quickstock saving two cows" to be divided between the children of deceased, son, Isaac and his own
sons then living.

Gives "cyder barrels" farming utensils and pew in
the church to Nehemiah.

Gives his household furniture and two cows to Judith Chace and Anna Lealand to be equally divided
between them.

Directs that his books be equally divided among all
his children or heirs, and appoints Josiah Stiles executor.

The Will was proved up and allowed, by the Probate
Court of Worcester County, Nov. 5, 1793.

Oct. 17, 1 94, the following named persons as heirs of
Isaac Gale of Royalston, son of late Capt. Isaac Gale of
Sutton, received the amount due them, by the Will of
Capt Isaac Gale, of Josiah Stiles Ex :

Peter Gale, Bartholomew French, Jonathan Gale,
Isaac Gale, Henry Nichols, David Gale, Jonas Gale,

Otis Capron (husband of Judith Gale, deceased leaving
children) and James Gale.

:—children of Capt. Isaac Gale by his wife, Judith :

110. 1 *Isaac*,b. 1732 ; m. Mehetable Dwinel.

111. 2. *Judith,* b. April 12, 1734 ; m. Abel Chace.

112. 3. *Jonas,* b. Apr. 23, 1735 ; m.1st. Tamar Marsh ;
        2d, Hannah Bancroft ; 3d. Widow Rebecca Guy
        —had dau. Lydia who m. Josiah Styles of Mill-
        bury.

113. 4. *Nehemiah,* b. Feb. 12, 1736—7 ; m. Ruth
        Marsh.

114. 5. *Sarah,* bap. 1741 ; died young.

115. 6. *Elisha* b. Nov. 26, 1743 ; m. Mary Singletary.

116. 7. *Anna,* b. Dec. 4, 1746; died an infant.

117. 8. *Anna,* b. Nov. 11, 1748 ; m. James Leland, Jr.
        who was b. 1745, and d. 1801, at Hopewell, On-
        tario Co., N. Y.

(45.) IV. BENJAMIN ALLEN Jr., who m. July
1, 1731, EUNICE GALE, was b. Dec. 13, 1709, son of Benjamin Allen of Watertown and settled in Lincoln. He is
reported as having died previous to 1768 and his widow
m. (2d) Dec. 3, 1768, Abijah Steadman :—had children :

118. 1. *Eunice,* b. Jan. 28 1733 ; m. Mar. 8,1759, Jona-
        than Tower.

119. 2. *Lydia,* b. Mar. 29, 1735.

120. 3. *Beulah,* b. Apr. 16, 1737 ; m. June 6, 1761,
        Joseph Billings.

121. 4. *Benjamin,* b. Nov. 11, 1739 ; m. Feb. 1, 1766,
        Mary Brown, and had Pattee, who m. Feb. 10,
        1780, Joseph Billings Jr. He died Feb. 26, 1770
        and his widow d. May 3, 1773.

122. 5. *Abigail,* b. June 26, 1742 ; m. Feb. 2, 1764,

m; Abraham Wesson.

123. 6. *Phinehas*, b. Apr. 6, 1745 ; m. Mar. 6, 1769,
    Abigail Foster, who d. May 18, 1770.

124. 7. *Rachel*, b. June 25, 1747 ; m. Mar. 9, 1768,
    Edward Farwell, of Townsend.

125. 8. *Anna*, b. Sept. 20, 1749 ; m. (pub. Nov. 2)1771,
    James Stimson Jr., of Weston.

126. 9. *Lucy*, b. Mar. 20, 1753 ; m. Jan. 24,1781, Nath-
    aniel Jackson.

(46.) IV. SAMUEL PHILLIPS, Jr., who m. July
25, 1735, ABIGAIL GALE, of Wat., was b. Sept. 14, 1713, at
Wat., was the son of Samuel Philips, b. Feb. 20, 1679--
80, at Wat., and d. at Weston, Nov. 9, 1752 ; who was
the grandson of Rev. Geo. Phillips, the first minister of
Watertown, b. at Raymond in Norfolk Co., Eng., graduated at Cambridge College, Eng., 1613, came to America
with Gov. Winthrop and landed June 2, 1630, organized
the Wat. Church, July 30, 1630 and d. July 2, 1644.—
Samuel and Abigail had one child.

127. 1. *Abigail*, b. Mar. 7, 1736—7.

The parents were dismissed to Framingham church,
Mar. 5,1747—8, and soon after removed there.

(48.) (IV.) JOSIAH GALE, m. ELIZABETH——, and
settled in Sutton about 1750, where he had a large farm
and personal property in 1778 of the assessed value of
£330.   He made the campaign to Sheffield for the relief
of Fort Wm. Henry, Aug. 1757, with his brother Lieut.
Isaac Gale.—: Children.

128. 1. *Elizabeth*, bapt. May 24, 1741—2.

129. 2. *Josiah*, b. March 20, 1744 : m. Elizabeth Rice,
    and removed to Warwick.

130. 3. *Abraham*, b. July 29, 1745 ; m. Abigail Rice.
131. 4. *Amos*, b. March 3, 1747—8 ; m. 1771, Hannah
     Maynard of Grafton.
132. 5. *Henry*, b. March 22, 1752 ; m. Jan. 16, 1772,
     Elizabeth Drury of Worcester.
133. 6. *Rachel*, b. June 24, 1754 ; m. Ebenezer Phillips
     of Grafton, March 30, 1775.
134. 7. *Mercy*, b. Dec. 2, 1756 ; m. 1777, Benj. Carter
     of Grafton.
135. 8. *Abigail*, b. Feb. 8, 1757 ; m. Dec. 10, 1778,
     Samuel Leland of Grafton.
136. 10. *Paul*, b. Sept. 19, 1762 ; m. Huldah Holman
     of Sutton, Mar. 27, 1783, and settled in Als-
     tead, N. H.
137. 10. *Lydia*, b. Apr. 3, 1764 ; m. Jesse Pierce of
     Sutton, March 6, 1784.

    (63.) IV. JONATHAN KENNEY, of Sutton, m.
March 3, 1735, PRUDENCE GALE and had the following
children in that town :
138. 1. *Prudence*, b. 1737.
139. 2. *Nathan*, b. Nov. 4, 1741.
140. 3. *Violette*, b. May 1, 1744 ; m. Jonathan Gale,
     Apr. 21, 1768, and died without issue some five
     or six years after.
141. 4. *Rebeckah*, b. April 18, 1746.
142. 5. *Jonas*, b. Oct. 24, 1748.
143. 6. *Lucy*, b. Oct. 27, 1750.
144. 7. *A Babe*, b. and d. Aug. 16, 1754.

    (65.) IV. EBENEZER GALE, JR., of Oxford, m.
June 17. 1742., ELIZABETH KINEY, of Sutton.
    He made the campaign to Sheffield for the the relief of

Fort Wm. Henry, in Aug. 1757, in the company commanded by Capt. Edward Davis, of Oxford. He continued to reside in Oxford, at least, until after 1768, and was a quiet, respectable farmer.   --Children :

145. 1. *Hannah*, b. Dec. 22, 1742.
146. 2. *Jonathan*, b. July 12, 1744 ; m. Violette Kenny.
147. 3. *Lydia*, b. May 26, 1746.   .
148. 4. *Sarah*, b. Apr. 15, 1748.
149. 5. *Asa*, b. March 16, 1751.
150. 6. *Susannah*, b. March 15, 1753.
151. 7. *Lucy*, b. Feb. 25, 1755.
152. 8. *Molly*, b. Mar. 5, 1768.

(67.) IV. ABIJAH GALE, of Oxford, m. MARY GREGORY.

He removed to Oxford about 1740, and entered the King's service in the French and Indian War, April 1. 1758, served under Gen. Abercrombie in the unfortunate assault on Ticondaroga July 5, then made the campaign to Oswego under Col. Bradstreet and assisted in the brilliant capture of Fort Fontenac., now Kingston, Canada, Aug. 27 and returned home by the way of Little Falls, N. Y. and was discharged Nov. 9, of the same year. He received £14. 6s. 9d. wages for the campaign. The following spring he was impressed into the service, and on the Rolls was called 30 years of age, the only record we have of his age. He served in one of the divisions of the army against Canada and was discharged Dec. 3, of the same year. He continued to re-enlist each spring and served the Summer campaign until the close of the war in the fall of 1763.

Abijah spent the last of his days with his son Levi, in Hadley, where he died at a good old age, about 1806. —: Children :

153. 1. *Abijah*, b.——
> He entered the service of the Rebels at the first Lexington alarm in April 1775,then an '8 months man,' in Col. David Brewer's Reg. of Continentals of the same year and continued in service until his death by disease, at what period in the war is not known from any records to be found.

154. 2. *Jesse*, b.——
> He entered the service of the patriots of the Revolution, April 7, 1777, to serve during the war, and was killed in some battle or skirmish March 24,1780.

155. 3. *Abraham*, b.— ; d. at the age of 16 years.

156. 4. *Levi*, b. 1765 ; m. Anna Dickinson.

157. 5. *Enoch*, b. Sept 1, 1775 ; m. Jerusha Scott.

158. 6. *Mary*, b.—; m. Joel Fairbanks.

159. 7. *Lucretia*, b.—Never married. d. Dec. 26, aged '71. No further dates.

(69.) IV. DAVID GALE, of Sutton, m. March 9, 1756, ELIZABETH KENNEY of that town. David Gale removed to Warwick, between 1761 and 1764, where he was a prominent citizen.—: Children :

160. 1. *John*, b. Aug. 28, 1758 ; d. at Warwick,Nov. 2, 1776.

161. 2. *Huldah*, b. Feb. 10, 1760 ; m. at Warwick, Sept. 1777, Ephraim Town.

162. 3. *Judith*, b. Dec. 30, 1761 ; m. May, 1787 at Warwick, Asa Gould.

163. 4. *Olive*, b. Jan. 17, 1764 ; m. Dec. 1788, Josiah

Conant of Warwick.

164. 5. *Mary*, b. Feb. 28, 1766 ; m. Oct. 24, 1784, at
Warwick, Benjamin Conant.

165. 6. *David*, b. March 23, 1768 ; m. at Warwick,
Nov. 4, 1790, Mary Eddy. He probably removed to Windhall, Vt.

(72.) (IV.) JONAS GALE, m. MARY BENJAMIN,
the daughter of his guardian, Mar. 10, 1747 and soon after removed to Worcester, where he practised the trade
of a "jeweller", until about 1768, when he removed to
Holden, where he died Sept 21, 1784, and his tombstone
is still standing by his grave. Jonas served in the cam-
paignfor the relief of Ft.Wm.Henry,in Aug.1757,but I do-
not find his name among the soldiers of the Revolution
His Will was dated Sept. 20, 1784, only the day before
his death, if the dates are correct, in which he gives
1st. To wife Mary, the use of the real and personal estate, until the children became of age, if she remained a
widow, otherwise only one third of the use.

2d. To son *Joshua*, five shillings in addition to what he
had received.

3d. To daughter, *Mary*, £6. 13s. 4d., in addition as
aforesaid.

4. To son, *Jonas*, the jeweller's shop and £47. 2s. 7d.,in
addition as aforesaid.

5th. To daughter, *Sarah*, 16s. 6d., in addition &c.

6th. To son, *Isaac*, £55. 17s. 1d.

7th. To son, *Abel*, £74. 9s. 5d.

8th. To daughter, *Lydia*, £26. 11s. 7d.

9th. To daughter, *Susannah*, £26. 11s. 7d.

10th. To son, *Oliver*, £55. 17s. 1d.

All the legacies to be paid when son, Oliver, arrived at 21 years of age. The 5th of Oct. 1784, the Will was proved and wife Mary and son Jonas were appointed executors.

The Inventory and appraisment amounted to £640.-1s. 10d.—:Children :

166. 1. *Joshua.* b. May 28, 1750 ; m. Mrs. Molly Hubbard.
167. 2. *Mary*, b. Nov. 6, 1752 ; m. June 1, 1780, Wm· Parker, of Winchenden.
163. 3. *Jonas*, b. Dec. 15, 1754.
169. 4. *Sarah*, b. July 29, 1759 ; m. Nov. 21, 1780, Paul Raymond, Jr.. of Holden.
170. 5. *Isaac*, b. Nov. 30, 1761 ; m. Susannah Moore.
171. 6. *Abel*, b. April 17, 1764.
172. 7. *Lydia*, b. Jan. 20,1767 ; m. March 7,1786, Solomon Smith, of Holden.
173. 8. *Susannah*, b. April 30, 1769 ; m. Mar. 20, 1792, Ebenezer Wellington, of Boylston.
174. 9. *Oliver*, b. May 30, 1771 ; m. 1795, Esther Wellington, of Worcester.

FIFTH GENERATION.

(89.) V. DANIEL GALE, of Warwick, m. Sept. 8, 1743, SARAH, dau. of John Lamson, of Weston and removed to Sutton, where his first child was born. He volunteered for the relief of Ft. Wm. Henry, Aug. 1757, and made the campaign in the company in which his uncle, Isaac Gale, was Lieut. He removed to Warwick after 1762 and probably about 1770, where he died at a good old age.—: Children :

175. 1.   *Daniel*, b. Sept. 15, 1744 ; d. young.
176. 2.   *Jonathan*, b. Dec. 3, 1748 ; m. Mary Bancroft.
177. 3.   *Reuben*, b. March 3, 1751 ; d. unm.
178. 4.   *Sarah*, b. June 14, 1752 ; m. Samuel Melody of Guildford, Vt., Dec. 6, 1770.
179. 5.   *Daniel*, b. Nov. 18, 1753 ; m. Esther Rice.
180. 6.   *Esther*, b. July 13, 1755 ; m. Philip Goss, of Winchester, N. H. 1779.'
181. 7.   *Noah*, b. July 20, 1757 ; m. Rebecca Chace.
182 8.   *John*, b. Jan. 27, 1759 ; m. Patty Marble.
183. 9.   *Ephraim*, b. Apr. 1, 1760.
184. 10. *Richard*, b. Sept, 19, 1762 ; m., had several children and, with a second wife, removed to Canada some fifty years ago.

(90.) V. HENRY GALE, of Weston, m. Feb. 22, 1745, ABIGAIL, dau. of Joseph Smith, of Lexington. He lived in Weston until 1768, when he sold his real estate and probably removed to another town.

He entered the King's service, as corporal, May 19, 1755, and was discharged at Mendon, Dec. 11, of the same year ; belonged to the trainband, at Weston, April 18, 1757, re-entered, in King's service, April 2, 1759, from Weston, and served until Jan. 30, 1760, when he re-enlisted and served under Col. Frye, in the campaign of 1760, in Nova Scotia, and was finally discharged, Jan. 30, 1761. His sons served with credit in the war of the Revolution, after which we lose track of the family.—

They probably removed to N. H., if they survived the
w ar.—:Children :

185. 1. *Esther*, b. Feb. 14, 1746.

186. 2. *Ephraim*, b. Oct. 25, 1748.

187. 3. *Joshua*, b. Jan. 30. 1751.

188. 4. *Henry*, b. March 20, 1753.

189. 5. *Nathan*, b. Feb. 5, 1755. Feb. 7, 1781, Nathan enlisted from Lexington for three years. He is de-
scribed on the muster rolls as a "farmer, age 25, statue
5 feet 11 inches, complexion dark, eyes black." Receiving his bounty, he signed the following receipt :

"These Lines May Certify that I the Subscriber Have
enlisted for the Town of Lexington for the Term of three
years unless Sooner Regularly Discharged and have Rec'd
of the Town as a Bounty two Hundred Silver Dollars in
paper Money at Seventy five for one.

Lexington Feb. 20th, 1781, Nathan Gale."

The foregoing receipt is not in the hand writing of the
signature. It well illustrates the depreciation of the Continental Currency——seventy-five dollars being then
worth but one dollar.

Finding no further trace of Nathan or his brothers, it is
possible that they all perished in the Revolution.

(91.) (V.) THADDEUS GALE, of Westborough,
m. March 9, 1744—5, LYDIA AMSDEN, of Westborough,
where he settled, soon after, where his children were
born and where he died, previous to 1794, the date of his
widow's will.

Thaddeus was a sergeant in Capt. Ephraim Dolittle's
Co. and served in the campaign of 1755 and was in the
battles of Sept. 8, at Lake George ; also in the Revolution.
he entered an artillery Co-, as gunner, in 1775, which was

commanded by Capt. Edward Crafts and served in different companies the most of the time during the war.— Whether he died in the service or subsequent, the records, of Westboro do not show. His widow, LYDIA GALE made her Will at Westboro, June 26, 1794, and gave all her estate to daughter Lydia, wife of Samuel Bellows, except as follows:

To grand daughter, Bernice, a wooden box.

To grand daughter Esther Gale,   £4,

To grand son, Thaddeus Gale,   20s.

To grand daughter, Sarah Gale,   20

To grand daughter, Abigail Gale,   20

and made son-in-law, Samuel Bellows, executor. She died Feb. 16, 1795 and the Will was proved in Court, March 3, 1795. The town records only show the births of the first two following names and the balance are added from other sources of information :

190. 1. *Jacob*, b. May 30, 1746.

191. 2. *Abraham*, b. Aug. 30, 1747 and died Sept. 18, 1748.

192. 3. *Amsden*, b.——; m. Jan. 1772, Elizabeth Henderson.

193. 4. *Lydia*, b.——; m. April 20, 1783, Samuel Bellows, of Weston ; had children :

1. *Bernice*, b. March 2, 1784 : m. 1807, Wm. Williams. 2. *Huldah*, b. March 8, 1785, d. unm., 1828. 3. *Luke*, b. June 21, 1789 ; d. unm. 4. *Edward*, b. Dec. 23, 1792 ; m. 1823, Hannah Sophia Hawes, of Westboro, and had 3 children.

The descendents of Mrs. Lydia Bellows, now in Westboro, are unable to state what become of the family, but have a faint racollection that two sons or grandsons died of the asthma. At any rate, the writer can get no further information relating to the family, than what is above given.

The grand children spoken of in the Will are probably the children of Amsden, as his name appears among the volunteers who marched from Westboro to Concord, Apr. 19, 1775, "on an alarm which was occasioned by a Brigade of Ministerial Vengeance." His Reg., was under Maj. Gen. Ward.

(93.) (V.) ABIJAH GALE, of Westborough, m. June 23, 1748, ABIGAIL AMSDEN, of Westborough, to which town he immediately removed from Weston.

Abijah entered the service of his King in June, 1756, in the "French and Indian" war and served through the most part of that war, and was in some of the hardest battles. In 1757 he was in that part of the company not surrendered to the French at Ft. William Henry, and was marked as having, with 132 others in Col. Frye's Reg., deserted on the 12th of August, three days after the surrender of the Ft. As they were never punished for the desertion, but Abijah re-entered the service again the following spring, it was probably considered only as a "red tape" desertion, and really justifiable under the circumstances.

The old iron soldier finally, died, June 18, 1804, in peace, amidst his numerous family, so unostentatiously that the town records do not even mention the time of his death.

His first wife, Abigail, d. Feb. 27, 1771, and he m. SUSANNAH ALLEN, of Weston, Nov. 14, of the same year

who d. Jan. 14, 1831, aged 91 years. His Will recites:
"Abijah Gale of Westborough, yeoman, being advanced in age" &c. He dated his will April 16, 1804,
and 'gave to his wife, Susanna, her dower of ⅓ of the estate and one cow, $40, one looking glass, one case drawers and "40 dining chairs she brought with her." meaning, probably, at their marriage.

2d. Gives to his "five sons Nahum, Amsden, Lewis,
Cyrus and David all real and personal property except"
as follows : To "*Nahum* 1 pew and horse stable at
meeting house" &c., ⅓ use of them to widow during her
life.

To son *Elisha*, $5, which, with what he had already
given him, was his proportion.

To son *Isaac*, $35, same as Elisha.

To daughter *Eunice* $100, half in furniture and balance
in cash.

To daughter *Susannah* $100, same as Eunice.

To Abijah Nicholls, deceased, heirs at law, $7.

To grand daughter *Nancy* $50; probably daughter of
Abijah Gale, Jr., who died Jan. 20, 1801.

The Will was proved and allowed Aug. 7, 1804, and
Nahum appointed executor. The Inventory amounted
to, Real estate $6,166, and personal estate $933,19, being of the total sum of 7,099.

This amount, with what he had already settled on his
oldest children, indicates that he was one of the most
wealthy men in town.

He was a Hotel keeper and kept a popular stopping
place for judges and lawyers between Worcester and
Boston ; many anecdotes, of which, he used to tell in the
latter part of his life. He was fond of Jokes, and tradi-

tion says that when his wife left one Sabbath for church she instructed Abijah to "put the pot boiling for dinner," and sure enough he put the pot in a five pail kettle, filled the kettle with water and had the pot boiling in good earnest when the good wife returned.

Being a good business man, he was continually pressed with town offices; hence we find him Constable 1764; on the committee to hire a schoolmaster, in 1768; surveyor of boards and shingles, and on a committee to put in four new pews in the church, 1769; surveyor of highways in 1770; one of a committee of seven, in 1773 "to take into consideration ye rights as stated by the committe of Correspondence of ye town of Boston and of ye infringements and violations of ye same." After naming the grievances of the Colonies this Committee say: "it appears that every member of this committee, qualified to act in town affairs, should at all times have a proper sense of them, more especially as ye Future happiness of his Family, as well as himself depends greatly on their being Removed. For no *Dought* ware tyranny is exercised opposition becomes a Duty. As our fathers could, so can we plead our Loyalty, we have been and now are ready to spill our dearest blood in Defence of our King, Religion and Constitutional Laws, we cannot but look upon it as a hard Trial, yea greater than we can bear, if we cannot be said to give full proof of our Loyalty, otherwise than by sacrificing those Right and Liberties which we prize beyond life itself." In the same year he was chairman of a Committee to sell "Pue Spots" round the church. In 1775, he was one of the Committee of Inspection and Observation" recommended by the Continental Congress.

In 1777, was Chairman of a Committee "to make a re-monstrance to the General Court concerning the state money being put on loan " &c.

In 1778, was Chairman of the Committee to consult to-gether on the plan of Government sent out by Congress. He reported that : "We are of the opinion that the Protestant Religion is not duly guarded in said constitu-tion. Also we think it might be well to acknowledge the Superintendence of Heaven in the Stile :By adding these words : (under God) after the words Shall be, which re-mark we humbly submit to the town for acceptance."

The same year he was Chairman of a Committee "to give instruction to our Representative concerning ye Con-stitution"; and on another Committee "to settle with those who had been in the military service of the United States " ; and also Moderator of the town meeting.

In 1779, he was Chairman of the selectmen and the same the following year (an important office in those days.) After the latter date, he was occasionally Mod-erator and on Committee.—:Children :

194. 1. *Amsden*, b. March 17, 1748—9 ; and d. April 2, 1749.
195. 2. *Abijah*, b. May 1, 1751 ; and d. June 11, 1751;
196. 3. *Sarah*, b. Aug. 15, 1753 m. Edmond Entiswall, Dec. 6, 1777, and d. Oct. 16, 1778.
197. 4. *Abigail*, b. Dec. 22, 1755 ; m. Malachi Nichols.
198. 5. *Abijah*, b. April 26, 1759, and d. June 20, 1801 unm.
199. 6. *Asa*, b. April 26. 1761; d. unm.
200. 7. *Nahum*, b· Dec. 19, 1772 ; m. Anna Forbes, at Needham, Jan. 28, 1850.

201. 8. *Eunice*, b. April 30, 1774; d. at Needham, Jan. 28, 1850. unm.

202. 9. *Elisha*, b. May 13, 1775, and d. Apr. 25, 1776.

203. 10. *Jacob Amsden*, b. April 21, 1777 ; d. unm.

204. 11. *Elisha*, b. June 22, 1778 ; m. Eliza, and lived in Roxbury.

205. 12. *Sarah*, b. Sept. 11, 1779 ; and d. Aug. 22, 1780.

206 13. *Isaac*, b. Nov. 17, 1780 ; m. Anna Norcross and lived in Roxbury.

207. 14. *Susannah*, b. March 31, 1782 ; m. Jonah Forbush in 1806 ; d. without issue.

208. 15. *Luis*, b. July 14, 1783 ; unm.

209. 16. *Cyrus*, b. Oct. 7, 1785 ; m. Eliza Davis, sister of Hon. John Davis, of Worcester, Senator in Congress.

210. 17. *David*, b. Feb. 2, 1788 ; m. Betsey Wallen.

(94.) (V) JONATHAN GALE, m. 1st. ABIGAIL BEAL, of Sudbury, May, 30 1750, who died without issue, and m. 2d. MARGARET, dau. of Wm. Crawford, of Shrewsbury, March 10, 1757, and settled in the latter town.—He was a member of "the 2d, foot Co. of Shrewsbury," and among the "alarram men," Apr. 8, 1757, and served in the Revolution, in 1778, on the North River, in 1779 in Rhode Island, and in 1780, among the troops raised by the town of Shrewsbury to "re-inforce the Continental Army." Jonathan d. Nov. 22, 1799.—Children :

211. 1. *Abigail*, b. Feb. 9, 1758 ; m. in 1781, James Stiles, of Princeton, and had son John.

212. 2. *Eli*, b. June 3, 1760 ; m. Feb. 1785, Anna

E1

Brown, of Worcester.

213. 3. *Jonathan*, b. Sept. 26, 1762 ; m. Sarah Wellington.

214. 4. *Rhoda*, b. Nov. 26, 1764, m. Geo. Andrews.

215. 5. *John*, b. July 31, 1767 ; m. Eunice Bond.

216. 6. *Elizabeth*, b. July 31, 1767. Betsey Gale, of Boylston, made her Will, May 18,1829 and gave her sister Rhoda, wife of Geo. Andrews,of Westboro, $4.

The Baptist Church of Shrewsbury, $5.

One half wearing apparel to Abigail, wife of James Stiles and the other half to Sally, wife of Geo. Eager, Martha, wife of Luther Drury and "Eunice Gale, dau. of my deceased brother Jonathan Gale to be equally divided between them."

A Gold neclace to Betsey Plimpton dau. of brother Jonathan.

The balance of her property to Abigail Stiles and "my nephew John Stiles, of Boylston."— John Stiles appointed executor.

217. 7. *Martha C.* b.—; m. Luthur Drury, May 5,1822, of Shrewsbury and had *William Sherman*, b. Sept. 28, 1823 and *Dolly Lincoln*, b. June 16, 1826.

218. 8. *Sally*, b. —; m. George Eager.

(97.) V. ELISHA GALE, of Princeton, m. May 20, 1762, Sarah,dau. of James Jones, of Weston. Sarah was b. at Weston, Aug. 3, 1737 and survived her husband. Elisha, entered the King's Service, Sept. 15, 1755 and was in the expedition to Crown Point of that year, and acted as clerk in the Co. commanded by Capt. Jonathan Baldwine. He was discharged Dec. 14, 1755, having served 13 weeks, and received for his services, besides travelling expenses, £5 10s. 9d. He belonged to the "Train Band" at Weston, April 18, 1757, and removed to Princeton after his marriage where his children were born. His Will was dated June 25, 1774; he died July 4, 1774, and the Will was proved and allowed July 11, 1774.

By his Will he gave his wife, Sarah, the use of all his property until his dau. Anna became 7 years of age and then ⅓ only.

To his sons, Luther and Calvin and the survivor of them, ½ of all real estate.

To his daughters, Sally, Clarissa and Anna and the survivors of them, the other half.

The Inventory called him a "Blacksmith" and appraised his estate as follows:

"Homestead farm,	£280.		
"The other farm in Princeton,	193	6s.	8d.
"8 acres in Hubbardton,	2	8	
"In door moveables,	19	16	8
Total. £650 17s. 1d."			

Among his personal property, named, was his blacksmiths tools and stock, and farm stock and implements and "one pair of leather breeches," &c.—Children:

219. 1. *Luther*, b. Jan. 3, 1765; was a tanner and d. at Lennox, March 5, 1846.

220. 2. *Calvin*, b. Sept. 23, 1767.

221. 3. *Sally*, b. Dec. 10, 1769; m. Dec. 27, 1789, Elisha Hobbs, Jr.

222. 4. *Clarissa*, b. Feb. 1, 1772; m. Nov. 15, 1795, Dr. Ephraim Wilson.

223. 5. *Anna*, b. April 29, 1774; m. Oct. 7, 1792,

Nathan Perry.

(103.) (V) SAMUEL GALE, of Waltham, m. July 17, 1755, *Anna*, dau. of Dea. Samuel Fiske, of Waltham, who was grandson of John Fiske, b. in England, about 1619 and one of the early settlers of Mass. Anna d. June 2, 1800.

Samuel, was in Capt. Abraham Pierce, Co. of Waltham, "called out," says the muster roll, April 19, 1775 "to the Concord and Lexington fite in defence of the Liber_ties of amarica." His son, Samuel, was in the same ex_pedition. He was allowed 6s. 9d. for three days service and 28 miles travel. What further service this father performed, during the war, there is no very definite record found, but being within two hours march of Boston, the Waltham Co. probably stood as "minute men," until after the evacuation of Boston by the British troops, the 17th of March, 1776. He was probably the Samuel Gale who served under Capt Ward, from Jan. 22, to Aug. 19, 1776, for 6 m. and 26 days, with extra wages for service in Boston, 25 days, £3 3s. 0½, where he was discharged. This, however, might have been his son, Samuel, before he entered Capt. Fuller's Co.

Samuel occupied the old homestead and May 9, 1792, made his Will, giving ⅓ of his property to his wife, Anna. To daughter, Anna, wife of John Cutting, £300, and all the balance of the property to be equally divided between his two sons, Jacob and Alpheus, who were appointed the executors. He d. March 6, 1793 and his Will was proved in court, March 13, 1793.

The Inventory and appraisment, dated April 20, 1793, set the Real Estate at £2500, and all other estates at

£342 4s., makinging total of all estates £2842 4s.

According to the Assessment Roll, of Waltham, 1771, Samuel was assessed for an annual income on real estate of £40 per annum, for one negro slave, between 14 and 45 years of age, two horses, two oxen, twelve cows, 150 bushels of grain, 40 barrels of cider, and other articles in that proportion, usually belonging to a farm.—Children:

224. 1. *Samuel,* b. Sept. 11, 1756. He made the campaign with his father to Concord, April 19, 1775, after which he entered the patriot service and at · the close of the campaign of 1776, was returned on the muster roll of Capt. Fuller, in Col. Brooks, Reg., as among the missing after a battle, and is supposed to have been killed or mortally wounded at the battle of White Plains, Oct. 28, 1776· He was never heard of afterwards by the family.

225. 2. *Jacob,* b. April 14, 1758 ; m. Sept. 23, 1784. Lois Hagar.

226. 3. *Anne,* b. Feb. 28, 1759 ; m. Oct. 5, 1780, John Cutting; of East Sudbury.

227. 4. *Alpheus,* b.—1764 ; m. July 5, 1787, Lydia Hammond.

(110.) (V) ISAAC GALE, Jr., of Royalston, m. in 1756, MEHETABLE DWINEL, or DUNEL, of Sutton, removed to Royalston about 1770, and died there, May 19, 17-9. He served as sergeant, in the campaign of 1776 in the Northern Army at Ticondaroga, under Col. Samuel Brewer, but no evidence is yet found of any further service in the Revolution, nor in the French war of 1755.—He was called a "miller" and was the owner, when he died intestate of a saw and grist mill in Royalston, and a farm of nearly 200 acres. The return of the Appraisers dated Aug. 28, 1779, valued the whole estate at £11,662 13s. 4d. The debts and cost of the settlement of the estate were reported at £1082 18s. 4d., and the balance was divided among the widow and children, Peter, the oldest son receiving, according to the law then in force, a double share, and the widow one-third of the whole estate. The currency was then in an expanded condition and the administratrix in the settlement of her accounts reduced it at the rate of "20 for 1." to £2709 29.s 12d., the supposed hard money value, leaving the real value for the "estate to be divided £1629 11s. 8d. The figures are given as found in the ɟProbate Office, at Worcester, but do notseem to agree :—Children :

228. 1. *Peter*, b. Dec. 4, 1756 ; m. Prudence French.
229. 2. *Susanna*, b. July 14, 1758 ; m. Bartholomew French.
230. 3. *Isaac*, b. Dec. 10, 1759 ; m. Elizabeth Cutler.
231. 4. *Jonathan*, b. July 3, 1761 ; m. Rhoda Baker.
232. 5. *Jonas*, b.—; m. Zeulia Fox, and removed to Conn.
233. 6. *James*, b. March 9, 1763 ; died young.
234. 7. *Judith*, b. Jan. 2, 1765; m. Otis Capron, and d. after the birth of two daughters.
235. 8. *David*, b. April 24, 1767.
236. 9. *James*, b. Dec. 15, 1770 ; d. June 3, 1771.
237. 10. *James*, b. March 12, 1773 ; m. Elsea Schapmos.
238. 11. *Silas*, b. March 13, 1774 ; d. April 3, 1774.
239. 12. *Hannah*, b, April 26, 1775; d. 1777.
240. 13. *Delia*, b. Oct. 26, 1777 ; m. David Peck.

(III.) V. ABEL CHACE, of Sutton, m. JUDITH, dau. of Capt. Isaac Gale, of Sutton, Jan. 3, 1754. Mr. Chace was a prominent citizen of the town :—Children :

241. 1. *Abel*, b. Oct. 29, 1754 ; m. Anne Bond, of Sutton, Sept. 29, 1779- (See Bond's Gea. no. 499.)

242. 2. *Isaac*, b. June 26, 1756 ; d. Sept. 8, 1759.

243. 4i *Judith*, b. March 19, 1758 ; d. Sept. 28, 1799.

244. 3. *Judith*, b. March 27, 1760 ; m· Aaron Parker, of Ward, Nov. 27, 1782.

245. 5. *Isaac*, b. Sept. 12, 1761 ; m. Sarah Bond, of Sutton, Jan. 8, 1789, and settled in Westford Vt.

His son, Rev. Ira Chace, D. D., graduated at Middlebury College, Vt., in 1814, with the highest honors of his class. Desirous of entering the ministry, he studied at Andover Theological Seminary, where he graduated in 1817, and was the same year ordained a Baptist minister at Danverse and went as missionary to Western Va. The following year he was made a Prof. of Theology in a Seminary at Philadelphia. In 1821, this Seminary was removed to and incorporated with Columbia College at Washington, D. C.— Here Dr. Chace remained four years two of which he was acting President of the College.

Finding that this College did not meet his cherished wishes in educating young men for the ministry, he resigned his position and become one of the principal founders of the Baptist Theological Seminary at Newton, Mass., where he was made Prof. of Biblical Literature, Nov. 28, 1825, which position he held with great acceptability for twenty years, when he resigned and removed to Boston. Near the close of his life he returned to Newton, where he died in 1864, 71 years of age. He was an eminent critical scholar, an eloquent preacher and author of several books and many religious essays.

246. 6. *Sarah*, b. Jan. 15, 1763; m. Dea. Oliver Bond, Nov. 24, 1785, of Sutton, (See Bond's Genealogy no. 479) She d. Jan. 1834.

247. 7. *Emme*, b. Nov. 23, 1764.

248. 8. *Anne*, b. Sept. 7, 1766.

249. 9. *Persis*, b. March 22, 1768 ; m. Jonathan Richardson, May 7, 1789.

250. 10. *Jonathan*, b. Feb. 27, 1770.

(112) V. JONAS GALE, of Sutton, m. 1st. TAMER MARSH, who d. soon after, when he m. 2d, Hannah Bancroft, Sept. 20, 1757. She died, and he m. 3d, widow, Rebeckah Gay, Dec. 28, 1783. Jonas d. about 1807.

By the property assessment of Sutton. in 1778, Jonas was returned as then in possession of a good farm and stock of cattle.

He is spoken of by some one who still remembers him "as a man of fine personal appearance, dignified and manly bearing, regular features, nose slightly aquiline and fine complexion. According to the fashion of the times, he wore powdered hair, blue coat, yellow buckskin breeches, and white topped boots."

Jonas had but one child, Lydia, who m. and resided on the father's homestead : Child :

251. 1. *Lydia*, b. Oct. 20, 1758 ; m. July 11, 1776, Jonah Stiles, of Sutton. They resided on the farm of Jonas Gale in the same town and Jonas Stiles was many

years Justice of the peace.   Their children were :

252. 1.   *Barnum,* m. and settled in Amsterdam,N.Y.on
the Mohawk river, where he raised a family.

253. 2.   *Isaac,* killed by the bursting of a grindstone in
Armory villege.

254. 3.   *Lydia,* b. 1793 ; d. Aug. 10, 1830, unm.

255. 4.   *Charles,* b.—

256. 5.   *Cyrus* b.—

257. 6.   *Vernon,* m. Sept. 22, 1822, Lucy H. Goddard,
of Grafton.   He kept a public house in Middlebury and finally removed West.

Jonah Stiles d. Dec. 15, 1822, and Lydia, his wife,
Sept. 27, 1810.

(113.)   (V.)   NEHEMIAH GALE, of Millbury, m. June
24, 1760, RUTH, dau. of Stephen and Ruth (Waters)
Marsh of Sutton, occupied the old homestead of his father,
Capt. Isaac Gale, took care of his father and mother, from
Oct. 1, 1776,to the time of their deaths and had the home-
stead.

On the military roll his name first appears as having
made the campaign with his father in the Expedition for
the relief of Ft. William Henry in Aug., 1757, and the
6th of April 1759 he enlisted in the regular service in the
Reg. commanded by Col. Timothy Ruggles and probably served on the Northern Frontier under Gen. Amherst during the balance of the war.   From the 14th to
the 17th of Sept. 1759, he was in the hospital at Fort
George, when he returned to his Reg.

In the Revolutionary War, he was an ardent patriot of
the fighting class, and on the Lexington alarm in April
1775, he drew his sword, as first Lieut. of the company of

Artillery, of Sutton, and marched with the company foɪ the relief of Concord and Cambridge ; and the following year served as a private, in the Reg. commanded by Col. John Holman, in the expedition to Providence, R. I.— He was also in the battle of White Plains, Oct. 28, 1776.

Being in possession of his father's farm and money at interest, he was in independent circumstances and brought into town the first Chaise that was introduced into Sutton. In the days of horseback riding, this vehicle was consid- ered as equivalent to "a Coach and four, and much aston- ished the natives. We do not claim this to be the "Dea- con's one hoss Shay" of the school books.

It is said he died while on a visit to his son, Dea. Solo- mon Gale, at Bennington, Vt., in 1820 and his wife Ruth d. Oct. 1814. Children :

257. 1　*Benjamin*, b. April 18, 1761 ; and d. unm. 17- 85, at Sterling. He was finely educated and a Physician.

258. 2.　*Solomon*, b. Sept. 12, 1763 ; m. 1st. Rachel Woodward, and 2d, Phebe Hays.

259. 3.　*Elizabeth*, b. Dec. 9, 1764 ; d. unm. 1806, of consumption.

260. 4.　*Jonas*, b. March 6, 1765 ; m. Elizabeth Grout.

261. 5.　*Ruth*, b. Oct. 12, 1767 ; m. Dec. 17, 1788, John Greenwood.

262. 6.　*Anna*, b. July 3, 1769 ; d. 1797, unm.

263. 7.　*Tamer*, b. Feb. 27, 1771 ; m. 1st. Henry Dwin- el, and 2d., Levi Page.

264. *Rufus*, b. July 5, 1773 ; m. 1st. Louisa Livermore, and 2d. widow Knox.

265. 9　*Nehemiah*, b. Jan. 4, 1775 ; d. young.

266. 10. *Isaac*, b. Sept. 1, 1777 ; m. Persis Stiles.

267. 11. *Andrews*, b. April 8, 1780 ; d. 1797.

268. 12. *Mehetable*, b. Sept. 9, 1782 ; m. David Chase.

(115.) V· ELISHA GALE, of Barre, Vt., m. Apr. 8, 1767, MARY, dau. of Hon. Amos Singletary, of Sutton and removed to Princeton, where the most of his chil dren were born, after which time he removed to Barre, Vt. where he died January 17, 1827.

When but a boy, Sept. 15, 1755, he entered Capt. Juduthan Baldwine's Co. and made the campaign with his cousin, Elisha Gale, to Crown Point in the French and Indian war. On the breaking out of the Revolution he was one of the fighting patriots, and on the Lexington alarm, April 19, 1775, he entered Capt. Boaz Moore's Co., and marched to Concord and Cambridge.

March 1, 1776, he was commissioned 2d, Lieut. in the Co. commanded by Capt. Joseph Sargent, in the third Continental Reg., commanded by Col. Nath. Tyler, and June 12, 1779, he was re-commissioned 2d, Lieut. in the Reg. commanded by Col. Josiah Whitney. His wife was b. in Sutton, June 21, 1747, and d. Oct. 30, 1835.

Children :

269. 1. *Sawin*, b. Nov. 21, 1767 ; d. Nov. 19, 1776.

270. 2. *Rhoda*, b. June 4, 1769 ; m.—Richardson, and d. Feb. 3, 1814.

271. 3. *Mary* or *Polly*, b. May 31, 1771 ; m.—Olds, and d. March 28, 1796.

272. 4. *John*, b. Aug. 5, 1773 ; m. Eunice Bancroft, of Warwick, Mass., 1801.

273. 5. *Elisha*, b. Sept. 1, 1775.

274. 6. *Achsah*, b. Nov. 7, 1777 ; d. Sept. 26, 1790.

275. 7. *Sawin*, b. Nov. 1, 1779 ; m. Betsey Blanchard.

276. 8. *Sukey*, b. Dec. 26, 1781 ; m.—Willey, d. Oct.
26, 1828.

277. 9. *Ann*, b. Dec. 26, 1781 ; d. in infancy.

278. 10. *Abraham*, b. April 22,1784,m. Clarissa Bancroft,
of Warwick, Mass.

279. 11. *Isaac*, b. April 22, 1784 ; m. Eliza Annis.

280. 12. *Mahaly*, b. April 1, 1788 ; m.—King, and d.
Dec. 22, 1832.

281. 13. *Lucy*, b. Dec. 19, 1791 ; m Claflin ; d. Sept. 15,
1863.

282. 14. *Amos Curtis*, b. Nov. 26, 1793 ; m. Rhoda
Royce.

(130.) V. ABRAHAM GALE, m. Nov. 28, 1769,
ABIGAIL RICE, of Worcester, dau. of *Absalom* Rice of
that town. Abigail was b. Oct. 7, 1746, and was mentioned in her mother's will, dated July 1, 1791, and also
in her father's will, dated June 8, 1771 and proved June
8, 1782.

Abraham, at the time of his marriage, was said to be
of Shrewsbury, but removed to Princeton about 1774.

A devoted revolutionary patriot, he went as Sergeant
in Capt. Boaz Moore's Company, April 19, 1775, on the
Lexington alarm, to Concord and Cambridge, was absent
9 days, marched 46 miles and received therefor £1 3s.
1d. The following March he was commissioned 2d,
Lieut. in the Company commanded by Capt. Ephraim
Hartwell, in the third Continental Reg. of Col. Nath.
Tyler, and re-commissioned as 2d, Lieut., June 17, 1779,
in the 12th. Company of the Regiment commanded by
Col. Josiah Whitney. In Sept. 1779, he was 2d, Lieut.
in David Moore's Company, in the Reg. of Col. John

Jacobs, in Rhode Island, near Providence. He was discharged from service at the close of that campaign, Nov. 25, 1799, which probably closed his nearly five years service in the Revolution.

On the Nov. 21, 1786, Abraham was Captain of a company of 60 armed "Regulators" from Princeton, which marched into Worcester, closed the Court House and compelled the Court to adjourn. They then returned home. On the 1st. of the following month, the same company, with many others from different parts of the State, assembled at Worcester, under the leadership of Daniel Shays, compelled the Court to adjourn, signed a petition that no courts be held until after the next session of the Legislature, in May, and were dismissed for home, about the 10th, Dec. (See account of Shay's Rebellion in notice of Henry Gale.) He removed to N. H. soon after the Rebellion and probably d. there. Children :

283. 1.   *Mary*, Feb. 7, 1772.
284. 2.   *John*, b. April 6, 1774.
285. 3.   *Abigail*, b. Aug. 5, 1776.
286. 4.   *Azubah*, b. Jan. 8, 1778.
287. 5.   *Betsey*, b. March 31, 1781.
288. 6.   *Abraham*, b, June 18, 1784.
289. 7.   *Lucy*, b. Dec. 19, 1786.

(131.)   V.   AMOS GALE, m. 1771, HANNAH Maynard, of Grafton and removed from Sutton to Alsted, N. H. where his first three children were born. He then went to Grafton where his fourth child was born, and thence to Princeton where his fifth child was born.

He appears to have served in the campaign in R. I., in the forepart of 1777, in Col. Josiah Whitney's Reg. of

Mass. troops, but the writer has no knowledge of what other Revolutionary services he may have performed from N. H. He was afterwards Captain in the Militia. Children :

290. 1. *John*, b. Oct. 4, 1773 ; m. Nancy—.

291. 2. *Deliverance*, b. Sept. 7, 1785.

292. 3. *Amos*, b. Aug. 24, 1777 ; d. in Charlestown or Charlton, April 12, 1856.

293. 4. *Josiah*, b. Aug. 4, 1780.

294. 5. *James*, b. Nov. 11, 1782.

(132.) V. Capt. HENRY GALE, of Barre, Vt., m. in Jan. 16, 1772, Elizabeth Drury, of Worcester, and settled in New Paris, afterwards call Ward and still later changed to Auburn, Mass. He was a church going man and the old church records still show that in 1775 he paid £14, for Pew No. 49 in the church of that town.

The war records of Mass. still on file in the office of the Secretary of State at Boston, shows that on the "Lexington Alarm" in April 1775, Henry promptly Volunteered as a private in the company commanded by Capt. John Crowl and marched to Cambridge for which he was allowed £1 4s. ½d. for 11 days and 100 miles travel. Again in the campaign of 1777 he served four months in the Northern Army in the company of Capt. Abel Mason Col. Cushing's Regiment and participated in the glorious victory over General Burguoyne in October of that year. In that campaign he served from Aug. 13, to Nov. 30, when his regiment returned home.

As early as 1771 the records of the town of Princeton show that Henry had in that town a good farm valued at £185, with three buildings and a good stock of cattle, and

ınd in 1778Henry removed to that town where he resided
ıntil he removed to Barre Vt. in about 1790.

In Princton he lived in comparative independence, and
ıeing a man of good education, occupied a high social po-
:ition, and after the close of the Revolution joined hearti-
y in the discussions of the day, how an independent [but
ıankrupt state might be galvanized into life and a circula-
ing medium in the shape ot money established. But
vhile these subjects were rackingthe brains of the wise and
;ood patriots, of the country, the amnesty proclamation
ıad restored to Boston and other large towns the wealthy
oyalists, who had left the state with the British army,
when they evacuated Boston.

These wealthy men having lost all sympathyfor the reb-
:l country and people on their return commenced indis-
:riminately the prosecution for the collection of their old
:laims, most of which had been outstanding during the
war. This alarmed the otherwise quiet creditors,and par-
:icularly as "Greenbacks" as a legal tender did not then
∍xist and any debtor to the amount of $5,could be ordered
ı0 jail. So great was the rush of business to the courts
lhat 2000 cases were said to have been entered at one
term of the court at Worcester.

: The people in alarm held public meetings and petitioned the legislature for relief.

The legislature setting in Boston under the influence
of Boston merchants and Boston lawyers, who were also
reaping a great harvest in high fees, refused the desired
relief under the plea that they had no power, a plea generally resorted too when there is a lack of disposition.

The people then petitioned to the courts that they adjourned over without granting the judgments, until some kind of relief could be afforded by the legislature, but the courts declared they would not be instructed in their duty by the people, while Judge Artemas Ward, in a speech of two hours long from the steps of the Court House in Worcester declared to the people that their "conduct was treason and the punishment of treason was death."

Thus the people of Worcester and other interior counties were, for two years, ground between two millstones, the courts and the jails, with nothing but bankruptcy and imprisonment staring them in the face.

To soldiers who had so lately vindicated their rights by their swords and had learned for seven years to treat the word "traitor" as a by-word, it was no hard affair to fly to arms, not to overthrow their government but simply to temporarily stop the courts in granting judgments in civil cases.

The people in many counties organized into companies, chose their officers, marched to the Court Houses and prohibited the holding of the courts. Henry Gale was captain of a company from Princeton and his brother Abraham, was Capt. of a company from Grafton. Daniel Shays, a brave officer in the Revolutionary war, became the commander or general leader. Thus matters run a short time when the Governor ordered out 4000 men and the "Rebels" disbanded, not however in Springfield until they were fired on and three men killed.

The "Rebels" studiously avoided bloodshed.

But this tragedy, in the best style of the books, was to terminate in a farce. Judge Artemas Ward, who was a military man, but no lawyer, had only vindicated his military arm leaving his judicial arm still in *limbo.* As

E2

the judge had boldly threatened the Rebels with the punishment made and provided for "treason," he caused indictments to be found against the supposed leaders in the different counties and convicted what did not slip through his hands by the verdict of the jury.

The writer has procured from the court records in Boston a copy of the indictment and judgment, the material part of which is as follows :

"At the Supreme Judicial Court of the Commonwealth of Massachusetts began and holden at Worcester on the last Tuesday of April A. D. 1787"&c.

"The jurors for the Commonwealth of Massachusetts upon their oaths present that Jacob Chamberlain of Dudley in the same county, Gentleman, Henry Gale of Princeton in the same county, Gentleman, Josiah Jennison Jr. of Spencer in the same county Yeoman, being members and subjects of the Commonwealth afforesaid," &c. * * "that upon the 5th day of Sept. 1786 and on diverse other days and times as well before that time as since at Worcester within the said county of Worcester falsely and traitorously did devise and conspire to levy war against this Commonwealth and then and there with a great number of rebels and traitors against the Com'th, afforsaid, viz : the number of 500 whose names are yet unknown to the jurors being armed and arrayed in a warlike and hostile manner, viz : with drums beating fifes playing and with guns, pistols, bayonets, swords, clubs and diverse other weapons as well offensive as defensive did falsely and traitorously prepare, order wage and levy a public and cruel war against the Commonwealth, &c., and then and there with force and arms aforsaid wickedly and traitorously did assault, imprison, captivate, plunder, destroy,

F1

kill and murder diverse of the leige subjects of the said Commonwealth," &c, &c.

Under this indictment Jacob Chamberlain and Henry Gale were arrested and put upon their trial. They plead not guilty and put themselves on "God and their country." The court in its great clemency assigned to them James Sullivan and Levi Lincoln, Esq. as counsel two of the most noted enemies of the Rebels that were practicing at the bar ; the lawyers being all hostile to the "Rebels" to a great extent.

Thus organized Mr. Chamberlain was acquitted and Capt. Gale convicted of treason and sentenced to "be taken to the Gaol of the Commonwealth from whence he came and from thence to the place of execution and there be hanged by the neck until he be dead."

When the day of execution arrived the old soldier was, by the sheriff, marched to the gallows with great solemnity, the rope adjusted around the neck of the prisoner, solemn prayers said by the clergy and when all was ready to send the prisoner to eternity, the sheriff cautiously drew from his pocket the Governor's reprieve and read it to the gaping crowd and the prisoner was then withdrawn, and soon after fully pardoned.

This was the majesty of the law vindicated," Judge Artemas Ward's threats executed, the novelty of a "hanging bee" witnessed and an innocent man saved from death by the executive pardon based on the theory that laws must be general but that general laws sometimes convict the innocent of a crime.

The same procedure was had in other counties where the General had convicted "Rebels" of treason.

Judge Artemas Ward to the contrary notwithstanding,

the position of the "Rebels" that their acts were not treason, is still believed by many, as they did not wish to
overthrow the government but only desired to resist the
execution of the law for holding the courts for the time
being for private purposes. This would not be Treason
against the U. S. according to the case *U. S. vs Howie,
Paine,* 265, and the U. S, courts refused to make treason
of the resistance to the Fugitive slave law.

Indeed, the Governor in pardoning the "Rebels" in effect held the offence not treason but only a contempt of
the court.

Thus ended the "first Bebellion" but its effects on
Massachusetts did not end here, for a stampede for
the wilds of Vermont and N. H. immediately commenced, and thousands of the old soldiers who had won
immortality on the battle fields of the Revolution sought
in those new States for the enjoyment of those privileges
of which they had been denied in their native state.
With others, Henry Gale removed to Barre Vt. He was
a highly respected citizen of Barre Vt. for several years,
when he removed with a son to Brighton N. Y., where
he died August 13, 1836. He drew a pension from Government the latter part of his life for his Revolutionary
services.

Of his Revolutionary services we have only mentioned
such records as the writer found at Boston, but there are
several of his descendants who have heard him say that
he was sometime an officer in the Revolution and in several battles.—Children :

295. 1. *Lucy*, b. Jan. 20, 1772 ; d. young.
296. 2. *Ebenezer Brooks*, b. Nov. 10. 1773 ;
297. 3. *Betty*, b. March 4. 1775; d. Oct. 3, 1777.

298. 4. *Thomas Drury,* b. Dec. 3. 1778 ; d. Oct. 19.
1850.

299. 5. *Henry,* b. October 26. 1781 ; d. July 31, 1829.

300. 6. *Sampson,* b. Feb. 19. 1786; d. July 23,1736.

301. 7. *Justus W.* b. Feb. 20, 1788 ; d. June 12,1865.

302. 8. *Josiah,* b. July 5, 1793 ; d. Sept. 24, 1831.

303. 9. *Jonathan,* b. Jan. 1795 ; now living at Pittsford
N. Y.

(146.) (V) JONATHAN GALE, of Warwick m,
1st, at Sutton Violetty Kenney, April 21,1768; and removed
to Warwick where his wife died and he m. 2d, Dec. 1769
Lucy Temple. He probably removed to Vt.   Children :

304. 1. *Violette,* b. Oct. 8, 1770.

305. 2. *Lucy,* b. April 26, 1772.

306. 3. *Isaac,* b. Oct. 6, 1773.

307. 4. *Jacob,* b. Sept. 17, 1777 ; m. lived in Windham,
Vt., had a daughter *Huldah,* who m. W. Shep-
ard and lives at Wardsboro, Vt., Jacob d. about
1856.

(146.) V. ASA GALE, of—.He m.—twice. Probably
Asa moved to Chesterfield N. H. at an early day.   Children :

307. 1. *Ebenezer,* b. about 1777; m. Mary—lived in
Chesterfield N. H. and removed to Windham
Vt. about 1805.

308. 2, *Ivory,* b.—;half brother to Ebenezer, had a family
and lived in Townshend Vt.

(156.) V LEVI GALE, of Hadley m. Hannah Dickinson, of Hadley and settled in the latter town. He was

a true scion of the stock and noted for his physical strength. A story is told of him that a merchant of Hadley offered a barrel of beef to any man that could carry it home. Levi, being present, without remarks, picked up the barrel and started for home, whereupon the merchant gave him $5. to leave it. His father Abijah spent the last of his life with him, and died in Hadley in the fall of 1806. Children:

309. 1. *Alvan,* b. Sept. 9, 1793 : m. Sophia Reynolds.
310. 2. *Enoch,* b. Dec. 21, 1796 ; m. Eunice Fisher.
311. 3. *Martha,* b. Nov. 7, 1800.
312. 4. *Mary,* b. Jan. 12, 1802.
313. 5. *Harriet,* b. —; d. Oct. 13, 1822.
314. 6. *Levi,* b. June 8. 1808 ; unm. Lives in Piqua, Ohio.
315. 7. *Abraham,* b. —; m. May B. Adams.
316. 8. *Emeline,* b.—
317. 9. *Hannah,* b.—
318. 10 *Miranda,* b.—

(157.) V ENOCH GALE, of Charlton, m. 1st, JERUSHA SCOTT of Ward, now Anburn, Jan. 21, 1802. She d. Aug. 30, 1805 aged 22 years and four months, and Enoch m. 2d, SUSAN NICHOLS of Charlton, March 19,1807.

He made his Will dated Jan. 7, 1850 and gave to his wife, Susan, the household furniture and ½ of all real estate during her life, and she was to pay half of the expense of supporting her Mother Lucretia Nichols.

2d. Gave son, Franklin, $10.
3 d. daughter Jerusha Fuller wife of Aaron Fuller $50.
4th. Gave sons William and Sylvester and dau. Irene Lamson, wife of Horace Lamson, and Susanna and Mary

Gale the residue of the estate.

He died Jan. 14, 1850 aged 74 years and his Will was Probated Feb. 5, 1850. Children:

319. 1. *Franklin*, b. Aug. 25, 1802.

320. 2. *Mary*, b. July 20, 1804 ; d. Sept. 15, 1805.

321. 3. *Jerusha*, b. Nov. 24, 1810 ; m. Aaron Fuller of Springfield, Sept. 1835.

322. 4. *William*, b. May 4, 1813 ; m. Emiline Dodge of Charlton Dec. 2, 1832.

323. 5. *Irene*, b. Nov. 6, 1815 ; m. Horace Lamson of Charlton Oct. 12, 1843.

324. 6. *Susan*, b. June 13, 1818 ;

325. 7. *Sylvester*, b. June 20, 1823 ;

326. 8. *Mary Jane*, b. Jan. 11, 1826 ;

327. 9. *Ellen Amanda*, b. June 11, 1828 ; d. Jan. 19, 1832.

SIXTH GENERATION.

(176.) VI. JONATHAN GALE, of Warwick, m. Feb. 14, 1775, MARY BANCROFT, of Warwick. He was a prominent man in Warwick and was seven years one of the Select men. He early entered the Revolutionary service and made the campaign from Warwick to Cambridge at the Lexington alarm April, 20, 1775, was absent three weeks and received for wages £2 5s. 6d. He also served two other campaigns during the war, the last of which terminated in the battle of Saratoga and the surrender of the British army under General Burguoyne.

He died at Warwick much lamented Jan. 29, 1808, but his wife survived until Dec. 11, 1830. His grandson Rev. Dr. Amory Gale says of him that he "was a very worthy exemplary and upright man, possessed of a strong mind, was very kind, social and benevolent ;—in a word he was what they called an ⸢honest good man." Children :

328. 1. *Amory*, b. July 13, 1776 ; m. Lucinda Rich.

329. 2. *Polly*, b. Feb. 19,1778 ; m. Jan. 28, 1798 Martin Stephens and d. 1840.

330. 3. *Jonathan*, b. Nov. 27, 1779 ; d. Oct. 28, 1808 ; m.1822 Polly Stephens and lived in Maine.

331. 4. *Ira*, b. Aug. 28, 1782 ; m. Clarissa Sargent of Putney Vt.

332. 5. *Sarah*, b. Oct. 20, 1784; m. Jan. 6. 1805 John Stearns of Warwick, d. Jan. 20. 1857.

333. 6. *Daniel*, b. May. 12, 1787 ; m. Clarissa A. Ball,

334. 7. *Phebe*, b. Sept. 11, 1789 ; m. 1st Dec. 9, 1806 Urich Green and 2d Nehemiah Houghton.

335. 8. *Melinda*, b. Jan. 20, 1793 ; d. May 7, 1799.

336. 9. *Melinda*, b. Feb. 18, 1800 ; m.•J. W. Chase of Royalston.

(179.) VI DANIEL GALE of Petersham, m. Esther Rice, who was b. Dec. 29, 1755 and d. 1848.⸴

He served as an "8 months man" in the Reg. of Col. Jonathan Ward at Cambridge, in 1775, was at the battle at White Plains Oct. 28, 1776, and served in Col. Job Cushings Reg. from Sept. 5, to Nov, 29, 1777, and was probably at the capture of Burgoyne at Saratoga. Children:

337. 1. *Luther*, b.—

338. 2. *Jesse*, b.—

(181.) VI NOAH GALE, of Salem, m. Rebecca Chase, a widow, of Plymouth, whose maiden name was

Rebecca Dunham. By her first husband she had Joshua Chase, who resided in Plymouth many years.

Noah entered the Revolutionary service Jan. 27, 1777, served in the northern campaign under Gen Warner and was at the battle of Bennington Aug. 16. The following spring he served three months in Maj.Reed's,detachment, after which he served on board of Privateers from Salem, the most of the balance of the war.

After the close of the war he followed the sea, and finally with his oldest son was lost in a terrible storm,at sea. Children :

336. 1. *Elijah*, b.— lost at sea when about twenty years old.

340. 2. *Stephen*, b.—m. Martha Hersey of Hingham.

341. 3. *George*, b.—m. Joanna Glazier of Ipswich.

342. 4. *Daniel*, b.—m. Elizabeth Winslow.

443. 5. *Noah*, b.—; d. at sea unm.

344. 6. *Richard*, b.—m. Mehitable Heart of Salem, and d. without issue, at Sea near the Cape of Good Hope, on his return home, as first officer of the Brig Ann of Salem. He was *Powder Monkey* on the privateer Grand Turk from Salem, in the war of 1812, then 11 years of age. He was once taken prisoner from a prize and carried to Halifax.

(182) VI JOHN GALE, of Warwick m. PATTY MARBLE, of Warwick, Feb. 22, 1787. He was a Blacksmith and died in 1820. Children :

345. 1. *John*, b. Nov. 29, 1787 ; d. Aug. 28, 1790.

346. 2. *Noah*, b. April 18, 1789.

347. 3. *Visa* or *Lovisa*, b. June 24, 1791 ; m. Parker Atwood, and lives in Shorham Vt.

848. 4. *John,* b. Jan. 11, 1793 ; m. lived in Boston and d. Sept. 21, 1835 leaving a wife and three daughters.

349. 5. *Sally,* b. Oct. 13, 1794.

350. 6. *Abram,* b. Aug. 24, 1796,

351. 7. *Oliver Marble,* b. Sept. 22, 1798, m.—lives in Milford, has one son at home, two in California and one in the army, in 1865.

(200) VI NAHUM GALE of Westboro, m. Nov. 15, 1792 HANNAH FORBES of the same town. He resided some time in Auburn and was there in 1812. Children :

352. 1. *Hannah,* b.—m. June 22, 1814, Ebenezer Maynard of Westboro, and had children:

1. *Mary Bruce,* b. April 29,1815, m. 1843, Hannibal Aldrich. 2. *Hannah Forbes,* b. June 15, 1817 ; d. unm, Dec. 23, 1853. 3. *Julia,* b. May 7, 1819 ; d. July 16, 1842, unm.

4. *Emily,* b. Jan. 13, 1821 ; m. Levi S. Hemmenway of Shrewsby. 5. *George Lucus,* b. Oct. 9. 1822; m. 1st, Ellen Fellows; m. 2d, Melissa Van Velch. 6. *Henry Augustus,* b. Nov. 19, 1828, 7. *Henry Merick,* b. April 27, 1837.

The Father of this family d. in 1839 and the Mother in Dec. 1855.

353. 2. *Lyman,* b. Dec. 1794 at Dedham ; m. June 9. 1818. Azubah Baird, of Auburn, and d. at Grafton Sept. 28, 1850 ; had 1. *Azubah Maria,* b. Aug. 26,1824; m. March 14, 1848, Mr. Thomas

365. 2. *George*, b. March 24' 1808 ; m. April 12 1848
Pauline N. Thomas and d. at Roxbury Nov. 22,
1855. He was Registrar in Worcester. in 1848.

366. 3. *Fanny W.* b. Oct. 1812 ; d. Jan. 1813.

367. 4. *Aarriet*, b. Sept. 1816; m. Joseph Sturges of
Boston and had 2 sons and 1 daughter.

368. 5. *Isaac*, b. 1820.

369. 6. *Anna E.* b. Sept. 1824 ; d. May 1834.

370. 7. *Henry*, b. Feb. 1827 ; m. in Amesbury, June 19
1851, Harriet Tibbets' both of Amsbury. He
was, called a "shoe-cutter."

371. 8. *Abby J.* b. Jan. 1829 ; m. Sept. 27, 1850,James
F: Brown of Boston and has three sons.

372. 9. *Albert*, b. Jan. 9, 1832 ; d. Oct. 16. 1853.

373. 10. *Edwin*, b. Jan. 9, 1832, twin with Albert m.
Isabella Damon of Natic.

(209) VI HON. CYRUS GALE, of Northboro, m.
1st Eliza Davis, who was born Oct. 15, 1794 and d. Feb.
15, 1821, when he m. 2d,Sarah Patrick,who was b.March
16, 1795 and d. Dec. 4, 1849 and he m. 3d,Susan G. Holbrook, Feb. 17, 1852, who still survives with her aged
husband.

In early life Mr. Gale was a Provision dealer and
wholesale and retail Grocery merchant in Boston, and
during the war of 1812 Captain of a company of Militia
in that city. In subsequent life Capt. Gale has been Post
Master, Select man and for fifty years a justice of the
peace. He has also been two terms a member of the
Legislature and one term a member of the Governor's
council. For several years past he has occupied a farm
in Northboro, where he enjoys, in comparative wealth,the

consciousness of a well spent and useful life, and where
he is highly respected by an educated and christian community.   Children :

374. 1.   *Fredrick W.* b. June 22, 1816 ; m. Mary S.
Utley of Boston.

375. 2.   *Hannah D.* b. Jan.14, 1820 ; m. George Barnes
and had *Anna* ; d. July 15, 1051.

376. 3.   *Cyrus,* b. Nov. 25, 1820 ; d. Feb 17, 1821.

377. 4.   *Cyrus,* b. March 5, 1724 ; m. Dec. 5, 1850, Ellen M. Hubbard ; he is a merchant in Northboro.

378. 5.   *George A.* b. Feb. 19, 1827 ; d. Sept. 10, 1857.

379. 6.   *Sarah E.* b. Oct. 31, 1831 ; d. May 18, 1839.

380. 7.   *Walter,* b. Nov. 13, 1833.

381. 8.   *Susan M.* b. June 16, 1833 ; d. June 22, 1842.

(210) VI DAVID GALE, of Providence R, I.
m. April 4, 1813, Betsey Wallen of that place.   She was
b. July 24, 1791.   David was a House Carpenter by trade,
and lived in Northboro from Sept. 1816 to 1823, when he
removed to Providence R. I. where they lived in 1864.
Children :

382. 1.   *William Henry,* b. June 11, 1814 ; m. Abbey
Potter Baker.

383. 2.   *Lawson Wallen,* b.Oct 24,1816 ; m. Mary Howard.

374. 3.   *Phebe Ann,* b. Sept. 6, 1818. *

375. 4.   *David Edwin,* b.Aug. 6,1820 d. Aug. 17,1851.

376. 5.   *John Wallen,* b. Sept. 14, 1822 ; m. Adalaide
R. Calder.

377, 6.   *Mary Elizabeth,* b. May, 3, 1828 ; m. Thomas
Philips Jr. of Providence R. I. a Hard Ware

   * NOTE—Error in numbering.

Dealer.

378. 7. *Susan Allen*, b. Jan. 2, 1830 ; m. July 21,1858, Joseph B.Gurney a Lumber dealer in Providence R. I. and had son, *Joseph Gale*, b. May 19, 1863.

379. 8. *Ellen Frances*, b. June 1, 1832 ; m. Oct. 19, 1858, William H. Alexander of Providence R. I. by occupation a Jeweler.

380. 9. *Andrew Jackson*, b. July 30, 1836 ; m. Nov.24, 1862 Lizzie Bush Pearce of Bristol R. I. and had dau. *Lillian Pearce* b. Feb. 21, 1864. Andrew is a merchant at Providence. R.I.

(212) VI ELI GALE,of Worcester m.in Feb. 1785. ANNA BROWN of Worcester in which town he resided from marriage until after 1793.

May 15, 1777, then but 17 years of age, he enlisted from Shrewsbury in Capt. Pierces Co. in the 15 Reg. commanded by Col. Bigelow, during the war. He was occasionally promoted from private to corporal and in Dec. 31, 1788 held the post of Sergeant. Child :

381. 1. *Polly*, b. Nov. 4, 1786.

(213) VI JONATHAN GALE, of Shrewsbury afterwards of Roylston m. April 8. 1786 SARAH WELLINGTON of the latter town. She d. Dec. 11, 1815 aged 46. Jonathan died previous to 1829. Children :

382. 1 *John Green*, b. May 18, 1787.

683. 2. *Dana*, b. Jan. 14, 1789 ; m. Mary McClellan.

384. 3. *Sally*, b. May 24, 1791; m. Eager.

385. 4. *Curtis*, b. July 9, 1795. Still lives in Roylston.

386. 5. *Betsey*, b. Aug. 17, 1797. m.—Plimpton.

387. 6. *Martha Crawford*, b. Jan. 21, 1801.

388. 7. *Jarvis H.* b. Aug. 26, 1809 ; m. Polley Hat-

chett.

389. 8. *Eunice,* b. Aug. 14, 1811 ; m. Edwin Prentiss.

(215) VI JOHN GALE, of Stratford Con. m. Eu- ,
nice, dau. of Dea. Jonathan Bond of Westboro. She d.
in 1799 leaving one son. John was killed by being
thrown from a carriage.

In these statements,we have followed Bond's Genealogy, but some of the family say that Eunice died in Brimfield Mass. and that the son was b. there, and have no
knowledge that John ever lived in Conn. Child :

390. 1. *Jotham,* b. Sept. 1796 ; m. Clarrissa Gould.

(225.) VI. JACOB GALE, m. Sept. 23,1784, Lois,
daughter of Joseph Hagar, of Waltham, whose great
grandfather was the English ancestor who settled in Watertown and m. Mar. 20, 1644–5, Mary Bemis.

Jacob first entered the Patriot Service March 4, 1776,
in the language of the muster roll : "called out by Col.
Samuel thatcher in his Regiment wich the march was at
the request of Generall Washenton at the taken Possion
of dorchester hills and found our own Provisions for 5
days forth fifth sixth seventh and eight days of march
1776." This Roll is in the hand writing of Samuel Holden, Justice of the Peace. He next entered what was
called "the Ticonderoga service," April 15, 1776, in the
Co. commanded by Capt. Jonathan Danforths, in Col.
Whitcom's battalion, and was reported as on the sick list
in camp, Nov. 27, 1776, at Ticonderoga. He was probably discharged soon after.

He occupied the old homestead mansion at Waltham,
and he and his wife, being very devoted Methodists,made
the "Gale mansion" the home of the Methodist traveling

preachers for that region of country up to the death of
the widow, which occurred Feb. 16, 1851 ; soon after
which time,the old mansion passed into the hands of Gov.'
Banks, the Maj. General commanding the Army of the
South West in 1864, and has ever since remained Gov.
ernor Banks homestead.

Jacob having lost his only child by death, made his
Will to keep the estate in the family, Sept. 21, 1728 by
which he gave his wife Lois, after paying his debts, the
life use of his whole estate but to · be divided after her
death as follows :

To Samuel his nephew, son of his brother Alpheus
Gale all real and personal estate subject to the payment of
the following legacies :

To Samuel's brother Jacob,			$500,
To	do .	sister Sally.	200,
To	do	sister Lydia,	200,
To	do	sister Caroline,	200,
To Niece, Mariah Garfield,			500,

Mariah was niece to Jacob's wife and daughter of Joseph and Susanna (Hagar) Garfield,was b. March. 7,1802
and lived much of the time with her Aunt Lois.

Jacob died probably in Nov. and the Will was proved
in court Dec. 2, 1828 and the widow appointed executrix.
Child :

319. 1. *Samuel*, b. Feb. 7, 1785 and d. in 1796.

(227) VI ALPHEUS GALE, of Waltham, m.July
5, 1787, LYDIA daughter of Jonathan Hammond, a prominent citizen of Waltham, and Select man from 1765 to
'74, Jonathan was of the fifth generation of William
Hammond, born in Cavenham, Suffolk Co. England,

1575, settled in New England, 1634 and became one of the proprietors of Watertown 1642. Lydia was b. Oct.9, 1767 and d. April 6, 1810.

Alpheus, then in his 16 year, volunteered as a private in Capt. Edward Fuller's Co.Col.William McIntosh's regiment March 19, 1778, which was stationed at Roxbury, but was discharged April 5, of the same year.

He became a very active business man and was long regarded as the richest man in Waltham, but his rather sudden death about the first of Aug. 1823 revealed the fact that his name had been signed so often to other men's notes, which were then brought against his estate that the estate, inventoried and appraised ot $22,138,28, only paid 89 cents and 5 mills per $1,

The widow, a second wife, only received $300, out of the estate.

It was to remedy, in part, this misfortune that Jacob Willed his property to his brother Alpheus' children. Children :

392. 1. *William*, b. July 6, 1788. He graduated with honor at Harvard College in 1810, read law, was admitted to the bar, settled in Boston and became one of the most brilliant democratic lawyers of the city. But a disappointment in love, the death of his father and the bankruptcy of the estate, so effected his mind that he became intemperate and died a drunkard in 1839.

393. 2. *Nancy*, b. May 23, 1791 ; d. June 30, 1808,

394. 3. *Sally*, b. Aug. 12, 1794 ; she lived unm. at no. 41 Irving St. Boston in April 1864, with her two sisters, looking well.

395. 4. *Lydia*, b. June 26, 1797 ; d. Oct. 9, 1798.
396. 5. *Samuel*, b. Feb. 7, 1799 ; m. widow Fish.
397. 6. *Lydia Hammond*, b. Oct. 24, 1801 ; m. May
    21, 1863 Henry O. Byram of Boston and lived
    at no. 41 Irving St. in 1864.
398. 7. *Jacob*, b. Dec. 31, 1803 ; m. Mary Mabin.
399. 8. *Caroline*, b. June 1, 1806 ; is deaf and dumb,
    but is educated. She lives with her sister Sally,
    and remains unm.

(228) (VI) PETER GALE of Barre Vt. born at
Sutton Dec. 4, 1756 and m. April I5, 1779, at Royalston,
PRUDENCE FRENCH. He served his country in the Revolution, in the Continental Army during the campaign
of 1778, in the Reg. commanded by Col. John Jacobs,
and was allowed £28 19s. 8d, for service 6 months and 8
days and 120 miles travel ; and was on the muster rolls
as "of Royalston." The writer cannot locate the place of
service of that Reg. for that Campaign, but from the
memorandum on the muster roll; "Midleton Aug. 27,
1778" he infers that it might have guarded the lower
Connecticut river from the British, then occupying N.Y.
city. The Reg. however, might have been at the seige
of Newport R. I. under Gen. Sullivan.

In Feb. 1793 Peter Gale removed his family to Barre
Vt., a month before the organization of the town, and became the 14th family in the town ; and there purchased a
tract of wild land including a part of "Cobble Hill," that
has since furnished granite for the building of the State
House at Montpelier Vt.. and commenced pioneer life in
earnest. The snow was then six feet deep in the heavy
forest of that region.

Peter,having been brought up acquainted with farming, machinery, and mills, was well fitted to pioneer life, and could perform almost any variety of work. Accordingly, we find him clearing land of the native forests, putting in crops, building his house and barn, sheds and fences and often assisting his less ingénious neighbors in fitting up their cabins and erecting mills. He soon had a good farm under cultivation, and put up for himself a fair sized two story frame house with square roof, and also erected for himself a large barn. The , house was visited by the writer in 1840 and was in a good state of preservation,but was soon after superseded by a small tidy granite house built by Mr. Wheeten, the then proprietor of the farms.

The fifteenth of August 1817,Peter joined with his son Peter in the purchase of the "Walnut Bow Farm" in Colchester Vt. where he moved his family,but unfortunately, he was attacked with the Fever and Ague soon after he took possession of his new farm and died in Nov. 1818.

He was a man of fine physical proportions, strong mind, of social disposition and great energy of character. His widow survived him and returned with the family to the homestead in Barre Vt. She was born at East Bridgwater, March 17, 1756 and was the daughter of Micah and Ruth French, Micah was born at Braintree and was the son of Thomas (b. 1657)who was the son of John and Ruth French, that were residents of Braintree previous to 1641 and emigrants from England.   Children :

(400,) 1. *Peter*, b. Jan. 26, 1780 ; m. Hannah Tottingham of Westminster.

401. 2. *Jonathan*, b. March 7, 1782 ; d. Mar. 11, 1782.

402. 3. *Micah*, b. Feb. 27, 1783 ; m. Hannah Turner

Beard of Gardner.

403. 4. *Samuel*, b. Feb. 20, 1785 ; d. April 18, 1785.

404. 5. *Prudence*, b. Jan. 26, 1786 ; m. 1st Norcross who went south for his health and d. in Alabama, 2d m. Stephen Field of Waterbury Vt. about 1832 ; had no children. She d. April 11, 1840, at Waterbury, Vt.

405. 6. *Rhoda*, b. Feb. 1, 1788 ; m. John Emory of Barre Vt. and had *Orlinzo* and *Clarissa*, and d. soon after.

406. 7. *Mehetable*, b. Dec. 30, 1789 ; m.—;d. 1826.

407. 8. *Judith*, b. June 15, 1792 ; d. Aug. 10, 1796.

408. 9. *Anna*, b. Oct. 5, 1794 ; m. Thomas Town.

409. 10. *Isaac*, b. Sept. 13, 1796 ; m. Sally Page.

410. 11. *Ira*, b. Nov. 15, 1798 ; d. Nov. 23, 1798.

411. 12. *Jonas*, b. April 28, 1800 ; m. Abadil Allbe.

(230) (VI) ISAAC GALE, m. Nov. 19, 1782, ELIZABETH, dau. of Jonathan Cutler of Royalston who died Sept. 27, 1826, aged 90 years. In the settlement of his father's estate, Isaac had for his share ½ of the dwelling house, ½ of the saw mill and ¼ of the grist mill, and was a prominent citizen of Royalston until his death which occurred Jan. 12, 1826. His wife Elizabeth was b. Oct. 29, 1762 and died Dec. 23, 1826.—Their Children were :

412. 1. *Mehetable*, b. Oct. 5, 1783 ; and m. Nov. 13, 1802 David Holman, but had no children. She d. Oct. 16, 1847.

413. 2. *A son* and *daughter*, twins, b. March 12, 1785, and son d. 23d, and dau. 25th, Dec. of same year.

414. 3. *Hannah*, b. Oct. 29, 1788 ; d. Nov. 13, 1789.

415. 4. *Isaac*, b. Sept. 5, 1790 ; m. Rhoda Jacobs.

416. 5. *Jonathan*, b. Sept. 5, 1790, twins with Isaac ;

m. Sept. 2, 1817 Martha Pierce.

417. 6.   *Elizabeth*, b. Oct. 28, 1797 ; m. Dec. 10, 1816, Charles Bruce and d. March 3, 1831. She had chil. Otis b. Oct. 5, 1820 and *Martha*, b. Aug. 7, 1822.

418. 7.   *Otis*, b. Sept. 1, 1801 ; m. Elmira Sherwin.

419. 8.   *Cynthia*, b. Sept. 1, 1801, twins with Otis, m. Jan. 9, 1827 Elijah B. Newton, add d. Apr. 3, 1829. She had chil. *Charles Otis*, b. March 28, 1829.

420. 9.   *Sally*, b. June 27, 1806 ; m. Jan. 16, 1827, Carlton Bartlet, but had no children ; she d. July 5, 1863.

(231) VI JONATHAN GALE, of Royalston m. 1st, May 11, 1786 RHODA BAKER. She d. Dec. 6, 1818 aged 56, and he m. 2d SUSANAH MATHEWS Sept. 9, 1819. He d. Aug. 19, 1833, but the widow still survives and resides at Auburn N. Y.

He entered the 3d Reg. as a volunteer from Royalston, in the Revolutionary service, and received from that town a bounty of $50. His widow now draws a pension for his Revolutionary services. Children :

421. 1.   *Isaac*, b. Feb. 23, 1787 ; m. Tamar Goddard.

422. 2.   *Abigail*, b. June. 27, 1789 ; m. Moses Tylor, of Richmond N. H.

423. 3.   *Rhoda*, b. 1791 ; d. 1792.

424. 4.   *Jonathan*, b. 1793 ; d. 1795.

425. 5.   *Rhoda*, b. July 15, 1798 ; m. Nathaniel Godard Esq. of Millbury.

426. 6.   *Jonathan*. b. July 10, 1800 ; d. July 17. 1817.

427. 7.   *Dulcina*, b. Aug 29, 1802 ; m. Cyrus Davis of

Royalston.

428. 8. *Juda*, b. Sept. 13, 1804 ; m. Rev. Whitman Metcalf, of Nonday, N, Y.

429. 9. *Roxana*. b. April 29, 1807 ; m. Lorenzo Davis of Royalston. He moved to Putney, Vt. where he d. in 1860.

430. 10. *Lucy*, *W.* b. June 22, 1821 ; m. Benj. Humes and d. March 22, 1852.

431. 11. *Susan E.* b. June 18, 1823 ; m. Benj. Humes ; she d. Sept. 22, 1858.

432. 12. *Hannah*, *M.* b. Jan. 1, 1825 ; m. Wm. Brierly of Auburn N. Y.

433. 13. *James F.* b. April 27, 1827 ; and now resides in Worcester, and is a machinist.

(237) (VI) Dr. JAMES GALE, m. 1800. Elsea Schapmos, of Cairo, Green County, N. Y. in which town he had previously settled as a practicing physician. His wife d. in Nov. 1817, after the birth of six children, and sometime after her d. he m. 2d, widow Rebecca England, and removed to N. Y. city, where he d. in Nov. 1823 but had no children by his second wife.

Dr. Gale was an influential man in the region of Cairo, and left a family of considerable prominence at the present day. Children :

434. 1. *William*, *S.* b. Jan. 2, 1801 ; m. Hannah Folon.

435. 2. *Richard*, b. Nov. 1802 : m. Sarah Murdock.

436. 3. *Helen*, b.— still unmarried and resides with her brother-in-law and sister Mr. and Mrs. Read.

437. 4. *Hester*, b.—m. Thos. W. Read Esq. a native of England, an excellent scholar, to whom the writer is indebted for the history of Dr. Gale's fami-

ly as here given. They resided in Catskill Green County, N. Y. and have one daughter Kate.

438. 5. *Nancy*, b.—m. Benjamin Van Orden and resides in Catskill, but have no children.

439. 6. *Christiana*, b.—m. Samuel Goodsell of Conn. and resides in West Camp, Ulster Co. N. Y. They have the following children of ages from 25 to 16 years: *Hester*, *Van Orden*, *Helen*, *Sherman*, *Elsea*, and *Nancy*.

(240) (VI) DANIEL PECK, m. in 1795 DELIA GALE and resided in Royalston. He died Oct. 5, 1839 and his widow Sept. 2, 1848. Children :

440. 1. *Rectyna*, b. Feb. 13, 1796 ; m. March 4, 1817.

441. 2. *Chancy*, b. March 2, 1797 ; m. had a family and was residing in Boston in 1864.

442. 3. *Pomeroy*, b. Feb. 16, 1799 ; m. raised a family and d. in Aug. 1854.

443. 4. *Harriet*, b. Sept. 13, 1800, m. Oct. 11, 1821.

444. 5. *Mary*, b. Oct. 19, 1802 ; m. March 1830 ; d. Sept. 15, 1838.

445. 6. *Lyman*, b. Feb. 11, 1804 ; m. Jan. 21, 1829 ; d. Dec. 1, 1862.

446. 7. *Sullivan*, b. March 27, 1806 ; m. May 29, 1831.

447. 8. *Hannah F.* b. May 30, 1809 ; m. May 1829 ; d. May 13, 1851.

448. 9. *Elvira*, b. May, 19, 1811 ; m. Oct. 1837.

449. 10. *Elsea S.* b. March 11, 1813 ; d. June 26, 1838.

450. 11. *Delia*, b. Jan. 19, 1815 ; m. Sept. 1835.

451. 12. *Huldah C.* b. Feb. 9, 1817.

452. 13. *Augusta M.* b. April 13, 1820 ; m. Nov. 1840, d. Sept. 6, 1847.

(258) VI. Dea. SOLOMON GALE, of Bennington
Vt., was m. 1st, 1787, to Rachel Woodard of Sutton who
was b. 1767. She d. Dec. 27, 1799, when he m. 2d, July
6, 1800, Phebe Hays, who was b. Feb. 13, 1779 and d.
Oct. 10, 1847. Solomon d. Aug. 13, 1845. After his first
marriage he removed to Stratton Vt. and soon after to
Hoosick N.Y. and then to Bennington Vt. where he probably was located at the time of his death. He was a very
devoted member of the Baptist Church and for several
years a prominent Deacon in that church. The date of
his removal to Bennington is not known by his descendants, but his son Isaac was born there in 1801 and it is
believed that he resided there at last from that time to his
death. Children:

453. 1. *Nehemiah*, b. Aug. 24, 1788 ; m. Oct· 10, 1810,
Lucy Parker and d. June 9, 1844.

454. 2. *Esther*, b. July 15, 1795, m. Jan. 23, 1815, Ira
Wood . Her husband is dead and she resides in
Boston.

455. 3. *Betsey*, b. Dec. 29, 1798 ; d. June 20, 1820.

456. 4. *Isaac*, b. June 17, 1801 ; m. Jan. 1824, Lydia
Gardner. ·

457. 5. *Solomon*, b. Jan. 10, 1803 ; d, Oct. 25, 1805.

458. 6. *Sabrina*, b. Jan. 2, 1806 ; m. April 1, 1831, Elijah Harrington.

459. 7. *Laura*, b. Jan. 28, 1808 ; m. May 3, 1829, Eli-
as Johnson. She had a son ꝑin U. S. Navy in
1865.

460. 8. *Solomon*, b. Oct. 10, 1810 ; m. Dec. 28, 1835,
Emily Stone.

461. 9. *Harriet D.* b. Sept. 14, 1814 ; m. Sept. 1848,
Austin Jones.

462. 10. *Ansel Hays*, b, Feb. 16, 1817 ; m. Jan. 8, 1850, Amanda E. Spencer.

463. 11. *Maria*, b. May 10, 1819 ; m. Nov. 20, 1836, James Wager.

(26) VI JONAS GALE, m. Nov. 1, 1795 ELIZ-ABETH G ROUSE, of Westboro, Jonas d. at Millbury Nov. 21, 1814 and Elizabeth at Washington D. C. June 8, 1850. He occupied his father's homestead, and was highly esteemed for his many virtues. Children :

464. 1. *Nancy*, b. Aug. 11, 1796 ; d. Nov. 22, 1814.

465. 2. *Lucy*, b. May 3, 1798 : m. Oct. 8, 1820 ; Dr. Benjamin Pond M. D. of Westboro, who d. June 7, 1857. she d. Feb. 3, 1830. They had *Joseph C.* b. April 28, 1829 ; and d. Jan. 25, 1830.

466. 3. *Leonard D.* b. July 25, 1800 ; m. Anna E. Smith.

467. 4. *Philenia*, b. Aug. 3, 1802 ; d. March 2, 1804.

468. 5. *Philenia*, b. March 6, 1804 ; d. Jan. 23, 1815.

469. 6. *Benjamin A.* b. April 3, 1806 ; d. Jan. 29, 1808.

470. 7. *Jonas R.* b. March 30, 1808 ; m. Cynthia M. Adams.

471. 8. *Elizabeth Grout*, b. July 29, 1810 ; and in 1855 resided unm. at Washington D. C. and in 1864 in Brooklyn N. Y. Elizabeth has a good Education and conversational powers and has devoted much attention to genealogy, and particularly to the ancestors of her mother. She has also sacrificed her health and personal happiness to the attentive care of her aged mother who died in 1850.

(263) VI. HENRY DWINEL, who m. TAMER,

dau. of Nehemiah Gale of Millbury, in 1790, was b. at
Sutton, Feb. 22, 1762. He entered service in the Revolutionary war in 1778, was at the battle of Stony Point,
. at West Point when Andre was hung, and then served
in the south during the balance of the war. He resided
in Sutton until 1800 and then removed to Albany N. Y.
where he d. Oct. 17, 1805. After his death, TAMER, m.
2d Levi Page of Coventry, Ct. Jan. 10, 1810. She d. at
N. Y. city Feb. 12, 1853 aged 82 years. Children :

472. 1. *Elbridge Gerry*, b. July 25, 1791 ; m. Sarah
S. Nichols of Waterbury Ct., in 1811, and removed fo N. Y. city in 1816 where he d. in 1827.
He studied medicine in Albany N. Y. and had a
large practice until his death, had the following
1. *John*, d. in infancy. 2. *John Henry*, b.
1812.; m. Harriet Baldwin. 3. *Sylvester
Nichols*,—d. 1861. 4. *Elbridge Garry*, b.—
m. Mary Lawton. 5. *Harriet*. 6. *William*,
an Episcopal minister at Red Bank N. J. 7.
Charles, b. 1826 ; d. 1834.

473. 2. *Hannah*, b. Nov. 23, 1793 ; m. Enos Baldwin
of Albany N. Y.

474. 3. *Harriet*, b. 1795 ; m. Stephens Van Schaick of
Albany N. Y.

475. 4. *Nancy*, b. 1796 ; m. John L. D. Matthias of
Rochester, N. Y.

476. 5. *Henry Gale*, b. in Albany N. Y. Sept. 17,1804;
m. Aug. 5, 1845, Anna Maria Newcomb, of Albany N. Y. He removed to N. Y. city in child-
hood where he has ever since resided, and in
1864 was at 51 St. Marks Place. He graduated
M. D. in the Medical Dept. of the University of

N. Y. city in 1826 and has ever since practised
Medicine.   In 1862 he published the geneaology
of the Druniel or Dunnel Family.   Had children:
1. *Hahneman,* b. Oct. 29, 1846 , d. young. 2.
Harry Newcomb, b. July 17, 1848. 3. *Ellen
Berry,* b. Aug. 17, 1855 ; d. Nov. 10, 1860.

477. 6.   *William* (*Page*), b. Jan. 1811; was a distinguished artist in Italy in 1855. and in 1864 lived
in N. J.

478. 7. *Mary,* b. 1813 : d, Nov. 1818.

(264) VI Dr. RUFUS GALE, of Madison m.about
1797 Lovisa Livermore of Leicester. and soon after removed west, first to Genesee N. Y. and afterwards to Indiana and settled at Madison on the Ohio river.   The
country being new he passed down the Ohio to Madison
in an ark the style in those early days.   His first wife
died Dec. 1800 and he m. 2d Widow Knox but had no
children by her.   Rufus became a wealthy land holder
and in the latter part of his life a Thompsonian Physician.
We have no farther record of him.   In the Livermore
geneology he is called Abner Gale.   Child:

479. 1.   *Elmond,* b. about 1798.   He married at Madison, Ia. and had a family.   His business was bny-
ing and packing pork.   We have no records of
his family nor of him.

(266) VI ISAAC GALE, of Sutton, m. 1803 Persis
Stiles dau. of Joshua and Abigail (Gale) Styles of Princeton.   They resided some five years in Sutton and a few
years in Douglass, where in 1818 they removed to Madison in the State of Indiana.   Isaac died in the latter state
Jan. 21, 1831 and his wife Jan. 26, 1847.   Isaac did not

remain long in Madison but removed and settled at or near Columbus, Bartholoeew Co. Ia. where he probably died. Children :

480. 1. *Harriet Stiles,* b. July 14, 1804 ; m. Geo. Cummings and d. Sept. 14, 1827.

481. 2. *Sophrona,* b. Sept. 21, 1806 ; d. Sept. 5, 1807.

482. 3. *Alonzo,* b. March 24, 1809 ; m. 1st, Matilda Robinson, who d. March 12,1835 when he m. 2d, Ruth Jacobs, May 10 1835, no children by 2d m. By the first marriage he had 1st, *Virgil P.* b, May 23, 1832 ; 2d, *Joseph Elona,* b. Aug. 23, 1834.

483. 4. *Joseph Edwin,* b. Feb. 24 1811 ; d. May 28, 1831, unm.

484. 5. *Andras Waters,* b. May 24, 1813 ; and d. same year, May 30.

485. 6. *Martha Ann,* b. July 12, 1814 ; m. Joseph Robinson, Feb. 8, 1836, had six children.

486. 7. *Mary,*
487. 8. *Maria,* } b. 1817 ; d. 1818.

488. 9. *Josephine Fasset,* b. Aug. 21 1820, d. 1826.

(272) VI. JOHN GALE, of Barre Vt. m. EUNICE

Bancroft at Warwick Mass. in 1801. Children :

489. I. *Clarissa,* b. Sept. 11, 1802.

490. 2. *Gardner,* b. March 13, 1804.

491. 3. *Luthera,* b. June 2, 1806.

492. 4. *Augusta,* b. Sept.9,1808.

493. 5. *John,* b. Nov. 25, 1811.

494. 6. *William,* b. Feb. 28, 1813.

495. 7. *Maria,* b May 5, 1814.

496. 8. *Lewis,* b. July 22, 1817.

497. 9. *Eunice Sabrina,* b. Sept. 17, 1824.

(275) VI. SAWIN GALE. of Barre Vt. m.Jan. 12, 1804 BETSEY BLANCHARD of Barre Vt. who was born Dec. 12, 1784. He was a prominant Farmer in that town and d. May 24, 1846, his wife d.Feb. 16, 1842. His first two children were born in Williamston Vt.where they lived a short time. Children :

498. 1. *Francis*, b. Feb. 14, 1805, m. Patience Scott.
499. 2. *Pressen*, b. March 17, 1807 ; m. Sarah Earl.
500. 3. *Polly*, b. March 17, 1807.
501. 4. *Elvira*, b. Dec. 22, 1819 ; d. Feb. 25, 1821.
502. 5. *Clark* b. May 29, 1822 ; m. Cornelia M.Brooks.
503. 6. *Calista*, b. May 29, 1822.

(278) VI ABRAHAM GALE, of Barre Vt. m. at Warwick, Jan. 10, 1808 CLARISSA BENCROFT of the latter town, who was b. at that place Aug. 22, 1789. She. d. March 12, 1842, and he m, 2d, Nov. 20, 1843, at Barre Vt. Hannah Elmer. He d. Nov. 1, 1862.

Abraham lived in Craftsbury Vt. where his first child was born; at Irasburgh Vt. when the second was born soon after which, he settled at Barre Vt when he died. Children :

504. 1. *Fred*, b. April 10, 1809.
505. 2. *Julius C.* b. July 9, 1811 ; m. Almira C. Drury.
506. 3. *Royal C.* b. May 28,1815 ; m. Chastina Twing,
507. 4. *Louisa M.* b. Oct. 5, 1818 ; m. Denison Taft.
508. 5. *Clarissa M.* b. May 18, 1821 ; d. July 20, 1825.
509. 6. *Emily L.* b. Aug. 18, 1823 ; m. Edmond Pope.
510. 7. *Clarissa M.* b. Nov. 3, 1827 ; m. Jude Town.
511. 8. *Lucy A.* b. Jan. 8, 1830 ; m. George W. Smith.
512. 9. *John B.* b. Nov. 28, 1832 ; d. April 1833.

(279) VI ISAAC GALE, of Goshen Vt. m. Eliza

1st, Annis, March, 1806, of Randolph Vt. Children:

513. 1. *Squire*, b. 1807,—; d, March 1, 1844.

514. 2. *Silas D.* b. Sept. 5, 1809 ; m. at Goshen Vt. Mariah Blood, d. April 4, 1861.

515. 3. *Isaac*, b. April 11, 1811 ; m. Dec. 5, 1833, Mary Ann Fitts of Goshen, Vt.

516. 4. *Curtis A.* b. April 11, 1816 ; m. April 21, 1839, at Pittsford Vt. Hariette Mead.

517. 5. *Elisha Warren*, b. June 25, 1820, m. Oct. 27, 1842, Olive Relief Harrison.

518. 6. *Augustus*, b.—

519. 7. *Martha*, b.—; d. Dec. 12, 1851.

(282) VI AMOS CURTIS GALE, of Stanstead, Canada East, m. Dec. 4, 1818 RHODA ROYCE, in Sharon, Vt. She was b. in Marlow N.H. Nov. 24, 1787. They removed to Williamstown Vt. where they resided until about 1825 when they removed to Stanstead, Canada. Children:

520. 1. *Laurena*, b. Aug. 15, 1819 ; m. 1st John H. Miller, Dec. 6, 1837, who d. Sept. 1845, when She m. 2d Lemuel Stevens, of Stanstead Ca. Oct. 1849; Child. 1st *Elisha*, b. Aug. 9, 1840. 2. *John A.* b. Sept. 19, 1844 : 3. *Charles*, b. Oct. 6, 1850.

521. 2. *Warren*, b. Oct. 21, 1821.

522. 3. *George*, b. Feb. 28, 1824 ; m. Dorothy Davis.

523. 4. *Martha*, b. April 13, 1828 ; d. May 28. 1833.

524. 5. *Mary*, b. April 13. 1828 ; d. April 23, 1828 ; twin with Martha.

525. 6. *Mary*, b. July 8, 1831.

526. 7. *Eunice*, b. July 8, 1831 ; d. July 2, 1833.

527. 8. *Andrew*, b. March 8, 1836.

(284.) VI. JOHN GALE, of Plattsburgh, N. Y. m.
.and lived in E. Troy, Vt., 1800, where he discovered the
bed of iron ore which has been extensively worked since.
He removed to Plattsburgh, N. Y., probably about the
commencement of the war of 1812, and at the time our
army was stationed there in 1814, he baked bread for the
the army under a contract. Subsequently he removed to
Ohio where he d. about 1840. John's wife d. soon after
the war. Children :

528. 1. *John*, b. 1800.
529. 2. *Stillman*, b. ; probably d. at Plattsburg.
530. 3. *Martin*, b.—; lives at Cleveland, Ohio.
531. 4. *Abram Rice*, b. June 2, 1811 ; m. Harriet Coop-
    er.

(290.) VI. CAPT. JOHN GALE, of Barnard, Vt.,
m. NANCY—. He lived sometime in Marlow, N. H., and
then removed to Barnard, Vt. Children :

532. 1. *Amos*, b. at Marlow, N. H. 1797 ; d. at. Low-
    ell, Oct. 15, 1847 ; called a "laborer."
533. 2. *Emery*, b.—
534. 3. *John*, b.—
535. 4. *Gilman*, b.—
536. 5. *Milton*, b. at Marlow, N. H., Jan. 12, 1809 ;
    m. Margaret M. Gault.
537. 6. *Josiah*, b.—
538. 7. *Jeremiah*, b.—
539. 8. *Daniel*, b.—
540. 9. *Addia*, b.—; m. Paul Crowell.
541. 10. *Louisa*. b.—; m. Charles Greenlief.
542. 11. *Hannah*, b.—; m. C. P. Adams.

(296.) VI. EBENEZER BROOKS GALE, of
Barre, Vt. m. He was a prominent citizen of Barre, Vt.
and d. there Sept. 13, 1846. Children :

543. 1. *George,* b. July 7, 1799 ; m. Harriet Stone.

544. 2. *Brooks,* b. April 2, 1802 ; m.—and had *De-*
witt C. b. Oct. 31, 1832, and *Horace H.* b. Oct.
3, 1845.

545. 3. *Orlando Converse* b. July 8, 1810 ; m. and had
Converse A. April 1.1855. There were also three
daughters,but we have failed to obtain their names,

(307.) VI. EBENEZER GALE, of Windham, Vt.
m. MARY— and moved to Vt. about 1805. The widow
was alive in 1865 and resided at Weston, Vt. She dic-
ated the following record : Children:

546. 1. *Gordon Hutchins,* b. Dec. 20, 1805 ; m. Orpha
Holbrook.

547. 2. *Emiline,* b. June 9, 1810 ; m. Nov. 9, 1842.

548. 3. *Gardner,* b. Feb. 5, 1812 ; m. June 30, 1836.

549. 4. *Rosetta Ann,* b. June 3,1814 ; m.Nov. 29,1843.

550. 5. *Elijah,* b. April 20, 1816 ; m. June 7. 1842; d.
Sept. 9, 1847.

551. 6. *Ira Willard,* b. July 27,1818 ; m. May 3,1848.

552. 7. *Esther,* b. Sept. 20, 1820 ; m. Sept. 19,1849.,

553. 8. *Mary Lomira,* b. Dec. 5, 1822 ; m. Nov. 25,
1847.

554. 9. *Ebenezer Warren,* b. Nov. 22, 1824 ; m. Mar.
12, 1849.

555. 10. *Nelson Barton,* b. Oct. 23, 1826, m. Dec. 4,
1850.

(309.) VI. ALVAN GALE, of Northampton, m.
1816, SOPHIA Reynolds. Children :

556.   1.   *William D.* b. March 7, 1818.
557.   2.   *Susan, B.* b. Jan. 28, 1820.
558.   3.   *Harriet,* b. Aug. 8, 1822.
559.   4.   *Charles,* b. Dec. 29, 1823 ; d. Sept 21.
560.   5.   *Mary Ann,* b. March 5, 1828.
561.   6.   *Sophia,* b. Aug. 16, 1830.
562.   7.   *Charles A.* b. Nov. 24, 1834.
563.   8.   *Annie M.* b. May 23, 1839.
564.   9.   *Otho Gregory,* b. March 4, 1842.   He enlisted
            in the U. S. service in the late rebellion and was
            wounded on the Rapidan.

(310.)   VI.   ENOCH   GALE, of Piqua, Ohio, m.
Eunice Fisher, of Walpole, N. H., June 3, 1822.   He is
a respectable farmer in Piqua, Ohio, but formerly resided
in Hadley.   Children :
565.   1.   *George Fisher,* b, March 16, 1823 ; m. Mary
            D. Williams.
566.   2.   *Mary,* b. Feb. 12, 1825 ; d. 27th of next month.
567.   3.   *Julia Maria,* b. Jan. 27, 1826.
568.   4.   *Alvan T.* b. Feb. 5, 1828.
569.   5.   *Hannah,* b. April 6, 1830 ; d. Oct. 4, 1836.
570.   6.   *Edward,* b. March 25. 1832 ; d. Nov. 26.
571:   7.   *Edwin D.* b. Sept. 26. 1833 ; d. Oct. 25, 1834:

(315.)   VI.   ABRAHAM GALE, m. Mary B. Adams
of Watertown.   Children :
572,   1,   *Harriet,* b,—
573,   2,   *Oliver Perry,* b.—
574,   3,   *Levi,* b,—
575,   4,   *Wakeman,* b,—

(322)   VI.   WILLIAM GALE, of Charlton, m, Dec.
2, 1832, Emiline Dodge, of the same town,   Children :

576. 1. *Helen Amanda,* b. Oct. 5, 1833.
577. 2. *William Franklin,* b. July 30, 1837.
578. 3. *Susan Emiline,* b. Oct. 6, 1844.
579. 4. *Lorinda Augusta,* b. May 14, 1847.
580. 5. *Mary Ella,* b. March 27,1852 ; d. Feb. 4,1854.
581. 6. *Emogene,* b. April 29, 1856.

(319,) Vl, FRANKLIN GALE,of Columbus,Ohio,
m. He is an attorney at law.

SEVENTH GENERATION.

(328.) VII. Maj. AMORY GALE, of Warick, m.
Sept. 24, 1797, Lucinda Rich and d. Sept. 20, 1852.
He was a prominent man, in the town, three years one
of the Selectmen and Major in the militia. Children:
582. 1. *Amory,* b. Oct. 15, 1800 ; m. Martha Leland,
of Warwick.
583. 2. *Jacob R.* b. July 1, 1802 ; *m.* Alma Leland.
584. 3. *Jonathan,* b. May 8, 1804 ; d. Aug. 7, 1846.
585. 4. *Lucinda,* b. Sept. 13, 1808 ; m. Jonas Ben-
craft and lives in Winchester, N. H.
586. 5. *Charles,* b. June 9, 1811; d. Aug. 3, 1814.
587. 6. *Mary,* b. July 5, 1814.

(331.) VII. IRA GALE,of Atlas, Mich, m. in 1809,
Clarissa Sargent, of Putney, Vt., sister of Judge Sargent, of Washington D. C., the Com. of Customs in
in the U. S. Treasurer's Office, in 1864.
After the death of his father, Ira occupied the Homestead at Warwick for a few years and then transferred it
to his oldest brother, Amory, and afterwards carried on

H1

609. 5. *Mary*, b. 1823; d. June 23, 1844 at Northampton, was a teacher.

(338) VII JESSE GALE of Petersham, m. *Hannah* —. His family was probably b. in Heath. We have only two of the family. Children:

610. 1. *Martha M.* b. 1811; d. Feb. 23 1858.
611. 2. *Hannah A.* b.—; m. Nov. 27, 1845 Parmaly Carlton, a farmer.

(340) VII Dr. STEPHEN GALE of Portland, Me. m. Martha A. Hersey of Hingham. Children:

612. 1. *Albert H.* b.—
613. 2. *Edward T.* b.—
614. 3. *Stephen* b.—
515. 4. *Martha E.* b.—
616. 5. *Elizabeth H.* b.—
617. 6. *Mary C.* b.—

(341) VII GEORGE GALE, of Salem m. Joanna Glazier, of Ipswich in 1813, and d. in 1819. He served in the war of 1812, against England and was wounded in the side at the explosion of a magazine at the capture of York, Upper Canada, on the 27, April 1813 at the same time that Gen. Pike, the comander of our forces was killed. Children:

618. 1. *Sarah Ann*, b. June 8, 1815 .
619. 2. *George Winslow*, b. April 20, 1817.
620. 3. *Rebecca Dunham*, b. April 20. 1819 .

(342) VII DANIEL GALE, of Plymouth m. 1st ELIZABETH WINSLOW. She had one dau. and d. when he m. 2d. ——Samson :

The family removed to Ill. where the father, mother and

Vt., where Daniel d. Aug. 27, 1847. Clarissa d. at Warwick, April 6, 1820. Children :

599. 1. *Hannah H.* b. Jan 13, 1808 ; m. 1829, Clement S. Johnson. They had five children but only a son and daughter alive who are married and living in Corunna, Mich., near their father.

600. 2. *Charles D.* b. March 15, 1809 m. June 1850, Harriet L. Moore and lives in Sterling Mass. They have sons *Edward* and *John.* Charles is a farmer.

601. 3. *Horatio H.* b. Feb. 6, 1811 ; m. Aug. 22, 1839, Fidelia D. Cushing.

602. 4. *Clarissa L.* b. Feb. 2, 1813 ; m. Jan. 1, 1834, Alonzo L. Baker.

603. 5. *Absalom B.* b. Dec. 31, 1814 ; m. Nov. 20, 1848, Louisa Atherton. She d. and he m. Ellen Whitney of Harvard, where he resided in 1865. He had by Louisa. sons *Henry* and *George.*

604. 6. *Elizabeth L.* b. Nov. 13, 1816 ; d. March 27, 1818.

(337) VII LUTHER GALE, of Heath. He had wife, Sarah, if we have the records correct, for we could obtain nothing of the descendents. His family were born in Heath. Children :

605. 1. *Otis,* b. 1806 ; d. in Heath Sept. 29, 1856.

606. 2. *George C.* b. —; m. Nov. 10, 1858, Lucy A. Farnsworth.

607. 3. *Daniel,* b.—; m. in Rowe, May 24, 1843 Nancy Dodge.

608. 4. *Elizabeth S.* b.—; m. Sept. 7, 1849, Levi S. Rust, of W. Springfield.

627. 2. *Prudence Ames,* b.—
628. 3. *Abner Havens,* b.—
629. 4. *Hannah,* b.—m. in Ashland June 12, 1860, George E. Whitemore.

(357) VII ELISHA GALE, of Worcester m. Nov. 3, 1831, at Shrewsbury, ABIGAIL CUTLER WHITNEY, who was b. Jan. 25, 1813, and d. Oct. 16, 1864. He moved from Shrewsbury to Worcester in 1836. Children :

630. 1. *Eliza Abigail,* b. Jan. 26, 1834 ; d. Dec. 4, 1840.
631. 2. *Lomira Ellen,* b. Jan. 18, 1836 ; m. Nov. 14, 1861, Marcus Morton Mills, of Springfield.
632. 3. *Sarah Adaline,* b. March 24, 1839 ; d. Feb. 6, 1856.
633. 4. *Caroline Abby,* b. Oct 28, 1841.
634. 5. *Alfred Denny,* b. Oct. 18, 1843.
635. 6. *Mary Utley,* b. Sept. 14, 1846; d. Jan. 20, 1852.

(358) VII JOHN WHITTEMORE, of —— m. LOUISA GALE, who was b. March 1804. Children :

636. 1. *Susan* b. 1831; m. William Moulton and had *Susan.* b. 1856. *Anna* b. 1858 ; *Alice,* b. 1863.
637. 2. *Thomas,* b. 1834 ; m. Louisa Rice of Framingham and had Arthur, b. 1859 ; *Fredrick* b. 1862.
638. 3. *George,* b. 1836.
639. 4. *Marie,* b. 1840.
640. 5. *Caroline,* b. 1842.
641. 6. *John,* b. 1846.

(361) VII REV. NAHUM GALE, D.D. of Lee; m.

. . . . Ashland, June 18, 1869.

. . . . LEWIS CATE, of Worcester m. Nov.
. . . . A . . . . ELIZA WHITNEY, who
. . . . d. Oct. 16, 1864. He moved
. . . . Worcester . 1846. Children :

. . . . Edward G. . . . . b. . . ; d. Dec. 5,
. . . .

. . . 2. . . . . . b. Jan. 18, 1836; m. Nov. 14,
. . . . Marcus Morton Mills, of Springfield.

. . . 3. . . . . . . b. March 24, 1839 ; d. Feb. 6,
. . . .

. . . . b. Nov. . 1842.
. . . . 1843.

. . . . 1846; d. Jan. 20.

. . . . WHITMORE, of . . . . .
. . . . March 1864. Children .

. . . . 1846 . . . . . William Morse . . .
. . . . 1868 . . . .

6. . . . . . . b. 18 . . . . . . Abba Rice, of Framingham.
. . . . April 24, b. 1862.

835 . . . . . 1859.
3. . . . .
. . 5. . . . . . . 1842.
. . . .

only Yours
Nahum Gale

Aug. 10, 1843. MARTHA TYLER of East Windsor, Conn. who was b. Nov. 22, 1819, and was dau. of Rev. Bennet Tyler D.D. He prepared for college in Philips Academy, Andover, and entered Amherst College, where he graduated A. B. with honor in 1837. At East Windsor Theological Seminary, he took his Theological course and was ordained pastor of the Congregational Church at Ware, in 1842, where he continued until Aug. 1851, when he was called to the Theological Professorship, at East Windsor of Ecclesiastical history and Pastoral duty. In Aug. 1853 he resigned this post and was installed pastor of the Congregational Church at Lee, Mass. where he still remains.

He is called a good scholar, a sound Theologian and preacher of considerable eloquence and was honored by the degree of D.D. by William's College in 1858. Dr. Gale is a good writer and is the author of two question Books on Scriptural Biography, "Conversion through Personal Efforts," "The first year of the Pilgrims," and a "Memoir of the life of Rev. Bennet Tyler D. D." his father-in-law, prefacing Dr. Tyler's Theological Lectures. Dr. Gale has published, at the request of others, ten of his own sermons and public addresses. He was made one of the trustees of William's College in 1861 and his aid is generally solicited for the benevolent enterprises of the day. Children :

642. 1. *Edward Tyler.* b. Jan. 1845 ; d. Feb. 18, 1855.

643. 2. *William Cowper*, b. June 22, 1850.

644. 3. *Mary Williams*, b. Jan. 28. 1853 ; d. Feb. 15. 1855.

645. 4. *Bennet Tyler*, b. June 18, 1856.

(374) VII FREDRICK W. GALE, Esq. of Worcester, m. 1st. MARY S. UTLEY of Boston, who d. soon and he m. 2d. SARAH WHITNEY of Cambridge Feb. 16, 1852. On the 19th of the same month he made his will in which he provided

1. For the payment of all debts.

2. Gave the Orphan Home of Worcester $500.

3. Gave half brothers, Cyrus, George and Walter $500.

4. His niece, Marianne, dau. of Geo. Bamis of Northboro $500.

5. To John Crawford Wyman of Worcester $1000.

6. To Geo. Mondell of Washington D. C. $1000.

7. To M. Johnson Mondell of Boston, in trust for Harriet Eddy, $500.

8. To same, in trust for Mrs. Mary Lawton of Hardwick $500.

10. In case he left a wife and child or children the legacias to be void and the whole estate to go to wife and children.

He sailed to Europe with his wife Sarah and his dau *Florence* where he made a delightful tour but returning in the Steamer Arctic they were all lost at sea Sept. 27, 1854. The Will was proved and allowed! by the Probate Judge at Worcester, Dec. 5, 1854, but the property finally passed to his father Capt. Cyrus Gale.

Fredrick graduated at Harvard College, was admitted to the bar, and, for several years was a successful lawyer of St. Louis, Missouri. He then returned and settled and practised law in Worcester until he left for his European tour. He was an accomplished scholar, a sound lawyer and a gentleman of comprehensive mind, and his unfortu-

nate death shocked the whole community. Children ;
646. 1. *Elizabeth*, b. —; d. at 3 years of age.
647. 2. *Florence*, b. —; d. at sea Sept. 27, 1854.

(380) VII MAJ. WALTER GALE, of Northboro.
In July 1861 Mr. Gale enlisted as a private in Co. "C."
of the 15th Reg. of Massachusetts Vols. and was soon
after promoted to sergeant, Jan. 17, 1862 he was promoted to 2d Lieutenant, Oct. 24, 1862 to Captain and July
14, 1864 to Major, when he was ordered home in command of the Regiment, their three years term having expired.

Major Gale was in all the battles in which the Regi
ment was engaged during the three years and was twice
wounded.

We cannot better show the gallant services of Maj.
Gale, than by quoting from the report of the Adjutant General of Mass. for 1864, the services performed by the Reg.

"This Regiment (15th.) left the State August 8, 1861.
It was first engaged at Ball's Bluff, October 21, 1761
at battles of the Peninsula, Antietam and Fredricksburg
in 1862, and at Fredricksburg, Gettysburg, Bristow Sta-
tion and Robertson's Tavern in 1863. The history of
this regiment was brought up to Dec. 20, 1863, in my R
port of last year." * * * "On or about the 1st of May,
[1864] the campaign opened. A field return on that
day gave the strength of the Fifteenth Regiment present
for duty, as about three hundred officers and men ; of
t his number, two hundred and seventy-five were rank and
file." "In the battle of the Wilderness the regiment lost
about one-half its numbers in killed and wounded." "The
simple statement that in all the marches and battles from

the Rapidan to Petersburg, in which the second Corps was engaged, the Fifteenth Regiment bore its part, is in itself sufficient history."

"On the 22d of June, the regiment, dwindled down to five officers and about seventy muskets, confronted the enemy near the Jerusalem plank road, before Petersburg. A break or gap in the line of battle allowed the enemy to throw a large force on the flank and rear of the Second Division, Second Crops. Hidden from view by a dense undergrowth, the manoeuver was not comprehended until too late. The first intimation of the position of affairs, was a demand from the enemy to surrender. Taken thus by surprise, and overwhelmed by numbers, the remnant of the regiment was captured almost entire. Fonr officers and about sixty-five men were marched off prisoners of war; one officer and five men escaped to tell the story. This officer being wounded the same day, and shortly after the disaster above mentioned, the few remaining, increased somewhat by the arrival of convalescents were placed for a few days in another command, until officers of the regiment who had been wounded in the campaign, and who were on their way to the front from hospital, should arrive.

"On the 12th day of July, the regiment was ordered to proceed to the city of Worcester, Mass., to be mustered out of service, its term of three years having expired. One company, not mustered in until August 5, 1861, was left in the field; the balance, increased by detachment of sick and wounded men whose condition was such as enabled them to travel, men on detached service, etc., entered the city of Worcester about one hundred and fifty strong. The reception these men received will never be forgotten as long as life and memory shall be granted them."

"His excellency, Gov. Andrew, and staff, together with his honor Major Lincoln, and the city Authorities of Boston, welcomed the regiment home, thanking the men in eloquent words for the part they had borne in their country's struggle, and alluding with tender respect to the honored dead who had fallen in the fight. Both state and city were represented in the military escort and processions. The city, decorated with flags, wore a holiday aspect, and the crowded streets and welcoming shouts gave proof of the heartiness and spirit of the people."

The 28th of the same month the regiment was formally mustered out of service and Major Gale returned his sword to its scabbard.

(382) VII WILLIAM HENRY GALE, of Providence R. I. m. Oct. 25, 1846, ABBY POTTER BAKER, who was b. Nov. 22, 1817. William, by occupation is a builder. Children:

648. 1. *William Henry*. b. Nov. 22, 1847.
649. 2. *Charles Sheldon*, b. May 19, 1849; d. young.
650. 3. *Lydia Sheldon*, b. July 2, 1851.
651. 4. *Cyrus*, b. July 2, 1858.

(383) VII LAWSON WALLEN GALE, of Providence R. I. m. Nov. 6, 1843 MARY HOWARD, who was b. April 8, 1822. He is by occuparion a Butcher. Children:

652. 1. *Mary Josephine*, b, March 24, 1845; m. Feb. 8, 1864 George Webster of Providence R.I.
653. 2. *David Lawson*, b. April 6, 1852.
654. 3. *Ella Frances*, b. Sept. 5, 1853.

(376) VII JOHN WALLEN GALE, of Providence R. I. m. Dec. 3, 1846 ADELAIDE R. CALDER. who was b. June 8, 1827. Children :

655. 1. *Addie Calder*, b. Oct. 3, 1848.
656. 2. *Frank W.* b. Oct. 4.
657. 3. *George H.* b. Dec. 31,1862.

(383) VII DANA GALE, of Columbus Ia. m. May 1823, MARY, dr. of Dea. John McClellan of Sutton, Mary was b. June 28, 1796 and was second cousin to the very able and noted Maj. Gen. Geo. B. McClellan of the war of the great rebellion.

Dana emigrated to Indiana in 1819 and settled at Columbus, Bartholomew Co. when the country was a wilderness. Dana's house was the second one in the place and and no other one within ten miles. He spent four years in the country clearing land and part of the time teaching school when he returned to Mass. and married, and took his wife by sail vessel to Philadelphia, thence by stage to Pittsburg, and thence down the Ohio in a skiff to Madison Ia.

Dana became a prominent man of his county, and died at Columbus Nov. 29, 1861 leaving about $8000 which he willed mostly to his four younger sons. His first wife Mary died Nov. 30, 1836 and Dana m. 2d, Jan. 7, 1838 Sarah P. Lundbeck, of New Jersey, who was b. June 8, 1813, she died Feb. 3, 1847. Children :

658. 1. *Joseph Fasset*, b. Sept. 21, 1824 ; m. Jan. 1856 L. Sloan, and had *John Dana, Mary Jane*, and two others which are dead.
659. 2. *James McClellan* b. Dec. 20, 1825 ; m. Susan B. Boomer.

660. 3. *Jonathan Dana*, b. June 19, 1829; m. Dec.
1853 Leannah Parks, and had 1, *Mary Emma*,
b. May 23, 1855 ; 2d, *Dana* b. Sept 1856 ; d.
May 1857 ; 3, *George Frederick*, b. Feb.22,1859.

661. 4. *William John*, b. Dec. 3, 1838. In 1862 enlisted in the 12th Ill. Reg. twice taken prisoner
and served through the war.

662. 5. *George Washington*, b. Feb. 22, 1840, enlisted
in Feb. 1864 and d. in the service, of chronic Di-
arrhea in Sept. 1864.

663. 6. *Mary Jane*, b. Nov. 6, 1842 ; d. in Nine days.

664. 7. *Jarvis Heard*, b. Dec. 3, 1842, enlisted in 1862
in 12th Ill. Reg. and was in Gen. Sherman's campaign to N. C.

665. 8. *Henry Clay*, b. Aug. 30, 1844, d. Oct, 1. 1845.

(388) VII Dr. JARVIS H. GALE of Columbus
Ia. m. 1833 POLLY HATSHETT, who d. 1847 and Jarvis m.
2d, MARGARETT QUINN in 1849. Jarvis came west with
Dana his brother and lived with him until twenty years
of age when he learned to be a milwright and machinest.
Ho built some mills for others and three for himself. The
first burned, and the others undermined and went off in
freshets. These losses used up his property and he then
practiced a few years as a Thompsonian Physician.

In 1851 he removed to the extreme frontier of Iowa
into Fox Co. 100 miles N, W. of Ft. DesMoines, where
in Aug. 1352 he accidentally shot himself while out in
the lot shooting Prairie chickens. Children :

666. 1. *Adalinda Persis*, b. Nov. 1834 ; m. Davis in
1853.

667. 2. *Angeline L.* b. in 1836 ; m.— Bay.

668.　3.　*Elvira*, b. 1839.

669.　4.　*Martha*, b. 1846 ; m. Sept. 1864.

(390)　VII Col. JOTHAM GALE, of Millbury, m.
1817 Clarissa Gould of the same place. He came to
Millbury about 1812 and died March 15, 1857. He was
a prominent citizen of his town, a gunsmith by trade and
the town records says he was b. at Brimfield in 1793.
Such is the statement of his son, also but Bond's genealogy
places his birth-place at Stratford Conn. Children :

670.　1.　*Eliza*, b. May 1818 d. 1859.

671.　2.　*Jonathan G.* b. Aug 16, 1821, m. April 17, 1842,
　　　　Dorothy M. French, and has children; 1, *Geo. F.*
　　　　b. 1845 2. *Albert J.* b. 1850.

672.　3.　*Leander*, b. Jan. 1824, b. 1862 ; m. Feb. 2, 1845,
　　　　Martha P. Pierce.

673.　4.　*Julia Ann*, b. 1829; m. Jan. 1st, 1850, Sum-
　　　　ner R. Parker of Millbury.

674.　5.　*Charles S.* b. 1835 ; m. Nov. 21. 1854, Mary
E. Sawyer, both of Millbury.

(396)　VII SAMUEL GALE, of Albany N. Y. ;
m. 1844 a widow Fisk. He d. at Albany about 1848.
Children :

675.　1.　*Caroline Henrietta* b. 1845.

676.　2.　*Agnes*, b. 1847.

(398)　VII JACOB GALE, of Albany N. Y. m.
1839, Mary Mabin of Deleware Co. N. Y. and settled in
Albany where he owns and carries on a garden to supply
the city. Children :

677.　1.　*Lydia Hammon*, b. 1840 m. Rev, Charles
　　　　Shrimpton, of Stratford, Canada West.

878. 2. *Eugene* b. 1848.
879. 3. William Bardford, b. 1854. Several other
children were born but are now dead and their
names were not obtained by the Author.

(400) VII PETER GALE, of Waterbury Vt. m.
Jan. 27, 1805 HANNAH TOTTINGHAM of Westminster
Mass. HANNAH was daughter of Nathaniel! (b. June 10,
1740) and Esther (Brown) Tottingham, Son of Elisha (b.
Oct. 18, 1713) and Sarah, (Lawrence) Tottingham; Son
of Eliah, (b. Feb.28,1652 at Woburn Mass.) and Rebecca
Tottingham; Son of Henry and Ann Tottingham supposed
to have emigrated from near London and settled at Woburn previous to 1646. Henry was a devoted Puritan
and one of the bold petitioners for the liberty of Prophecy,
from Woburn, in 1653. Hannah had a vigorous mind,
fair common school education, an amiable disposition, was
an excellent mother, and a devoted christian of the Congregational church, and died strong in the faith and full
of hope, on the 24th of Feb. 1848, at Waterbury Vt.
  Peter Gale had a Massachusetts common school education up to 14 years of age, when he removed with his father to the wilds of Vt. after which his opportunities must
have been very limited. He, however, wrote a fair hand,
was a good reader and understood the rudiments of Grammar and Arithmetic. His memory was very retentive
and in old age he would repeat pages of his old "Parry's
Spelling Book and Grammar" that he had learned in boy-
hood days. On the establishment of the "Barre Library"
about 1800, he became a stockholder and industrious reader of history and biography, and possessing good conversational powers, was ever an intelligent and agreeable

companion, in social life. He united with the Congregational Church at Barre about the time of its formation and was very much devoted to the interest of religion until about 1830 when he became skeptical and the balance of his life was inclined to Deism. In moral life he was without a blemish to the day of his death, and his honesty was proverbial. Politically he was an old school Democrat, voted for Jefferson in 1804 and was an ardent supporter of Madison and the war of 1812. On the declaration of war he enlisted as one of the five "minute men" of Barre and was mustered into the U. S. service in the fall of that year and stationed at Swanton on the Canada line. Here he was attacked with the Measles which prostrated his health so that three months after his enlistment, he was discharged from the service, and sent home on foot, and as the small pay he had received from government was expended in his sickness, he begged his way home as a poor sick soldier. The incidents of that journey, of abuse from the Federalists and kind treatment from the Democrats, he often related to the Writer, to illustrate the party feeling of that day. When the British advanced to Plattsburg, he volunteered in the company from Burlington Vt. and reached that place in time to join in the battle of Sept. 13th, 1814 and was posted to guard the ford of the Saranac river.

On the 30th of April 1803, Peter leased of the School Trustees of Barre "the S. E. ¼ of the Second Division English School lot in Sd. Barre," as "long as water runs & timber grows" for the annual rent of $6,03½, and three years after he purchased of Ezekiel Wood an addition to his farm of about 14 acres, for $140, and received a Warrantee deed thereof.

H2

On this farm he erected substantial buildings and commenced life as a farmer,but his buildings having burned when the fire was running through the woods, and having lost his health in the service, he sold the farm for wooden ware in 1813 and removed to Burlington, where he opened a wooden ware shop and manufactured and sold such articles for several years. In 1817 he removed to Colchester Vt. where he and the most of his family were sick two years with the "fever and ague," then returned to Burlington and in 1824 removed to Waterbury Vt. and opened a new farm on the eastern slope of the Green mountains, in which town he died with "old age," Ang. 6. 1851, at the residence and under the attentive care of his daughter, Mrs. Henry. He lived to see his children all married and comfortably settled in life and then sunk to the earth like an "ear of corn fully ripe."

But the peculiarity of his life is yet to be stated, He was a natural mechanic. He could build a house, frame a barn, erect a saw-mill or set a horse-shoe. He often made ingenious articles of machinery and the latter part of his life experimented considerably on "flying machines," on the principle of the screw as a propeller, but [finally came to the very sensible conclusion that the air was made for birds but the earth for man. Although an attentive reader of the political newspapers of the day, he had no taste for political promotion and seldom would ˉaccept even a School District office. He had the following children :

680. 1. *Hiram*, b. Feb. 6, 1808 ; m. Sally Bryant.
681. 2. *Angeline*, b. Sept. 29, 1809 ; m. David Lord,
682. 3. *Matilda*, b. Aug.31,1811; m. James M.Henry.
683. 4. *Elvira*, b. Feb. 25, 1814 ; m. Elisha A. Town.

684. 5. *George*, b. Nov. 30, 1816; m. Gertrude Young.
685. 6, *Hannah*, b. Dec. 28, 1824; m. Samuel S. Luce.

(402) VII MICAH GALE, of Orange, Vt. m. Feb.
1, 1807 HANNAH TURNER BEARD, at Gardner Mass., who
was b. at Westminster Jan. 30, 1787, and resided in 1864
with her son G. Randall Gale at Orange, Vt. Micah, after his marriage, resided until about 1816 at Barre, Vt.
whence he removed and commenced farming in Orange,
Vt. when he died with cancer of the stomach Dec. 1, 1848,
leaving a respectable property. He was a very worthy
citizen and highly esteemed in the community where he
resided. Children :
686. 1. *Greenfield Randall*, b. Feb. 1, 1808 : m. Har-
         riet Newell Fifield.
687. 2. *Gustavus Orlinzo*, b. Dec. 7, 1809 ; m. Ma-
         hala Merrill.
688. 3. *Horace Palmer*, b. May 28, 1817 ; m. June
         11. 1840, Merandy Waterman of Orange, Vt. and
         had one child which d. in infancy. He is a
         farmer and still lives in Orange.
689. 4. *Sophrona Raymond*, b. April 12, 1855, m.
         1847 Anson Baley of Lowell, Mass. where he now
         resides as a merchant. They have children *Wal-
         ter* and *Carrie*.

(409) VII ISAAC GALE, m. Dec. 24, 1820, SALLY
PAGE of Burlington Vt. who was b. at Bradford Vt.
March 30, 1795, In 1821, Isaac removed to a farm in
Orange Vt. where he resided until 1843, when he removed to Barre, Vt. where the aged husband and wife, in
1865, were still enjoying the quiet of an unostentatious
life. Isaac served in the war of 1812 and received under

the act of 1855 a land warrant for 160 acres of land.
Children :

690. 1. *Lorinda*, b. Jan. 22, 1822 ; m. May 15, 1861
Denison Mora of Barre, Vt.

691. 2. *Sarah*, b. April 5, 1824 ; m. Elbertus T. Claflin Jan. 15. 1850, and had children, *Ellen* b. May
3, 1851, and *Elmer G.* b. Oct. 4, 1853. Elburtus
T. d. July 8, 1856.

692. 3. *Hawley*, b. Aug. 17, 1826 ; m. Anne Mower.

693. 4. *Susan P.* b. Feb. 10, 1829 ; m. June 19, 1855,
Harvey Marsh of Orange Vt. and has child :
Charles A. b. May 14, 1856.

694. 5. *Emma*, l. Sept. 25, 1831,

695. 6. *Caroline*, b. Dec. 24, 1833 : m. Oct. 16, 1855.
William L. Huntington of Montpelier Vt. where
he still resides and keeps a shop for the manufacture and sale of Harnesses. They have children :
Eva B. b. Aug. 1857 and *Flora A.* b. Sept. 3
1860.

696. 7. *Orrison I.* b. May 27, 1836 ; m. May 29, 1862,
Mary Anne Durkee of Williamstown Vt. b, June
28, 1837.

(411) VII Dea. JONAS GALE of Elmore Vt. m.
March 8, 1827, Abadil Allbe and lived, first in Hard
wick, Vt. nine years, second at Wolcott. Vt. nine years
where he was a Deacon in the Congregational Church, and
the balance of his life since his marriage in Elmore, Vt.
where he continued to reside in 1864. He is a man highly esteemed in social life and an independant Farmer.
Children:

697. 1. *Jasper N.* b. March 22, 1828, m. 1854 Mary
May Labarron and d. Aug. 20, 1855.

698. 2. *Lyman A.* b. Aug. 26, 1830 ; m. 1858, Elmira
     Wells and lives in Elmore, Vt.
699. 3. *Samantha A.* b. July 26, 1832.
700. 4. *Almeda A.* b. Aug. 27, 1835.
701. 5. *Justus F.* p. Sept. 21, 1837 ; was a volunteer
     in one of the Vt. Regiments and died in the ser-
     vice Sept. 19, 1863,
702. 6. *Charles T.* b. Aug. 27, 1845, and d. Aug. 30,
     1862.

(415) (VII) ISAAC GALE, of S. Royalston m. May
30, 1816, Rhoda Jacobs, who was born Aug. 12, 1794.
Isaac is a prominent farmer in South Royalston and the
one who inherited the sword of Capt. Isaac Gale; his great
Grand-father, which he so kindly donated to the Museum
of the Galesville University. Children :
703. 1. *Isaac,* b. June 17, 1817, and d. Jan, 15, 1854.
704. 2. *Joseph Jacobs,* b. April 27, 1822.
705. 3. *Julia Elizabeth,* b. Jan. 20, 1826, and d. April
     27, 1846.
706. 4. *Loving,* b. Feb. 15, 1828.
707. 5. *Oliver Hart well,* b. Aug. 19, 1833.

(416) (VII) JONATHAN GALE, of Royalston m.
Sept. 2, 1817 Martha Pierce d. Aug. 19, 1851. They
had children at Royalston :
708. 1. *James,* b. Jan. 17, 1818.
709. 2. *Mary,* b. Sept. 14, 1819.
710. 3. *George Pierce,* b. Jan. 22, 1822 ; d. Aug. 15,
     1851.
711. 4. *Jonathan Dana,* b. July 19, 1828.

418 (VII) OTIS GALE of S. Royalston m. May

18, 1823 ELMIRA SHERWIN. He was a prominent citizen and farmer in South Royalston in 1864 and very kindly collected and furnished the writer with the most of his information relating to the Gales of Royalston. Their children were:

712. 1. *Charles Augustus*, b. Aug. 15, 1824 ; m. July 14, 1851 Janett D. Bemas and has one dau. *Susan* b. Nov. 1, 1857. He resided in South Royalston in 1864.

713. 2. *Cynthia Newton*, b. March 4, 1829 ; m. July 14, 1851 Charles Wolppam, had no children and d. Oct. 12, 1861.

714. 3. *Otis Percival*, b. Sept. 4, 1849.

(421) VII ISAAC GALE, m. TAMAR GODDARD of Royalston March 10, 1813. He was a quiet industrious farmer and lived on his father's homestead in Royalston where he died Jan. 22, 1838. He attracted no particular attention of the world, but his personal virtues are developing in the high position to which his family has attained. Children:

715. 1. *David P.* b. Feb. 19, 1814 ; d. March 28, 1814.

716. 2. *Amory*, b. Aug. 24, 1815, m. Caroline E. Goddard.

717. 3. *Catharine L.* b. Jan. 12, 1817, m. 1844, Samuel G. Metcalf. She d. Dec. 6. 1844.

718. 4. *Jonathan P.* b. Jan. 12, 1819, m. March 22, 1854, Marian L. Kelsey. He d. Nov. 15, 1863.

719. 5. *Rhoda B.* b. July 19, 1821 ; m. June 26. 1845, Holden B. White. She d. Oct. 11, 1862.

720. 6. *Dulcena S.* b. Sept. 24, 1823 ; m. April 25, 1855, Leonard Rice.

721.   7.   *Samuel C.* b. Sept. 15, 1827 ; m. Susan A.
           Damon.
722.   8.   *Juda Anna*, b. Jan. 5, 1830 ; m. Calvin K.
           Witherby, Oct. 25, 1856.
723.   9.   *Harlow A.* b. July 29 1832 ; m. Elizabeth C.
           Griggs.
724. 10.   *Maria T. G.* b.April 15,1835,and d.Sept. 24,
           1848.

(425)   VII NATHANIEL GODDARD of Millbury
m. RHODA GALE Oct. 27,1820 and resides at Sutton,Mass.
He was b. at Royalston.   Children :
725.   1.   *Julia Ann,* b. April 25, 1822 ; m. May 29,
           1845,Henry W.Benchley and lived in Worcester.
           They had two children, *Charles Henry* and *Ju-
           lian Goddard,* but the latter d.July 30,1854.
726.   2.   *Maria,* b. Nov. 24, 1824 ; d. Dec. 16, 1834.
727.   3.   *Dolly Sapia,* b. March 24, 1828 m.Rufus Mas-
           son Jr. of Worcester, Sept. 1, 1858
628.   4.   *Ira Nathaniel,* b. March 1, 1830 ; m. Jose-
           phine C. Ryan, have son, *Henry M.* and live at
           Millbury.

(434) (VII) WILLIAM S. GALE, m. HANNAH
FOLON.   He died in April 1851, but his widow still resides in Hudson Columbia Co. N. Y.   They had the following children :
729.   1.   *Jane,* b.—
730.   2.   *Jacob Van Rennslaer,*b.—; m,has two children
           and in 1864 occupied a farm at German Town
           near Hudson.
731.   3.   *Harold Columbus,* b.—; m. Mary Elton, have

infant son and reside in Hudson N. Y.

732. 4. *Helen*, b.—; m. Amos Hovey have one infant daughter and reside in Hudson, N. Y.

Harold C. Gale and Amos Hovey under the firm of Gale, Hovey & Co. carry on an extensive Soap Factory at Hudson N. Y.

(435) (VII) Dr. RICHARD GALE, m. Sarah Murdock and settled in Rahway, N. J. and afterwards in Elizabeth, Union Co. N. J. where his widow resided in 1864. He was a Surgeon in the Navy until his marriage and afterwards a practicing physician until his death about 1844. They had children.

733. 1. *James*, b. —; m. Catharine Kelly, have four children and resided in 1864 at Elizabeth N. J.

734. 2. *William*, b. —; m. Elizabeth H. Seeper and have had one son who d. Jan.1864, five years and six months of age. William is a surgeon in the Navy and in June 1864 belonged to the Steamer "Adela" in the East Gulf Blockading Squadron, near Key West, Florida.

735. 3. *Helen*, b. ———Still unm. and resides in Elizabeth N. J.

736. 4. *Benjamin*, b. —— He enlisted early in the Rebellion, in the 9th Reg. N. J. Vols.. has been in several severe battles and finally was reported by Gen. Heckman as among the missing in the disastrous attack of Gen. Butler on Ft. Darling in May 1864.

737. 5. *Margaret*, b.—m. Thomas Forsyth and resides in Elizabeth, N. J.

738. 6. *Maria*, b.—was unm. in June 1864 and resided with her mother.

(453) VII NEHEMIAH GALE of LeRoy, N. Y.
m. Oct. 10, 1810 to Lucy Parker, who was b. near Boston Oct. 22, 1786. The winter subsequent to the marriage
they removed and located at Champion, Jefferson Co. N.
Y. At the commencement of the war of 1812 he enlisted
in the U. S. Service and was stationed at Sacket's Harbor
to guard the frontier where he was often engaged in
raids on the British and resisting them when made by the
enemy. He was in the attack on Prescott made by the
"Julia," mentioned in the history of Jefferson Co. At the
close of the war he settled in Houndsville in the same
county, which proved to be distinguished for 'nothing except continual Fever and Ague, where he or some of his
family were constantly on the sick list. In 1829 with
shattered constitution and decimated family he removed
to LeRoy and settled on a farm where he remained until
his death June, 9, 1844. Having assisted his father in,
early life in opening one of the iron ore beds at Bennington Vt. he became interested in ores and made several
discoveries of ore beds, since extensively worked.

He was proverbial for his honesty, an instance of which
mentioned in the history of Jefferson Co. proved fatal to
the U. S. Paymaster, Whittlesey, who claimed to have
been robbed of $30.000. Whittlesey marked a package of
the money and dropped it in the road expecting some one
would pick it up and put it in circulation, when he would
have a *prima facie* case against him of the robbery and
by hard swearing by Whittlesey, could be sent to states
prison. Unfortunately for the Paymaster Mr. Gale found
it in the road, and, instead of putting it in circulation advertised it. Whittlesey, in the meantime having given
notice of the robbery to government. The circumstances

raised a suspicion of fraud. Whittlesey and his wife were searched and the $30,000, less only the amount found by Gale, was found in the possession of the wife of Whittlesey. The wife drowned herself in Black river to cover her shame, and the husband was taken in charge by the government. In his religious opinions Nehemiah was devoted to the Christian denomination, and was noted for his piety.

His pecuniary circumstances became easy the latter part of his life, and his death was caused by the kick of a horse. His wife died of consumption Sept. 25, 1859. Children :

739. 1. *Almon W.* b. July 27, 1811 ; d. Oct. 4, 1828.
740. 2. *Solomon O.* b. Oct 25, 1812 ; m. Dec. 22, 1842 Jane Griffin, and lives at Watertown N, Y.
741. 3. *Alanzo M.* b. Dec. 26, 1813 ; d, Aug. 2, 1843.
742. 4. *Hylon P.* b. Feb. 27, 1815 ; d. Sept. 18, 1822.
743. 5. *Henry,* b. Nov. 21, 1819; m. Edith R. Griffin.
744. 6. *Charles V.* b. Aug. 21, 1827 ; m. Caroline E Barber.

(456) VII DEA. ISAAC GALE, of Morris Ill. m. Jan. 19, 1824, at Hoosick, N. Y., LYDIA S. GARDNER, of that town and settled on a farm in Bennington Vt. near the place of his birth. Isaac loved study and desired a liberal education but the circumstances of his father did not favor the plan, and he abandoned the idea, which was the source of regret the balance of his life. He was a pious member of the Baptist Church in Bennington, and succeeded his father as Deacon in that church.

In the summer of 1856 he removed to Beaver Dam, Wis. where he went into trade, but the reverses of 1857

and 1858 made him a bankrupt, and he removed to Morris, Grundy Co. Ill., where his wife died Aug. 26, 1861,
and he stricken with grief was removed to Pavillion, Ill.
by his son Elbridge, but took to his bed and died there
the 6th of Sept. following, only eleven days after his wife.
The father and mother received every attention possible
from the son, Rev. Elbridge Gale, and other members of
the family, but death claimed his victims, and the two
soon met again in the land of the christian's rest. Dea.
Gale was greatly respected during his short residence at
Beaver Dam, Wis. Children :

745. 1. *Elbridge*, b. Dec. 25, 1824 ; was a Baptist min
          ister in Manhattan Kansas, in 1865.

746. 2. *Pheba*, b.—

747. 3. *Mary*, b.—

748. 4. *Isaac*, b, June 2, 1832 ; m. Julia Dutcher,
          March 1, 1854, is a farmer in Waukesha, Wis.
          has dr's. *Martha D.* and *Mary F.* and son, *Al-
          fred Isaac.*

749. 5. *Nelson G.* b. Aug. 14, 1837 ; m. Jan. 26, 1860,
          Ann Haymond, and has dr.*Jennie L.* b. July 30,
          1863, is a farmer and lives at Morris, Ill.

750. 6. *Harriet N.* —

751. 7. *Ansel H.*—

(462) VII Dea. ANSEL HAYS GALE of Sandusky Ohio, m. Jan. 8, 1850, Amanda E. dr. of Hiram
Spenser Esq. of Greenfield, Huron Co. Ohio. who was
born July 3, 1829.

Ansel received good primary education and read law
five years with Gov.John S. Robinson of Vt. and was admitted to the Bar about 1843.   He then spent four years

in the office of Hon. D. L. Seymour of Troy N. Y.and in the Spring of 1848 left for the west. After traveling through portions of the west he concluded to'throw up the profession of the law and go into trade and settled at Sandusky Ohio. where he opened a Hardware store. In 1861 he purchased a sheep farm in Iowa and the following year sent out 1000 sheep and stocked the farm which is conducted by a tenant. He is by faith a Baptist and Deacon of a Baptist Church in Sandusky, and has been master of the Masonic Lodge No. 50 for the last three years.

Originally he was an old School Democrat but after the commencement of the late rebellion he joined the Union party of Ohio and was "firm in the faith that the Rebellion would be crushed, was an early believer in the necessity of emancipating the slaves and introducing them into the army" and "in favor of enfranchising the blacks at once. He has been successful in business and is one of the live men of Sandusky. Children :

752. 1. *Mana Wager*, b. Oct 6, 1851.
753. 2. *Spencer Hays*, b. Aug. 29, 1853.
754. 3. *Laura Johnson*, 5. June 11, 1855.

(460) VII REV. SOLOMON GALE, of Tolland Conn. m. Dec. 28, 1835, *Emily Stone* of Stamford Vt.

He was converted to religion in June 1831 and in Aug. following was baptised and admitted into the Baptist church in the town of Hoosick N. Y. where he then resided. Desirous of entering the ministry, he the same fall, commenced his Academical studies in Bennington Vt., and at a subsequent time studied Theology under Prof. E. B. Smith in the Baptist institution at New Hampton N. H. and was finally ordained April 28, 1836.

In 1841 he was pastor of the Baptist Church at Bristol Vt. and in 1865 had charge of the church at Tolland Conn. but the writer has no further knowledge of the location of his ministry. He is a sound theologian, an eloquent preacher, and has been a successful iustrument in the conversion of souls to the Kingdom of Christ, having baptised on an average one each month from the com mencement of his ministry. He has never had any children and the energies of his life have been devoted to the spread of the Gospel and the salvation of the world.

(466) VII Dr. LEONARD D. GALE, of N. Y city, m. Aug. 21, 1835, Anna E., dau, of Capt Lewis Smith of N. Y. who commanded a war vessel in the war of 1812.

The Doctor graduated A. B. at Union College, in July 1835, and A.M. in Course, M. D. in 1830 at the College of physicians, in N.Y. was appointed in 1831 assistant Prof. of Chemistry in the College of Physicians; in 1832 Prof. of Geology and Mineralogy in the N. Y. University where he remained until 1839 when he was appointed Prof. of Chemistry and acting President of Jefferson College, at Washington Miss. where he remained two years, then returned to N. Y. and opened the manufacture of Sugar of Lead, which he continued until 1846 when he was appointed by Government the Chief Exam.iner of Patents in the Patent Office at Washington D. C. which post he held until 1857 a period of 11 years.

In 1862 he returned to N. Y. City from Washington where he resided in 1864 and had an office as a practical Chemist.

Dr. Gale is a man of fair talents, a member of the Episcopal Church and an exemplary Christian. In 1865 he was secretary of the N. Y. Association for the advancement of science, connected with the Cooper Institute. Children:

755. 1. *Clara Augusta*, b. Aug. 21, 1837 ; m. William Henry Allen in 1858 and has son *Clarence Gale.*

756. 2. *William Lewis*, b. March 14, 1841 and d. March 18, 1842.

(470) VII Dea. JONAS RUSSEL GALE of Delavan, Ill. m. Sept. 28, 1829, *Cynthia Maria Adams* of Southboro, who was born May 19, 1807. He received a good primary education and at the age of eighteen went to N. Y. city and entered the factory of Enos Baldwin and learned the business of manufacturing Planes &c, where he remained until of age, and then went into the same business at Providence R. I. with one S. R. Cummings. In 1836 he sold out and removed in September to Alton Ill. In the·spring of 1838 he was one of the 40 who were placed to guard the press of Elijah Lovejoy, the abolitionist. It was landed and placed in the third story of a warehouse. The next morning Mr. Lovejoy, was shot by the mob.

Dea. Gale having already commenced a farm in Delavan, to avoid the excitement of the times he removed on to his farm and became a successful farmer. In 1853 he joined with his neighbors and erected a Baptist Church for the Baptist society over which he was Deacon ; and being the only one of much property the main burden fell upon him. After exhausting the amount raised for the Church at Delavan, Dea. Gale and his wife returned east and raised the balance among their friends to com-

plete the building. Mrs. Gale however, did not long survive the completion of her cherished object, but died Feb.
27, 1855 of a disease of the spine.

Dea. Gale m. 2d. April 16, 1856 *Rosina L.* daughter
of Dr. H. L. Latham, of Whitehall,Ill. but formerly from
Long Island.

Deacon Gale was a pioneer settler at Delavan and by
his activity and zeal, he has acted a prominent part in
establishing christian civilization in southern Illinois. In
1862 his son Charles L. enlisted in the 75 Ill. Reg. and
was in the battles of Perryville and Stone river. Henry R.
enlisted about the same time in the 115 Reg. and was in
the battles of Chicamauga, Rocky Face,Dalton, and Nash-
ville. Both returned without a wound or scratch and
were in good health in May 1865. Children :

    757. 1. *Charles Leonard,* b. Aug. 30, 1830 ; m. Sept
          21, 1854, Carrie Cheaver, and had 1. *Emma A.*
          b. July 15, 1856. 2. *Edgar W.* b.Dec. 4. 1860 ;
          d. Feb. 18, 1864.

    758. 2. *Henry Russel,* b. Jan, 19, 1834 ; m. Dec. 17,
          1857 ·Marian L. Stillman and had 1. *Clara E.* b.
          July 10, 1860 ; d. Oct. 22, 1860. 2. *Henry A.*
          b. Jan. 11, 1862.

    759. 3. *Cyrus Adams,* b. Nov. 9, 1838 ; d. Feb. 10,
          1839.

    760. 4. *Cornelia Ella,* b. July 11, 1857.

    761. 5. *Anna Eliza,* b. Jan. 4, 1860 ; d. Dec. 17, 1860.

    762. 6. *George Sylvester,* b. Nov. 10, 1862.

    763. 7. *Jeannie Belle,* b. March 25, 1865.

    (496) VII LEWIS GALE, of Barre, Vt, m. Chil-
dren :

764. 1. *Clarence A.* b. Aug. 19, 1843.
765. 2. *Cortland A.* b. April 29, 1845.
766. 3. *Martin P.* b. Nov. 20, 1846.
767. 4. *Elgin J,* b. Sept. 7, 1850.
768. 5. *Burton L.* b. Jan. 25, 1859.

(498) VII FRANCIS GALE, of Forksville Ill. m. March 15, 1830. Patience Scott of Williamstown Vt. He was a farmer, in Barre Vt. until 1845, when he emigrated and settled in Wawconda Ill., and from there, about 1857 removed to McHenry and the Spring of 1864, again removed to his present residence. His wife d. in McHenry Ill. March 7, 1864. Children :

769. 1. *Sarah E.* b. Nov. 24, 1832 ; m. Burges T. Huson of Wawconda Ill. March 28, 1852.
770. 2. *Wesley,* b. March 12, 1835 ; d. Jan. 10, 1860.
771. 3. *Alice C.* b. July 31. 1843 ; d. May 18, 1856.

(499). VII PRESSON R. GALE, of Stowe, Vt. m. 1st. SARAH EARL who d. after the birth of the first child when he m. 2d. EMILY BLANCHARD, who d. Dec, 5. 1834 and he m. 3d, March 1835 LUCY MARY ADAMS his present excellent wife who was b. in 1817. Children :

772. 1. *Eliza,* b. Nov. 19, 1829.
773. 2. *Emily,* b. Aug. 31, 1834 ; m. Wm. Reed of Brookfield Vt. They have had four children two of which are still alive.
774. 3. *Betsey,* b. Nov. 27. 1835 ; m. March 30, 1857, Dr. R. Staiton and has three children.
775. 4. *Ellen,* b. Feb, 23, 1837.
776. 5. *A. Son,* b. and d. 1839,
777. 6. *Anjeline,* b. Dec. 17, 1840; m. Mr. Butts of Stowe Oct. 12, 1860 ; has son *Charles R.* b. July 2,

1863.

18. 7. *Sawin*, b. Dec. 25, 1842; is clerk in a store in Salem, Mass.

179. 8. *Albert*, b. Aug. 30, 1844, Volunteered in the 2d. Vt. Reg. in 1863.

780. 9. *Pressen*, b. June 13, 1846.

781. 10. *Daniel*, b. May 23, 1848.

782. 11. *John*, b. April 23, 1850.

783. 12. *Frank*, b. April 17. 1852.

784. 13. *Emma*, b. Sept. 28, 1854.

785. 14. *Clara*, b. Oct. 10, 1856.

786. 15. *Kate*, b. Oct. 5, 1858.

787. 16. *Fredie*, b. June 12, 1862, d. March 1, 1864.

788. 17. *Girty Adell*, b. Feb. 28, 1864.

(502) VII CLARK GALE, of Forksville, Ill. m. Jan. 26, 1856, CORNELIA M. BROOKS. Children :

789. 1. *Clarissa C.* b. Nov. 30, 1856.

790. 2. *Ira B.* b. March 7, 1859.

791. 3. *Hugh L.* b, July 8, 1863.

(505) VII JULIUS C. GALE, of Barre, Vt. m. 1st. Jan. 27, 1831, Almira C. Drury of Barre Vt. who d. Jan. 30, 1850 and he m. 2d, June 25, 1850 Abby S. Emmons of Lowell. He resided in Barre Vt. until after 1842 Was in Williamstown Vt. in 1845, removed from there to Lowell Mass. and finally died in Lynn, Mass. Part of his life his occupation was "a Yankee Pedlar," and the balance a Hotel Keeper. He d. at Lynn May 14, 1859 and was called in the record "Inn Keeper." Children :

792. 1. *Ellen M.* b. Feb. 8, 1832 ; m. Jan. 1, 1851 George Clark of Lowell and d. Dec. 8, 1855 at South Danverse.

793. 2. *Delia A.* b. Dec. 10, 1834 ; m. Feb, 3, 1856, at Lynn Mass. Nahum H. Newhall and d. in same town Feb. 14, 1861.

794. 3. *Almira E.* b. Nov. 2, 1835 ; d. April 1, 1850 at Barre, Vt.

795. 4. *Romeo E.* b. Sept. 18, 1837 ; d. Sept Sept. 23, 1850, at Lowell.

796. 5. *Fred M.* b. Dec. 29, 1839.

797. 6. *Carrie A.* b. Sept. 24, 1842 ; m. April 8, 1858, John B. Cozzens of Lynn.

798. 7. *Emma D.* b. July 28, 1845 ; m. Dec. 13, 1863, Albert P. Wood of Barre, Vt.

(506) VII ROYAL C. GALE, of Barre Vt. m. Dec. 5, 1839, CHASTINA TWING of that town. Children :

799. 1. *Almeda T.* b. March 14. 1843 ; m. May 10, 1864, Edwin J. Woodbury of Barre Vt.

800. 2. *Elanor L.* b. Sept. 4, 1845. She writes a good and intelligent letter and furnished the Author the Genealogies of the Abraham Gale family and descendants.

801. 3. *Sarah L.* b. Sept. 7, 1848.

(507) VII DENISON TAFT, of Barre Vt. m. Nov. 10, 1842, LOVISA M. GALE of the same town: She d. June 15, 1853, at Barre Vt. Children :

802. 1. *John A.* b. July 8, 1845.

803. 2. *Clara L.* b. Feb. 24, 1847.

804. 3. *Lucius D.* b. Dec. 1, 1852.

(510) VII JUDE TOWN, of Barre Vt. m. Jan. 1, 1852, CLARISSA M. GALE of that town. Children :

805. 1. *Fred G.* b. Jan. 16, 1853.

806   2.   *George J.* b. Nov. 25, 1854.
807.   3.   *Clara L,* b. Sept. 26, 1856.

(514)   VII   SILAS D. GALE, of Goshen Vt. m. at
Goshen Vt. Nov. 25, 1832, MARINDA BLOOD, and d. then
Feb. 12, 1861. He was by occupation a farmer. Children :

808.   1.   *Eugene C.* b. June 10, 1836; m. Nov. 27, 1856,
Sarah A. Wood, of Goshen Vt. In 1864 he
removed to Randolph Center, Columbia Co. Wis.
They had son, *George E.* b. Feb. 13 1858.
809.   2.   *Fanny Eliza,* b. Sept. 5, 1838, d. July 7. 1857.
810.   3.   *Sarah M.* b. Jan. 4, 1849.
811.   4.   *Ellen A.,* b. June 22, 1851.
812.   5.   *Elva A.,* b. June 22, 1851.
813.   6.   *Jonn S.,* b. Aug. 1854.
814.   7.   *Charles D.,* b. Nov. 4, 1856.

(515)   VII   ISAAC GALE, of Randolph, Wis. m.
Dec. 5, 1833, MARY ANN FITTS, of Goshen, Vt. in which
town he resided until 1862 when he removed to Randolph
Wis.   Children :

815.   1.   *Laura A.,* b. Dec. 9, 1834 ; m. Horton H. Luster, Jan. 1857, who d. same year, and she d. Aug
1861.
816.   2.   *Francis A.,* b. Feb. 10, 1836, was wounded in
the shoulder in the battle of Corinth and draws a
pension from the United States.
817.   3.   *Ansel J.,* b. June 20, 1841 ; d. Dec. 26, 1861.
818.   4.   *Lovina E.,* b. Jan. 9, 1843 ; m. Sept. 1861,
John Wilson, who volunteered in the army, and
was killed in the battle of Corinth Oct. 5, 1862.

819. 5. *Cyntha M.*, b. Nov. 20, 1845; d.Feb. 11, 1848·

820. 6. *Charles S.*, b. June 19, 1847.

(516) VII CURTIS A. GALE, of Forksville, Ill. m. April 21, 1839, HARRIETTE MEADE, who was b. at Pittsford Vt. March 7, 1816. He resided at Goshen Vt.· until 1846 when he emigrated to Ill. and settled at McHenry· From there he removed in March 1854 to Forksville, Lake Co. Ill. Children:

- 821. 1. *Franklin E.*, b. Nov. 28, 1841; d. Aug. 6, 1860.
- 822. 2. *Eleanor R.*, b. Sept. 11, 1843; d. June 29, 1863.
- 823. 3. *George A.*, b. Dec. 7, 1846; d. Sept. 13, 1848.
- 824. 4. *Adlah C.*, b. Jan. 6, 1848.
- 825. 5. *Martha A.*, l. Sept. 11, 1854.
- 826. 6. *Ward B.*, b. June 21, 1858.
- 827. 7. *Cora H.*, b. Sept. 11, 1861; d. Nov. 7, 1861.

(517) VII ELISHA WARREN GALE, of Wauconda, Ill. m. Oct 27, 1842, OLIVE RELIEF ! HARRISON at Brandon Vt. From his marriage to his removal in 1850 to his present residence, he resided in Goshen, Vt. He is an independent farmer. Children:

- 828. 1. *Warren Albert*, b. Oct. 22, 1843; Volunteered in the first Wis. Cavalry in Oct. 1861 and was killed at Whitewater Bridge, Mo. April 24, 1863.
- 829. 2. *Syrenus Isaac.* b, Jan. 1, 1846; Volunteered in the 17th Ill. Cavalry in Jan. 1864.
- 830. 3. *Ida Marion*, b. May 22, 1852.
- 831. 4. *Joseph Robinson Harrison*, b. Aug. 21, 1856.
- 832. 5. *Ada May*, b. May 22, 1860.

(522) VII GEORGE GALE, of Stanstead, Canada

East, m. Oct. 6, 1846, DOROTHY DAVIS of the same town.
She was b. Feb. 15, 1815. Children :

833.   1.   *Albert G.*, b. Dec. 31, 1848 ; d. Jan. 3, 1851.
834.   2.   *Adelbert H.*, b. April 29, 1854.
835.   3.   *Francis G.*, b. June 12, 1855.
836,   4.   *Flurella L.*, b. June 5, 1857 ; d. Aug.26,1863.

(528)   VII   JOHN GALE, of Waukesha,Wis. m.—
He lived in Cleveland Ohio, until the fall of 1836, when
he came out to Milwaukee Wis., and brought with him
the materials for three buildings which he put up in the
city. In 1837 he purchased of Calvin Harmon, the lot
on S. E. corner of E. Water and Wisconsin St. for $10,
000, and sold it back to Hammon 18 months after and
purchased at Prairieville, now Waukesha, 160 acres for
$6,000, the claim of Morris Cutler, on which most of the
village now stands. He afterwards sold three fourths of
the land to Judge Barber and one Lord of Ohio city.

Mr. Gale erected mills at Waukesha and at one time
was in partnership with the late Gov. Barstow, in the
grain and mill business. He died in 1851, and his widow
now resides in Milwaukee. He left two sons and five
daughters, but we only have the name of *Guy S.* who kept
a saloon on Walker's Point,Milwaukee in 1864 and has a
wife and one or two children :

837.   1.   *Guy S.*, b.—

(531)   VII   ABRAM RICE GALE, of Oconto Wis.
m. Jan. 21, 1839. HARRIET COOPER. Children :

838.   1.   *Stillman C.*, b. Jan. 1, 1840 ; d. Dec. 10, 1856.
839.   2.   *John C.*, b. Feb. 19, 1842 ; m. March 9, 1864.
840.   3.   *Martin R.*, b. June 24,1844 ; d. July 28,1846.
841.   4.   *Julia Ann*, b. June 1848; d. Sept. 17, 1849.

842. 5. *Jane Ann*, b. Jan. 12, 1851.
843. 6. *Franklin R.*, b. Dec. 30. 1853; d. Nov. 12, 1855.
844. 7. *William H.*, b. Sept. 28, 1856.
845. 8. *Harriet E.*, b. April 13, 1860.

(536) VII MILTON GALE, of Boston, m. 1883, MARGARET M. GAULT. He is a leather merchant in Boston, wealthy and occupies a high position in social life. He is said to be a member of the Methodist Episcopal Church. Children :

846. 1. *Charles W.*, b. Sept. 27, 1835.
847. 2. *George M.*, b. July 31, 1837.
848. 3. *Wilbur F.*, b. May 18, 1840.
849. 4. *Franceina*, b. Sept. 1842 ; d. 1849.
850. 5. *Howard M.*, b. Aug. 18, 1844.
851. 6. *Hasket H.*, b. Aug. 18, 1844, twin with Howard.
852. 7. *Milton*, b. June 29, 1850.

(543) VII GEORGE GALE, of Albion Michigan, m. Sept. 19, 1819. HARRIET STONE, who was born at Royalton Vt. June 13, 1801. In 1821, Mr. Gale removed to Lacadie, Lower Canada, and from there to Montreal, but returned to Barre Vt. in 1827. In Sept. 1835 he removed with his family west, and in the summer of 1836 settled in Moscow, Mich. where he afterwards established a Foundry. In 1852 he went to California where he remained three years. While in California he peeled the bark off of 116 feet in length, of one of the great pine trees, and shipped it to N. Y, where he set up 75 feet of it in the Crystal Palace in 1855. The tree was 350 feet high and 31 feet in diameter at the base. The bark was after-

wards shipped to England and now stands in the **Crystal Palace** near London.

Mr. Gale removed to Albion, Mich. in 1856 and established a Hardware Store, and was in that business associated with his son Orlando Charles Gale, in March 1866. He has been an active and successful business man. Children:

853. 1. *Laura I.* b. March 21, 1821 ; m. March 27, 1839 John R. Boulton, a farmer of Moscow, Mich, has I son and 2 daughters.

854. 2. *Orlando Charles*, b. June 3, 1823 ; m. Oct 16, 1847 Adaline C. Smith.

855. 3. *George H.*, b. Feb. 23, 1826 ; m. Nov. 5, 1855, Sarah Ellen Brown had *Nora*, b. Sept. 23, 1857.

856. 4. *Nathan Brooks*, b. Feb. 3. 1829, m. May 1853, Augusta Woolcott. She d. April 1857 ; had son *Athal W.*, b. Aug. 19, 1854.

857. 5. *Clara E.*, b. May 27, 1831 ; m. Sept. 26, 1853, Col. Elliot W. Hollingsworth.

858. 6. *Augustus*, b. Jan. 21, 1834 ; m. Annie Moseley Sept. 28, 1857 ; had *Frank Morley*, b. Oct. 29, 1858 ; d, May 1, 1863 ; *Clara Theresey*, Feb. 1, 1861 ; *Mabel Hayward*, b, Sept. 24, 1863.

859. 7. *Lucina H.*, b. March 4, 1836 ; m. Fredrick W. Sheldon, Oct. 11, 1858, a grocery merchant ; had *Clara N.* b. May 26, 1860 ; *James H.*, b. Dec. 27, 1863.

860. 8. *Horatio*, b. Nov. 6, 1838 ; m. Flora E. Blanchard Nov. 20, 1861 : had *Nellie B.*, b. Oct. 26 1862 and *Charles Blanchard* b, March 20, 1864.

861. 9. *Aurora*, b. Feb. 28, 1847 ; d. Nov. 14th of

same year.

(546) VII GORDON HUTCHINS GALE, of Townshend, Vt. m. ORPHA HOLBROOK, Nov. 22, 1832. Gorden d. Sept. 7, 1864, Orpha d. 1856. Children :

862. 1. *Burnell Belknap*, b. Oct. 8, 1835. He enlisted as a private in the 8th Vt. Reg. in 1861 and was accidentally killed on the Rail R. at New Orleans Aug. 16, 1862.

863. 2. *Eli Holbrook*, b. April 14, 1837. He graduated Batchelor of Arts at Middlebury College, Vt. Aug- 1862, and M.D. in the medical department of the University of Pa. at Philadelphia, in March 1865. He entered the military service as Cadet in Aug. 1861 and in May 1864 was appointed assistant surgeon to the 186 Pa. Vols. stationed at Philadelphia.

864. 3. *Alvah Thompson*, b. 1839 ; d. 1843.

865. 4. *Fernando Chamberlain*, b. Oct. 8, 1840 ; m. Oct. 1864, Fanny A. Taft of W. Townshend Vt.

(565) VII GEORGE FISHER GALE, of Philadelphia, Pa. m. March 20, 1851, MARY D. WILLIAMS, of that city.

George F. served five years in learning the trade of a printer and then went to Philadelphia where he commenced merchandising and in Feb. 1865 had a store at no. 6, Chestnut St. where he was doing a good business and growing wealthy Child :

866. 1. *James Alford*, b. June 19, 1852,

EIGHTH GENERATION.

VIII REV. DR. AMORY GALE, of East Medway'

m. in Nov. 1825, MARTHA dau. of Perley and Hannah
Leland of Warwick.

Dr. Gale commenced his studies with a view for the
ministry, but failing health at twenty induced him to turn
his attention to Medicine and he took his degree of M.D.
at twenty three.

After several years practice, he again turned his attention to the ministry, was ordained in Nov. 1844, and took
charge of the first Congregational Church at Norton. He
preached several years at Norton and a short time at
Barnstable, when his health failing, he resumed the practice of Medicine and purchased at the place of his present residence, a farm.

Dr. Gale was very successful in both of his professions
and is a man of considerable talent. Children :

1. *Caroline R.*, b. July 23, 1828 ; m. Alfred James of
   Fallsville, Ct. in Oct 1854, and has one son, *Edward Amory*, b. Dec. 9, 1854. They live in Boston.

2. *Martha L.*, b. July 24, 1832.

3. *Mary K.*, b. March 9, 1835.

4. *James Amory*, b. Oct. 3, 1837 ; m. Oct. 1861, *Jemima A.* dau. of Abijah R. Wheeler of E. Medway. He has one son, *Leland Amory*, b. Oct.
   1862. Dr. Gale took his degree of M. D. in
   1861, and was, in 1864, in the U. S. Army as a
   Surgeon.

5. *Annah H.*, b. July 24, 1840 ; m. March 1860, Lyman Adams Jr. of East Medway. They have
   dau. *Jane Annah*, b. March 1861, and *Carrie*, b.
   June 1863.

VIII JACOB R. GALE, of Warwick, m. May 29, 1831, *Alma Leland.* He was a prominent man in Warwick, having been six years one of the selectmen, long an acting justice of the peace. and three years a member of the Legislature of Mass. Children :

1. *Alma L.*, b, Sept. 8, 1832 ; d. Aug. 6, 1851.
2. *Charles R.*, b. May 9, 1835 ; m, 1864, Prudence Ann Smith, of Scipio, Mich. He has been School Committee 4 years and Selectmen of Warwick 3 years.
3. *Jasper A.*, b. Sept. 3, 1837.

VIII GEO. W. GRESWOLD, of Cornwall Vt. m· Oct. 1828, MARY WASHBURN GALE. Children :

1. *Polly E.*, b. July 10, 1829 ; d. Feb. 18, 1847.
2. *Elbridge H,,* b. June 8, 1831 ; m. Arabella Holt and has one daughter b. 1856.
3. *Clarissa E.*, b. Aug. 2, 1833, m. Alverdon Janes and has son *Alverdon* b. July 1859.
4. *Henry V.*, b. Feb. 13, 1836.
5. *Georgiette*, b· May 28, 1838 ; m.Edson Farnam,has one son and two daughters.
6. *Sarah E.*, b. Aug. 29, 1840.
7. *Margaret A.*, b. Nov. 28, 1842; m. Julius Barker of Leicester, Vt.
8. *Vincent R.*, b, May 26, 1845.
9. *Mary L.*, b. July 11, 1848.
10. *Kate E.*, b. May 4, 1851.
11. *George R.*, b. March 18, 1853 ; d. 1855.

VIII DR. ELBRIDGE G. GALE, of Atlas, Mich. m. POLLY RICH in 1835. He is now examining Surgeon of the 6th Dist. in Michigan and resides temporarily at

Flint, Mich.   Children :

1. *Perry Bascom,* b. Oct. 5, 1836 ; d. Jan 12, 1838.
2. *Adrian Perry,* b. May 5, 1839 ; m. Helen **Wilder** in 1858, and has children :
   1. *Perry W.,* b. July 5, 1859.
   2. *George W.,* b. Feb. 22, 1861 ; d. Nov. 1863.
   3. *Fredie Elbridge,* b. April 7, 1863.

VIII   CALVIN HYDE of Goodrich,Mich.m. CLAR-
ISSA S. GALE in 1838, both then of Hartland N. Y. Children :

1. *Edwin Faling,* b. May 1, 1839 ; m. Lydia Lath-
   em May 13, 1861.
2. *Sarah A.,* b. June 29, 1840.
3. *Ella L.,* b. June 18, 1857.

VIII   JOHN BENCROFT of Warwick, m. Oct. 2,
1836, NARCISSA S. GALE.   Both d. in Sept. and
Oct. 1844, leaving dau. an orphan child :
1. *Clarissa E.,* b. Feb. 15, 1844.

VIII   E. CHENEY EDDY, of Brighton, Iowa, m.
MARGARET GALE, in 1843.   Children ;
1. *George Spencer,* b. June 10, 1844.   He is Quarter
   Master Sergeant in the 30th Reg. Iowa Vols. in
   1864.
2. *Clarissa,* b. Jan. 20 and d. Jan. 21, 1858.

VIII   IRA BENCROFT GALE, of Atlas, Mich. m.
1st LUCINA MARTHES, who d. Jan. 13, 1860 and m. 2d.
Mrs. BETSEY BOYLE of Lapier, Mich.   Children :
1. *Mary L.,* b. Aug. 5, 1844.
2. *Flora L.,* b. Nov. 23, 1845.
3. *Clara M.,* b. Jan. 12, 1847 ; d. March 7. 1864.

4. *Francis M.*, b. March 11, 1851.
5. *Lucia Ann.* b. Jan. 21, 1854.
6. *Charles E.*, b. July 21, 1856.
7. *Elbridge G.*, b. April 13, 1858 ; d. March 11, 1864.

VIII DANIEL AMORY GALE, of Brattleboro, Vt. m. July 3, 1852, ROSETTA C. AUSTIN of Brattleboro, Vt. Children :
1. *E. Clarissa*, b. April 30, 1854.
2. *Mary R.*, b. Nov. 20, 1856.
3. *Lucia W.*, b. Nov. 1858.
4. *Eleanor L.*, b. Aug. 5, 1860.
5. *Kate Edna*, b. June 21, 1863.

VIII SAMUEL SARGENT GALE of Cornwall, Vt. m. Oct. 1, 1856, EMMA A. HARVY. Children :
1. *Dennis S.*, b. July 7, 1857.
2. *Hattie*, b. Oct. 14, 1858 ; d. Dec. 4, 1862.
3. *Clarissa M.*, b. Sept. 14, 1860 ; d. Dec. 8, 1862.
4. *Carrie Phebe*, b. Nov. 11, 1863.

VIII GEORGE WINSLOW-GALE, of Worcester m. Sept. 3, 1843, SUSAN GRAFTON GOODWIN, who was b, at Kennebunkport, Maine, March 18, 1818.

George W. is, by trade a manufacturer of paper, lived in 1844 at Newton lower Mills, then about ten years at Santa Teresa, near the city of Mexico. He returned to Kennebunkport, previous to 1858, and now resides in Worcester.

He is a good scholar, writes an excellent hand and furnished the Author, the genealogy of his grandfather's family. Children :
1, *Susie Goodwin.* d. Aug. 19, 1843.
2. *Mary Teresa*, b. Sept. 21, 1850.

3. *George Henry*, b. April 20, 1858.

VIII JAMES McLELLAN GALE of Bristol Ill.
m. March 4, 1856 Susan B. dr. of Rev. J. Boomer of
Mass. James made a trip to New Orleans in a flat boat,
then went to Mass. and obtained a legacy left him by his
grand father, and while in Mass. learned the art of De-
guerreotyping and practiced that art in Ill. for seven years
when he sold out and bought a farm adjoining the village of Bristol Ill. part of which he has since laid out as
an addition to the village. He is an enterprising citizen
of Bristol and has become wealthy. Children :
1. *Mary Inez*, b. Feb. 11, 1857 ; d. in October.
2. *James Arthur*, b. July 14, 1859.

VIII HAWLEY GALE, m. April 12, 1854, Ann
Mower of Barre, Vt., who was b. Nov. 25, 1826. Hawley removed to Barre soon after his marriage where he
was engaged in farming in 1864. They have children :
1. *Wilbur*, b. May 21, 1855 ; d. Dec. 10, 1858.
2. *Willis H.* b. Oct. 6, 1858.
3. *Mary M.* b. Sept. 4, 1862 ; d. Sept. 26, 1862.

VIII HENRY GALE, of Hermon N, Y. m. Jan.
12, 1848, Edith R. Griffin of Jefferson Co. N. Y., who
was born March 29, 1820. Henry first settled on a farm
but in 1855, rented it and removed into the Village of
Hermon. Children :
1. *Lucy*, b. May 8, 1849.
2. *Alanzo D.* b. June 30, 1851 ; d. Jan. 10, 1863.
3. *Henry P.* b. Dec. 13, 1859

VIII CHARLES V. GALE, of Russell N. Y. m.
Feb. 4, 1851, Caroline E. Barber, of LeRoy, N. Y.,

who was born July 16, 1827. In the spring of 1859 Charles located on a farm in the town of Russell St. Lawrence Co. N. Y. where he still resided in 1865, enjoying the thrift of industry, and the pleasures of domestic life. Children :

1. *Anne E.*, b. Nov. 7, 1851.
2. *Charles L.*, b. Aug. 28, 1853 ; d. while an infant.
3. *Orville*, b. Jan. 8, 1855.
4. *Edwin H.*, b. March 22, 1857.
5. *Mary D.*, b. July 15, 1859.
6. *Carry E.*, b. Nov. 15, 1861.
7. *Joseph Lynn*, b. Nov. 7, 1863.

VIII REV. AMORY GALE of Minneapolis, Minnesota, m. Feb. 9, 1847 CAROLINE E. GODDARD, and is said to be a man of fair talent and education, but the writer has no further information relating to him. Children :

1. *Amory Francis*, b. March 3, 1848.
2. *Lucy Maria*, b. Aug. 1, 1851.
3. *Charles Goddard*, b. Aug. 2, 1854.

VIII SAMUEL C. GALE ESQ. of Minneapolis, Minnesota, m. Oct. 15, 1861 SUSAN A. DAMON of that town He is a prominent lawyer of fair talent and education and of some wealth and furnished the writer with most of his information relating to his grandfather's family. Children :

1. *Edward Chenery*, b. Aug. 21, 1862.
2. *Alice*, b. Dec. 9, 1864.

VIII HARLOW A. GALE, of Minneapolis. Minn. m. June 13, 1859, ELIZABETH C. GRIGGS. He is an active business man, a merchant and Clerk of the District

Court for the county which he resides.   Child.

1. *Harlow Stearns,* b. June 1860.

VIII   ORLANDO CHARLES GALE, of Albion,
Mich. m. Oct. 16, 1847 ADALINE C. SMITH, who was b.
Oct. 18, 1829 in Monroe Co. N. Y. He is a successful
Hardware merchant and associated with his father in that
business and in a foundery ; also, a number of the "Pro-
vissional Board of Control" of Albion College.   Children :

1. *Mary Aurora,* b. Nov. 28, 1848. A student in
Albion College.

2. *George Henry,* b. April 11, 1851. A student in
Albion College.

3. *Alpheus Smith,* b. Aug. 1, 1853.

4. *Charles Nelson,* b. Dec. 2, 1855 ; d. Feb. 16, 1859.

5. *Hattie Belle,* b. Oct. 23, 1863.

VIII   COL. ELLIOT W. HOLLINGSWORTH, of
Albion Mich. m. Sept. 26, 1853, CLARA E. GALE, Col. H.
held a commission as Lieut. in the Mississippi Reg commanded by Jefferson Davis in the Mexican war,and was in
the battles of Monterey and Buena Vista. On the
breaking out of the Rebellion,he received the commission
of Lieut, Col. of the 19th Reg. Ohio Vols., and his Col.
being acting Brig. General, the most of the time he was
in command of the Reg. for nearly three years and in the
battles of Rich Mountain, Laurel Hill, Murfreesboro and
several others. He is now a successful Hardware merchant of Albion. They have no children.

VIII   HIRAM GALE, m. Jan. 1, 1833, SALLY, dr.
of Samuel Bryant Esq. of Waterbury, Vt. She was b.in

Vt. Feb. 12,1809. Hiram was an enterprising farmer on Waterbury river until about 1853 when he sold his farm and purchased the Saw and Grist-mills near by, on the same river, which he run up to the time of his decease. He died with quick consumption Sept. 24, 1857. He was a man of the most exemplary character, of good business talent and furnished most of the lumber used in constructing the bridges and depots of the Vt. Central Rail Road. Very kind and genial in his disposition,he was highly esteemed as one of the prominent business men in town.

In 1861,his widow removed with all her family, except the oldest son, to Galesville, Wis., where they resided in 1866. Children :

1. *Louisa Adelaide,* b. Oct. 20, 1833 m. Nov.1,1848, Oliver Adams of Waterbury Vt. and d. Sept. 18 1857. Oliver removed with the children in 1863, to E. Stockholm, St. Lawrence Co.N. Y. They had children: *Emma Louisa,* b. May 10, 1850 ; and *Hiram Gale,* b. April 5, 1853.

2. *Bowman Tottingham.* b. Feb. 3, 1835 ; m. Jane Gregg, June 26, 1856.

3. *Matilda Elenora,* b. May 10, 1838 ; d. Oct. 14, 1839.

4. *Hiram Alton,* b. Sept. 28, 1840 ; d. May 24, 1843·

5. *George Washington,* b. July 11, 1842. He enlisted as a private in the first Wisconsin Battery, under Capt. Foster in Sept. 1861, was promoted to corporal and served at Cumberland Gap in 1862,was in the first battle at Vicksburg under Gen. Sherman Dec. 1862, at the taking of Arkansas Post, in 1833, through the whole campaign of Gen-

eral Grant to the surrender of Vicksburg, July 4,
1863, in Texas under Generals Washburn and
McClarned and constituted part of the rear guard
at the celebrated retreat of General Banks from
Alexandria in April and May 1864. From the
time the Battery reached Alexandria to the arrival of the army on the Mississippi the Battery was
skirmishing with the enemy nearly the whole
time. He enjoyed good health through his whole
campaign and returned to Galesville Oct. 27,
1864 after the full service of his three years enlistment. In January 1866 he entered the Milwaukee Commercial College.

6. *Martha Elenora,* b. Sept. 14, 1844, m. Charles A.
Leith, Apr. 18, 1866.

7. *Hiram Randall,* b. Nov. 8, 1846. He enlisted
Jan. 25, 1865 in the 46th Reg. Wis. Vols. and
returned in the fall of the same year after the
close of the war. He then purchased a half interest in the Galesville Transcript is one of its ed-
itors and publishers.

8. *Almon Clark,* b. Dec. 13, 1851.

VIII DAVID LORD, m. Nov. 16, 1836, ANGELINE
GALE. He was a farmer in Waterbury and the son of
Rev. Samuel Lord. one of the first Freewill Baptists ministers in N. H., and one of the founders of that church in
the U. S. Angeline d. with cancer in the breast Sept. 8,
1858. David m. 2d, Betsey A. Kennedy of Bolton, Vt.
Aug. 16, 1860, and owned a farm in Bolton Vt. on the
bank of Winoska river, in 1864. Children :

1. *Alzina Angeline,* b. May 28, 1839.

2. *Lorin* `Bixby`, b. May, 15, 1841; m. Sarah E. Kennedy, Sept. 18, 1866.

3. *George Morton*, b. Sept. 19, 1843.

4. *Myra Jane*, b. Nov. 1, 1845.

VIII HON. JAMES M. HENRY, of Waterbury, Vt. who m. March 25, 1831, MATILDA GALE, was the son of Sylvester Henry Esq. an old and wealthy farmer in Waterbury and one of the early settlers in that town.

James was b. June 7, 1809 and was a young man of fair talent, whose superior social qualities made him the leader of all the balls and parties in town, and according to the customs of the times, contracted the habit of the moderate use of intoxicating liquors. After his marriage the habit increased and he became for a while disipated, but enlisted in the Washingtonian reformation, became an excellent temperance lecturer, and forever after a teetotaler. His father gave him a small farm and saw mill on Waterbury river, where he resided from the time of his marriage until about 1852, when he removed to the village, opened a Drugstore, and wholesaled patent medicines through nearly all New England, N. Y. and Canada, and thereby accumulated a considerable property. For several years, he was an acting magistrate and represented the town in the legislature for two successive years, (1860, '61). He was a lively and influential public speaker, and of very superior conversational powers. In politics he was a Democrat, but finally joined thr Republican party in the latter part of his life. As a politician his *forte* was to manage the wires, and several of the Governors, members of Congress and other high officials were indebted to him for their nomination and election. He d. with a disease of

K 1

the brain Dec. 28, 1863. The moral and Educational culture of the family mainly devolved on the mother, and she has nobly acquited herself in those duties. She has for some years, been a member of the Congregational Church. Matilda m. 2d, John Tenny Esq. and resides in Waterbury, Vt. Children :

1. *William Wirt*, b. Nov. 21, 1831 ; m. Mary Jane Bebee.
2. *John Francis*, b. Feb. 25, 1834 : m. Josephine Barrett.
3. *Delia Maria*, b. Oct. 20, 1835 ; m. Dr. Anderson R. Miller, of Kinston N. C, Sept. 19, 1857.
4. *Eliza Betsey*, b. Dec. 1, 1837 ; m. Emory D. Scagel of Waterbury, Vt. Dec. 28, 1861, a Druggist.
5. *Mary Sybil*, b. Dec. 2, 1839 ; m. Lyman B. Hinckley, Esq. of Chelsea, Vt, Nov. 21, 1861, an attorney at law.
6. *Sarah Ann*, b. March 1, 1842 ; m. Solomon Green, Aug. 12, 1861, a merchant of Richmond, Vt.
7. *James Edwin*, b. October 8, 1844. He graduated at Eastman's Commercial College at Poughkeepsie, N. Y. March 29, 1864. He enlisted as a private in Co. K. of the 17th Reg. of Vt. Vols. July 20, 1864 and was promoted to Second Lieut. The Reg. was ordered to Camp Rendezvous, Fair Haven, Conn. where it remained two months and was then ordered to the Front at Petersburgh, Va. Here the Reg. was stationed at Ft. Davis. The 2d of April 1865, the Regiment was ordered out at 2½ o'clock in the morning, to storm the Rebel Ft. Mahone. They met with a determin-

ed resistance, and were twice driven back, but on
the third assault they reached the fort when
Lieut. Henry, then one of the only two officers
left in the Reg., was shot through the body in-
front of an embrasure. He was carried off the
field and died a six o'clock P. M. Lieut. Henry
was highly esteemed in the Reg. as well as in social life.

8. *George Sylvester*, b. July 4th 1848. He also enlisted in the same Co. in the 17th Reg., participated in the charge on Ft Mahone, and was near
his brother Edwin when he was shot. George
escaped without injury during the balance of the
war, and was honorably discharged with his Reg.
after the close of the war.

VIII. Hon. ELISHA A. TOWN of Stowe, Vt. b. in
Waterbury, Vt. Sept. 25, 1804 ; m. May 5, 1836, ELVIRA
GALE, of Waterbury, Vt.

In 1836 and 1837 he represented the town of Mansfield,
Vt. in the Legislature of the state and for several years
was town Clerk and one of the selectmen of that town.
From the time of his marriage he has owned and carried
on a large dairy farm, devoted much attention to raising
Bees for honey, and occupies a high position as a chris-
tian Gentleman, and as a member of the Freewill Baptist
Church, of which his wife is also a member, Children :

1. *Nancy Elvira*, b. Aug. 29, 1837 ; m. March 5,
1862, Lemuel B. Smith Esq. the proprietor of the
lower mills in Stowe.

2. *Alfred Benton*, b. March 5, 1839 ; d. Jan. 24, 1843.

3. *Charles Elisha*, b. Nov. 8, 1841.

4,   *Daniel Benton,* b. Oct. 4, 1844.

5.   *Julia Matilda,* b. Aug. 28, 1850.

VIII Hon. GEORGE GALE LL. D., of Galesville, Wis., was b. at Burlington, Vt. Nov. 30, 1816, and m. at Elk Horn Wis. Dec. 5, 1844, GERTRUDE, dau. of Capt. George Young of the latter town. George's father removed his family to Waterbury, Vt. in June 1824 and commenced a new farm in the woods on the eastern slope of the Green Mountains. The facilities for an education was a common school, a mile down the mountains, which was made available. and the children all obtained a fair common school education including Arithmetic and Grammar. Until his sixteenth year George was regarded as a dull scholar, and made no more than the ordinary advancement in his studies, but excelled in his skill in hunting the Partridge and Woodchuck with his dog and gun, and in fishing for the speckled trout in the mountain brooks, to which sports he devoted every hour which he could obtain from his ordinary employment in clearing land and farming. But, in the summer of his sixteenth year, he borrowed of a neighbor, Walter Scott's Life of Bonaparte, which he read through very attentively and it had the effect of arousing his latent ambition, and he came to the very sensible conclusion that usefulness, fame and wealth, was not so much an accident, as an achievement reached by patient industry and talent, and that in that age of science and knowledge the successful competitor would probably be the one best instructed in the science and knowledge of the world.

From this time hunting and fishing ceased to be his favorite sport and he devoted, every leisure moment in reading approved authors in history, biography and travels, and after about two years he procured Flint's, treatise on Land surveying, and fully mastered its contents without an instructor and commenced practical Surveying with success. After surveying, he took up Navigation, Webber's Hutton's and Farrar's mathematics, Enfield's Philosophy, Henry's and Orfila's Chemistry, and works on Astronomy, Mineralogy and Geology, and at twenty-one years of age George had obtained a fair knowledge of the higher mathematics and Natural History.

Thinking it would be well to test his attainments by an examination, Mr. Gale, submitted himself to Mr. Jeremiah Flint, A.M. a graduate of Middlebury College in 1811, who had been his master, a part of two winters years before, in the common school, and after a fair examination Mr. Flint gave him the following certificate :

Waterbury March 10th 1838,

To all whom it may concern :

The subscriber has been acquainted with the Bearer, George Gale, for seven years and has frequently had him for a pupil. He loves study and has not loved it in vain. He is in a great measure self instructed, and by industry close application and perseverence he has, unquestionably, attained unto a more correct knowledge of Trigonometry, Navigation and particularly Surveying than most of our liberally educated young men. Such young men should be patronized, and, indeed they will be. The subscriber would not hesitate, a moment to employ him as a correct surveyor, in the common business of his avocation.

Jer. Flint.

In March 1839, Mr. Gale commenced reading law, in 1840 was appointed Post Master at Waterbury Center,

Vt. and in 1841 was admitted to the bar, emigrated west
and settled at Elk Horn, Walworth county, Wis. Here
he opened an office and entered into a successful practice
of the law. Unlike some others, he continued his law
studies with great diligence for four years, and became.in
fact, a well read lawyer.

Mr. Gale held several town offices among which was
Chairman of the Town Board of Supervisors for two years
and was also Chairman of the County Board of Supervisors for two years. In the fall of 1847 he was elected a
member of the Convention called to form the present
State Constitution and served on the judiciary committee.
The same fall, he was also elected District Attorney and
in the fall of 1849, a State Senator for two years. The
first year in the Senate, he was Chairman of the Committee of Privileges and Elections and the second year Chair-
tee of the Judiciary Committee. He was an active member of the Senate and made several speeches and reports
which were published.

July 4,1851, he received from the Governor of Wisconsin, the appointment of Brigadier General in the Militia.
The fall of the same year Mr. Gale removed to the Upper
Mississippi and settled at LaCrosse, and was the same fall
elected County Judge, for a term of four years, of La
Crosse county,and Chippewa county attached to LaCrosse
county for judicial purposes. As the county judge had
common law as well as probate jurisdiction, he was often engad two weeks at a term trying causes. This office
he resigned January 1, 1854. and April 1st 1856 was elec_
ted Circuit Judge for the sixth judicial circuit of Wisconsin composed of the counties of Buffalo, Clark, Jackson,
Monroe, Trempealeau, LaCrosse, Vernon and Crawford,

for the judicial term of six years, commencing Jan. 1, 1857.
When Mr. Gale first settled at LaCrosse he saw that
all Northwestern Wisconsin was entirely destitute of any
College, or other high institutions of learning, and he
urged upon the landed proprietors of that place to set aside
ten acres of land back of the Village and take the initia-
tory steps to establish such an institution, but they turned
a deaf ear and nothing of the kind was attempted. Mr.
Gale then conceived the idea, of not only starting a college, but a town, himself; and in 1853 purchased about two
thousand acres of land at the present location of Galesville,
including the waterpower on Beaver Creek, and in January 1854 procured from the legislature of Wisconsin, the
organization of the new county of Trempealeau, with the
location of the county seat at Galesville, and a University
charter with the same location. In June of the same years,
he laid out a small village plot and let a contract for the
erection of mills, but the mills (saw and flouring) were not
completed until 1856.

The Board of Trustees of the Galesville University,
was organized in 1855 and a College building commenced in 1858, and the preparatory department opened
for students early in May of the following year, and the
collegiate department in September 1861 ; and the first
college class graduated July 13, 1865. After the gradua-
tion of the class Mr. Gale resigned the Presidency of the
University when the Board unanimously adopted the
following offered by Rev. W. H. Brocksom of LaCrosse :

"Resolved, That the Board tender to Hon. George
Gale, LL. D. late President of this University, their pro-
found thanks for his able and faithful administration for

the period of nearly seven years as President of the Faculty and for over ten years as President of this Board.'

"Resolved further, That we tender to Hon. George Gale, LL. D., as its principal founder and patron, the Freedom of this University and the use of its Library as a token of our high appreciation of his long and efficient services, for which he has ev. refused all pecuniary consideration."

The Galesville University went into the hands of the Methodist Episcopal Church in 1858 and a majority of the Board of Trustees are appointed by the Church.

Mr. Gale removed from the then city of LaCrosse to Galesville in May 1857 and went on to a farm where he resided in 1866.

Although not a regular College graduate in course, yet Mr. Gale received from the Vermont University at Burlington, the degree of the Master in the Arts, in August 1857, and from the Board of Trustees of Galesville University, in July 1863, the degree of LL. D.

Mr. Gale's health partially failed in the Summer of 1862 and the three following winters he spent in the South and East, most of the time in the service of the Sanitary and Christian Commissions. During the months of February and March he had charge of the U. S. Sanitary Commission Depot on Morris Island S. C. for the seige of Charleston.

Mr. Gale has not entirely ignored literary labors, but in August 1845 started the "Western Star,"the first newspaper published in Walworth County, Wisconsin. which he sold out in less than a year, and in 1846, issued the first edition of his "Wisconsin Form Book" which was revis-

ed and re-published in 1848, 1850 and 1856, and 5500
copies sold in Wisconsin. He has also the manuscript
prepared and in press, of a book entitled "The Upper
Mississippi, or Historical Sketches of the Introduction of
Civilization into the Northwest," a work covering the period from 1800 to 1866 ; and has been the regular correspondent of the "Galesville Transcript," from March 1860,
for five years. The Gale Family Records have also cost
him a large amount of labor. Children :

1. *George*, b. Sept. 14, 1845, graduated A. B. at Galesville University July 13, 1865.
2. *William*, b. Oct. 23, 1848.
3. *Helen*, b. Dec. 5, 1850.

VIII SAMUEL S. LUCE, of Galesville, Wis., b.
at Stowe, Vt., Feb. 1. 1818 : m. Dec. 7, 1847, HANNAH
GALE, of Waterbury, Vt.. By trade, he was a house carpenter and Architect. After his marriage he removed to
Waterbury, and purchased a part of the Mills on Waterbury river, built most of the Depots on the Vt. Central
R. R., from Montepelier to Burlington, and in the spring
of 1857, removed to the place of his present residence,
where he superintended the erection of the present University Building and of the mansion of Geo. Gale.

In March 1860, he started the "Galesville Transcript,"
a weekly paper which he continued to edit and publish
until October 1865, when he sold it to Leith & Gale ; and
for four successive years, has held the office of Town
Treasurer, and six years the post of Secretary of the Board
of Trustees of the Galesville University. At the Commencement, in July 1864, the University gave him the
honorary degree of A. M..

Mr. Luce and his wife are both good writers of prose and poetry. In Nov. 1865, Mr. Luce was elected Superintendent of Schools for the County of Trempealeau.
Children :

1. *Flora Felicia*, b. Oct. 4, 1848.
2. *George Slayton*, b. March 17, 1850.
3. *Walter Scott*, b. March 28, 1861.

NINTH GENERATION.

IX. BOWMAN TOTTINGHAM GALE, m. June 26, 1856, JANE, dr. of John Gregg Esq., of Waterbury, Vt. and now resides, as a farmer, in the town of Stowe.
Children :

1. *Frank Warner*, b. June 18, 1857.
2. *Martha Louisa*, b. March 4, 1861.
3. *Mary Emogene*, b. Feb. 22, 1863.

IX GEN. WILLIAM WIRT HENRY, of Waterbury, Vt., m. August 5, 1857, MARY JANE, dau. of Lyman Beebe, of that town. About 1849, Mr. Henry went to California, where he remained about 7 years, enjoying all the ups and downs of California fortunes, has been alternately rich and poor several times. When he returned he entered into partnership with his father and brother John in the drug and patent medicine business, in Waterbury, and prosecuted a lucrative and successful business.

On the breaking out of the war of the Rebellion, William enlisted in the Waterbury company of Volunteers, and was elected and commissioned, June 20, 1861, First Lieutenant. The company went into the Second Vt.

Reg., as Co. "D." and the Regiment was sent to Washington, D. C., and was in the battle of first Bull Run.

Lieut. Henry was attacked with the measles at the commencement of the "advance to Richmond," but the prospect of a fight was superior to disease and he advanced with his company and participated in the battle of Bull Run, but the night after the battle he caught a severe cold, which nearly cost him his life. He was sick the balance of the fall and was mustered out of service for ill health, Nov. 4, of the same year.

Having regained his health the next year, he accepted the post of Major of the 10th, Vt. Vols., his commission bearing date, August 27, 1862. He was promoted Lieut. Col. of the Regiment, Oct. 17, of the same year and Col. April 26, 1864. The Regiment was put in what was called the Vt. Brigade and was in the Second Army Corps.

The Regiment advanced, under Gen. Grant, towards Richmond, in the spring of 1864, and was in that series of murderous battles to Petersburg. The Regiment was then sent to the Shenandoah Valley and fought another series of battles under Gen. Sheridan. Col. Henry led his Regiment through all these battles. except the last battle on the Shenandoah. which occurred when he was absent on leave. March 7, 1865, Col. Henry was *Brevetted* Brigadier General, by the War Department, for "gallant and meritorious conduct at the battles of the Wilderness, Spottsyvania, Coal Harbor, Monocacy and Cedar Creek." Gen. Henry had his right fore finger shot off at the battle of Coal Harbor, where he, with the 10th Vt. Reg., captured a North Carolina Regiment in their rifle pits.

On returning to Waterbury, Gen. Henry purchased the farm, half a mile west of the village, formerly the residence of the late Gov. Butler, but sold it last spring to the State of Vt., and the State has established upon it a Reform School. He was elected a State Senator from Washington Co. Vt., in Sept. 1865 and was re-elected to the same office in 1866. Children :

1. *Bertram Beebe,* b. Oct. 4, 1858 ; d. May 23, 1859.
2. *Mary Matilda,* b. March 11, 1860.
3. *Ferdinand Sherman,* b. August 9, 1862.

IX   JOHN FRANCIS HENRY, of Waterbury. Vt. m. Feb. 6, 1856, JOSEPHINE BARRET, of Madrid, N. Y. John obtained a good education and taught school two or three winters, after which he united with his father in the drug and patent medicine business at Waterbury, Vt. in which he has been very successful and has accumulated a respectable fortune. He has excellent business talents and occupies a high social position; and was appointed Post Master at Waterbury, Vt., in January 1865.— Has resigned the Post Office and is now a leading member of the firm of Demas, Barnes & Co., 21 Park Row, N. Y. Druggists. Children :

1. *Mary Ellen,* b. Nov. 22, 1856.
2. *William Barret,* b. May 6, 1859.
3. *John Francis,* b. Jan. 28, 1863 .

... State ... Gen. He ... purchased
... They ... ly for two
... first spoke to
... yed upon his
... ed a State Senator from
W ... ... and was re-elected to
free ... ... here.

... 1858 ; ... May 23, 1859.
... March 11, 1860.
... b. Aug. 19, 1862.

... 's HENRY ... of Waterbury, **Vt.**
... ... Romaine of Madrid, **N. Y.**
... ... and taught school **two**
... ... ated with his father **in**
... ... in Waterbury, **Vt.**
... ... and has accumulat-
... ... excelling business tal-
... ... and was appoint-
e ... ... in January 1865.
He ... ... was acting as a
ber of ... ... Co. 23 East Bay,
N. Y. Being ... ...

... ... 1856
... ... 1859.
... ...

Eng^d by A H Ritchie

Yours truly
John F. Henry

GENEOLOGY OF THE TOTTINGHAM FAMILY
IN AMERICA.

TOTINGHAM was the name of a very ancient and aristocratic family of London, Eng. and its suburbs, where there is still "Tottenham Court Road" an important street in London and "Tottenham," a town near the city.

The Totenhams had their well authenticated coats of arms in the Fendal ages and Burk gives the line of descent from several distinguished in the early history of England, but our limits will not allow us to copy.

Henry became a nonconformist of the strictest puritanic order and therefore came to America with his religious brethren for the enjoyment of that freedom of conscience which was denied him in his native land, and is the only one by that name that ever emigrated to America so far as the information of the writer extends.

He settled and purchased a farm near the village of Woburn Mass. which continued with his descendants until about 1845 when the proprietor, an old maid by the name of Rebecca, willed it to her hired maid.

We give in the following records of all the Tottinghams we have heard of in America except Henry Edwin Tottingham, whom the writer met at Waltham Mass. in 1864 who promised his family record but has neglected to furnish it. He was a second or third cousin to the writer, and was born near Ashburnham. He did not know the name of his grandfather.

In latter years the name has been written "Tottingham' in Mass. and Vt.

1. 1. HENRY TOTTENHAM, of Woburn, Mass., the an_ cestor of this family in America, settled there, at, or previ ous, to 1646. His wife, Anna, died Dec, 23d 1653 and he married 2d Alice Alger (or Eager) the 13th of **May** 1654. He was a member of the church and one of the Petitioners for the liberty of Prophecy Aug. 30, 16 53 and died April 5th 1728. By his wife Anna he had the following chidren :

  2. 1. *Nehemiah,* b. Aug. 23, 1646; who died, prob- ably unm. March 28, 1714.

  3. 2. *Eliah,* b. Feb. 28, 1652; m. Mary ——.

(3) II ELIAH TOTTENHAM, of Woburn, m. Mary; who d. about 1708 and he m. 2d, Rebecca—. Eliah d. Nov. 27, 1717. He had the following children :

4. 1. *Anah,* b. Sept. 24, 1685.

5. 2. *Mary,* b. April 18, 1688.

6. 3. *Sarah,* b. July 13, 1690.

7. 4. *Elisha,* b. July 22, 1696, d. young.

8. 5. *Elizabeth,* b. Feb. 8, 1699.

9. 6. *Alice,* b. June 10, 1701.

10, 7. *Arminell,* b. July 30, 1707.

11. 8. *Rebecca,* b. Aug. 4, 1710 ; d. unm. **April 28,** 1733.

12. 9. *Elisha,* b. Oct. 18, 1713 ; m. Sarah Lawrence.

13. 10. *Elizabeth,* b. May 4, 1722.

14. 12. *Phebe,* b. June 30, 1728.

15. 13. *Abigail,* b. —; d. Dec. 11, 1736.

(12). III ELISHA TOTTINGHAM, m. Sarah Lawrence May 27,1736, dr.of Nathaniel and grand daughter of Dea. Nathaniel Lawrence of Watertown.According to Bond's geneologies of Watertown, the Lawrences were lineal descendants of Sir. Robert Lawrence,who had arms conferred by Richard I. of England for his bravery in scaling the walls of Acre, A. D. 1191. Elisha d.at Woburn January 19, 1802, and Sarah, his widow, January 8, 1809, aged 93 years. They had the following children :

16. 1. *Elisha*, b. Feb. 18, 1737. He served the summer and fall of 1780 in the Continental army in Rhode Island, in Col. C. How's Reg.

17. 2. *Sarah,* b. Nov. 21, 1738 ; m. John Williams of New Marlborough Oct. 24, 1765.

18. 3. *Nathaniel,* b. June 10, 1740 ; m. Esther Brown of Lexington.

19. 4. *Ephraim,* b. April 9, 1743. On the 19th of April 1775, the day after the battle of Lexington, under Capt. Samuel Belknaps. he marched from Woburn to Concord and from thence to Cambridge, where he served for the next twenty-five days stopping the raids of the British into the country.

20. 5. *Moses,* b. July 22, 1746.

21. 6. *Jonathan,* b. Dec. 17, 1748. Served with his brother Ephraim, under Capt. Belknaps at Cambridge. Also, during the summer and fall of 1777 in the Reg. commanded by Col.John Robinson, in the continental service in Rhode Island. He d.Nov. 20, 1802, at Woburn, probably unm.

22. 7. *James,* b. July 14, 1751, and. was found dead in his bed Aug. 10, 1809.

23. 8. *Rebecca,* b. Nov. 15, 1753.

24. 9. *Abigail*, b. July 15, 1755, d. unm.Aug. 22,1810.
25. 10 *David*, b. Sept. 24, 1758 ; m. Dec. 1, 1785, Deborah Dixon of Cambridge.

(18) IV NATHANIEL TOTTINGHAM, of Woburn, removed to Westminster, early in 1770, where notice of
his intended marriage with Esther,(b. Dec. 1748,) dr. of
Daniel and Anne (Bright) Brown, of Lexington, were
published in June, 1770. They were married Aug. 16,
1770, at Lexington. He was a wealthy farmer at Westminster and d. there Dec. 12, 1793.   They had the following children :

26. 1. *Nathaniel*, b. May 31, 1771 ; m. at Westminster, May 5, 1814, Polly Tottingham, his cousin,
occupied the homestead of his father and died
without issue, Dec. 4, 1850.   He was long a
deacon in the Baptist Church at Westminster.

27. 2. *Elisha*, b. March 11, 1773 ; m. Clarissa Brown,
of Fitchburg.

28. 3. *Sally*, b. Jan. 9, 1775 ; m. Nov. 13, 1797, John
Maynard, of Westminster. He removed to Rutland, Vt., where he died,previous to 1830, leaving
his widow and 4 children, *Asa*, *Maria*, *Nancy*
and *Adaline*.   While living, he was an acting
justice of the peace for several years, in Rutland.

29. 4. *Anna*, b. Nov. 27, 1777 ; d. Sept. 27, 1779.

30. 5. *Asa*, b. Dec. 27, 1779 ; d. unm. Feb. 16, 1801.

31. 6. *Hannah*, b. Jan. 7, 1781 ; m. Jan. 27, 1805,Pe-
ter Gale Jr., of Barre, Vt. ; d. Feb. 24, 1848,
at Waterbury, leaving several children. (See
Gale Geneology,page 98.

K 2

32. 7. * *Josesph*, b. Sept. 14, 1783 ; m. June 16, 1806,
      Nancy, dr. of Dea. Wood of Westminster.

33. 8. *James* b. Dec. 29, 1785, m. and removed to
      Pittsford Vt. where he d. without issue March
      12, 1842. He left a fine farm on Otter Creek.

F (27) V. ELISHA TOTTINGHAM, of Westmin-
ster, Mass. m. June 20, 1813, Clarissa, dau. of Zacheriah
Brown of Fitchburg, Mass. Elisha was a good farmer
in Westminster and highly respected. He d, July 9,
1852 and his wife Clarissa March 8, 1861. He willed his
homestead to wife Clarissa, son Brown E. and daughters
Catharine, and Caroline E, who continued to occupy it.
Children :

34. 1. *Brown E.*, b. Feb. 22, 1815 ; d. of heart desease
      suddenly March 24, 1862 unm.

35. 2, *George W.*, b. Nov. 12, 1816 ; m. Susan Well.
      ington.

36. 3. *Nathaniel*, b. March 10, 1818, m. Harriet R.
      Page, Sept. 5, 1842, keeps a boarding house in
      Ashburnham Center, and has only son *Henry I.*
      b. May 20, 1847, who is clerk in a store in Fitch-
      burg, in 1864.

37, 4. *Catherine*, b. Dec. 14, 1820, unm. in 1864.

38. 5. *Caroline E.*, b. March 27, 1827, unm. in 1864.

(32) V. Dea. JOSEPH TOTTINGHAM, m. Jan.
16, 1806, Nancy, dr. of Dea. Wood of Westminster.
She was born at W. Feb. 16, 1786 and d. at Pittsford, Vt.
Nov. 8, 1841. Dea. Tottingham, settled at Pittsford, Vt.
soon after his marriage, purchased a large farm on Otter
Creek adjoining the Village, was a Dea. and very devoted
member of the Congregational Church, became quite

wealthy, was happy in all his family relations and . pecuniary circumstances, but finally became slightly deranged
and committed suicide by cutting his throat and died July
4, 1859.   He was one of the best man that ever lived and
his unhappy death was deeply felt by the surrounding
country.

When the writer visited him in 1856, he invited the
writer to visit the cemetry grounds of the Village and was
particular to point out the graves of several prominent men
of the town who had died violent deaths and was probably then laboring under the hallucination that he was to
be added to their number.   He made one campaign, in
the war of 1812.   They had children :

39.   1.   *Joseph Asor*, b. May 21 1808 ; d. Sept. 8, 1808.

40.   2.   *Angeline Wood*, b. 'Oct. 1, 1809 ; m. James
           Gorham.

41.   3.   *Bowman Brown*, b. March 12, 1812 ; m. Aman-
           da Hunt.

42.   4.   *Clarissa Columbia*, b. May 16, 1814 ; m. Rev.
           P. G. Cook and resided in Buffalo N. Y.

43.   5.   *Nancy Elizabeth*, b. April 26, 1816 ; m. Robert
           Ransom Drake.

44.   6.   *Norman Wheeler*, b. Aug. 12, 1818; He was
           for many years afflicted with bronchitis, was
           partner in a store at Elk Horn, Wis. for a few
           months in 1850 and finally d. unm. July 14,1859.
           He was a young man of much personal worth.

45.   7.   *Joseph Benjamin*, b. Dec. 11, 1820 ; m. Caroline
           S. Hall.

46.   8.   *Christopher Columbus*, b. Aug. 31, 1825 ; d.
           Nov. 7, 1826.

47.   9.   *Esther Ann*, b. Feb. 3, 1827 ; m. 1st. James

Kellogg. April 22, 1846, and had son *Joseph Tottingham*, b.Feb. 3, 1849, James d. July 2, 1851 and she m. 2d. Feb. 18, 1857, James A. Cheney of Rutland, Vt.

48. 10. *Mary Georgiana*,b. March 23, 1831 ; d March 31, 1832.

(35) VI GEORGE W. TOTTINGHAM, m. Aug. 26, 1838 Susan Wellington, and now lives near the Village in Westminster, and is a farmer. Children :

49. 1. *Franklin G.*, b. Oct. 8, 1842 ; d. Sept. 23,1843.
50. 2. *Mary S.*, b. June 12, 1844 ; d. Sept. 22, 1844.
51. 3. *George*, b. Aug. 26, 1845 ; d. Feb. 2, 1846.
*52. 4. *Waldo G.*,b. July 15, 1847.
53, 5. *Charles E.*, b. Oct. 26, 1849 ; d. Feb. 9. 1853.

(40) VI JAMES GORHAM, m. Dec. 9, 1829 Angeline Wood Tottingham, and resided in Pittsford, Vt. until his death which occurred Jan. 11, 1849. His widow still survived in 1865. They had children :

54. 1. *James Tottingham*, b. April 26, 1834 ; m. July 3, 1855 Addie N. Ives.
55. 2. *Mary E. W.*, b. Dec. 3, 1839 ; m. Sept. 28, 1859, Rollin S. Meachem.

41 VI BOWMAN BROWN TOTTINGHAM, m. Sept. 7, 1842 Amanda Hunt of Shoreham, Vt., in which place he has ever since resided as an extensive farmer. They have children :

56. 1. *Mary Jane*, b. July 13, 1843 ; m. Sept. 1862 William Horton.
57. 2. *Albert Edwin.* b. Dec. 3, 1844.
58. 3. *Lyman Hunt*, b. Sept. 12, 1848.

59. 4. *Ellen Angeline,* b. April 20, 1854.

(42) VI. Rev. PHILOS G. COOK A. M. of Buffalo, N. Y. b. Aug. 10, 1807, m. 1840 CLARISSA COLUM-
BIA, dau. of Dea. Joseph Tottingham. Philos graduated
A. B. at Middlebury College, Vt. in 1833 and at Auburn,
N. Y. Theological Seminary in 1848. He was a teacher
from 1833 to 1845. In 1862 he accepted the chaplaincy
of the 94 Reg. N. Y. Vols. and in August 1864 was near
Petersburg Va. in Genl. Crawford's Division of the 5th
army corps. Mr. Cook is ₁a gentleman of talent and of
fine scholarly attainments. Children :

60. 1. *George Tottingham,* b. Sept. 4, 1841. He en-
       listed as a private in the first Regiment raised at
       Buffalo, served two years, promoted to 2d Lieut.
       Severely wounded in the battle of Antietam an d
       transferred to the Veteran Reserve corps, with the
       same rank and was at Washington, D. C. in Aug.
       1864.

61. 2. *Clarissa Amelia,* b. Nov. 21, 1843. She grad-
       uated at the Buffalo Female Academy in 1862 and
       has been a teacher in an academy in Niagara
       county.

62. 3. *Philos Goodrich,* b. Dec. 16, 1845.

63. 4. *Mary Columbia,* b. March 4, 1848.

64. 5. *Henry Mills,* b. June 28, 1850.

65. 6. *Laura Elizabeth,* b. Jan. 18, 1853.

66. 7. *Joseph William,* b. Nov. 4, 1855.

43 VI ROBERT RANSOM DRAKE, b. Oct. 4.
1816 ; m. Feb. 29, 1844, NANCY ELIZABETH TOTTINGHAM-
He is a merchant and resides at Pittsford Vt. Children :

67. 1. *Ella A.,* b. June 2, 1845.

68. 2. *Robert H.*, b. March 8, 1847.
69. 3. *Charles E.*, b. Sept. 25, 1849 ; d. Oct. 26, 1850.
70. 4. *Emilie H.*, b. May 1, 1852.
71. 5. *Grace M.*, b. March 1, 1854 ; d. March 15, 1854·
72. 6. *James B.*, b, Aug. 20, 1856 ; d. Oct. 24, 1857.
73. 7. *Norman T.*, b. Sept. 16, 1858.

45 VI JOSEPH BENJAMIN TOTTINGHAM, m. Aug. 12, 1846, CAROLINE S. HALL. and resided in Pittsford Vt. until his death Nov. 21, 1853. Before marriage he taught school in Wisconsin a few months and speculated some in Wisconsin land. He was a young man of much moral worth. His widow married· about 1858 Mr. Hitchcock and resides in Pittsford, Vt. Children :

74. 1. *Nancy J.*, b. Aug. 15, 1850.
75. 2. *Mary E.*, b. Sept. 3, 1853.

HISTORICAL SKETCHES OF SOME OF THE DESCENDANTS OF REV. EVERARDUS BOGARDUS.

1. Rev. EVERARDUS BOGARDUS, m. June 21, 1642 ANNETYE JANSEN, of New York the widow of Roelof Jansen of that city. Mr. Bogardus was the first minister of the Reformed Dutch Church at New Amsterdam about 1633 and obtained a grant of sixty two acres of land on Manhattan Island, now New York city, which afterwards became the Trinity Church Property and which has caused so much noise in the world. He was a native of Holland and about 1647 sailed for Holland, probably on the business of his church, and with 80 passengers was wrecked off the coast of Wales and all perished. It is said that Col. Aaron Burr first discovered a defect in the title of Trinity Church to this property and some of the heirs of Bogardus have prosecuted suits against Trinity Church to recover the property but failed under the statute of limitations. During the excitement over this property special efforts were made to trace out the descendants of Bogardus and it was found that the number reached nearly 10,000, in 1840. The late Isaac Hallenbake Esq. of Albany county N. Y. was among those who interested themselves in hunting up these heirs, and about twenty years ago he gave the following list of descendants to Rev. Charles Waldron of Cohoes N. Y. Children:

2. 1. *William*, b.—

3.   2.   *Cornelius*, b.—

4.   3.   *Johannes*, b.—

5.   4.   *Peter*, b, — m. Winthe Cornbock.

(5)   Il PETER BOGARDUS m. WINTHE CORNBOCK. Child :

6.   1.   *Maurich*, b. —; m, Peter Jacobus Bosborne.

(6)   III PETER JACOBUS BASBORNE, m. MAURICH BOGARDUS.   Children :

7·   1.   *Trytye*, b.—; m. Isaac Truax.

8.   2.   *Fytye*,b.—.

9.   3.   *Annaty*, b.—.

10.   4.   *Martye*, b.—.

(7)   IV ISAAC TRUAX, m. TRYTYE BOSBORNE. Child :

11.   1.   *Aham*, b.—.

(11)   V AHAM TRUAX, m.   Child :

12   1.   *Annacher*, b.—; m, Richard Van Vranken.

·(12)   VI RICHARD VAN VRANKEN, m. in 1737, ANNACHER TRUAX.   They and one son and six daughters. Children :

13.   1.   *Moses*, b.—.

14   2.   *Annacher*, b. —; m. Van Arnam.

15.   3,   *Annamay*, b.—; m. — Rosa.

16.   4.   *Annahit*, b.—; m. — Winne of Albany N. Y.

17.   5.   *Annzjonnah*, b.—; m. Minderson.

18.   6.   *Annacastena*, b.—; m. — Rev.— Slingerland who lived in Madison Wis.

19.   7.   *Anamaughter*, b. —; m. Capt. Hendricks Waldron.

(19) VII Capt. HENDRICKS WALDRON, of
Albany, N. Y. m. Nov. 1771, Margaretta Van Vron-
cha. Capt. Waldron, according to the laws then extant,
executed a Bond with surety, to "our Sovereign Lord
George the Third" in a penalty of £500, conditioned that
there was no legal impediment to such marriage. Capt.
Waldron's occupation was running sail vessels from Albany to New York City.   Children :

20. 1. *Cornelius*, b.—; m. Hester Van Arnam.
21. 2. *Richard*, b.—; m. Catharine Peak.   .
22 3. *Jane*, b. — m.; Henry Van Arnam.
23. 4. *Moses*, b.—; enlisted in the war of 1812 as Capt.
     of infantry, and died at Sacket's Harbor. He
     sent his sword to his sister Nancy,
24. 5. *Nancy*, or *Anna*, b. Sept. 20, 1782, m. Capt.
     George Young.
25. 6. *William*, b.—; m. Elizabeth Winne ; d. about
     1825.
26. 7. *Christiani*, b.—; m. Jacob Hollenbeck of Alba-
     ny Co. N. Y.
27. 8. *Henry*, b.—; m. Julian Newman and settled in
     Albany N. Y.   .
28. 9. *Gertrude*, b. April 27, 1793 ; m. Ist——Barck-
     ley and had son *Henry*, and dau. *Henrietta*. Mr.
     Barckley d. and she m. 2d, Dr. Jonathan Johnson
     Feb. 2d. 1818, and had *Adaline*, b. 1818 ; *George
     Young*, b. 1820 ; *Eliza Mann*, b. 1822, *Jane
     Ann*, b. 1824 ; *Stephen C.* b. 1825 ; *John*, b. 18 27.
     Dr. Johnson d. May 25, 1860 and Gertrude'
     March 28, 1864.

(24) VII. CAPT GEORGE YOUNG, was b. at

Hagerstown Maryland. 1773, and m. Nancy Waldron, cf Schenectady N. Y. in 1800. His mother, Christiana was the daughter of Christopher Vought, a wealthy farmer of Hunterdon N. J. and married, Rev. John Young of Hunterdon, a Lutheran minister, who was put in charge of the Hagerstown church. Christiana died when her son George was only two weeks old and George was taken home by Mr. Vought, his grandfather, and brought up to manhood. Rev. John Young married again and had a family, one son of which was a judge in Ohio. The last notice which the writer has found of him is the following in a letter from Rev. H.M. Machlenberg to Rev. Dr. Frey. linghausen of the University of Halle, dated about 1783 :

"In Maryland, in a neighborhood termed *Conecocheague*, (now Washington county) is stationed the Rev. Mr. Young, who has charge of three Congregations, Hagerstown &c. He was examined and ordained several years ago, by our American ministerium, but during the present year met with a sad accident : namely, his horse fell and threw him headlong on the ground, on his way to church. He arose again uninjured, but then his horse kicked him and broke three of his ribs which have not been properly set, but have grown crooked so that he moves with difficulty and will scarcely be able to continue his pastoral labors,' (See "Hallesche Nachrichten," page 1413.) In a previous letter dated Dec. 6, 1782 between the same persons it is stated that "Rev. Young in M. D. is a man who labors with industry and fidelity, and faithfully discharges his duties, both in life and doctrine in several congregations' (same page 1425. The writer is indebted to Rev. Dr. S. S. Schmucker of Gettysburg College, Pa. for the foregoing extract and translations from the German work.

Christopher Vought was a Loyalist during the Revolutionary war and much of his property was confiscated to the U.S. After the war be removed to Nova Scotia when where he received a large grant of land and a pension for life of 365, crowns a year from the British government. He returned to the United States about 1794 and settled at Duanesburg where he had 2000 acres of land that had not been confiscated. Half of this land he gave to Capt. George Young who made it his residence for many years.

Capt. Young first commenced business at Schenectady, N. Y. as a merchant but subsequently went on to his farm built a large hotel which he kept over thirty years and then removed to Elk Horn, Walworth Co, Wis., where he settled in June 1843. He died in August 1844 from an injury received in falling from an oat stack.

Capt. Young was several years Capt. of an independent company of Cavalry, which was called into service of the United States in the war of 1812,

Mrs. Nancy (or Anna as she called her self) Young was in excellent health as late as July 1866. Children :

29. 1. *Christiana Vought,* b. Sept. 9, 1801 . d. unm 1850.

80. 2. *Margarett,* b. Nov. 30, 1802.

31. 8. *Mary G.,* b. Jan. 9, 1805 ; m. Lewis Freeman.

32. 4. *Jean C.* b. Nov. 13, 1806; m. John Pike.

33. 5. *Christopher Vought,* b. Oct. 26, 1888, d. young.

84, 6. *Gertrude,* b. Nov. 10, 1810 ; m. Hon. George Gale.

85. 7. *John Vought,* b. March 17, 1813 ; d. young.

36. 8. *Anne,* b. March 16, 1815 ; m. William Vanderpool.

37, 9. *George Henry*, b. March 8, 1817 ; m. March 21, 1838, Hester Hilton. Graduated M. D. at Castleton Med. College, Vt. in fall of 1837, and practices medicine at Elk Horn, Wis.

38. 10. *John*, b. July 28, 1819 ; m. Eliza Tygert.

39. 11. *Catharine*, b. Oct. 31, 1822 ; m. Thomas Liddle.

40. 12. *Jacob Hollenbeck*, b. Oct. 20, 1624, unm.—is a farmer at Elk Horn, Wis.

41 13. *Elizabeth*, b. August 15, 1826 d. Oct. 15, 1828.

42. 14. *William McKowan*, b. March 31, 1829, unm. He Graduated M. D. at the Chicago Med. College in 1853, and for several years has been Post Master and has also practiced medicine at Galesville Wis.

THE RECORDS OF THE
SECOND FAMILY OF GALES.

Among the different families of Gales in the United States, with whom the writer has become acquainted, he found extant almost uniformly, the tradition that their ancestors were four brothers, natives of England, who landed at Boston in the early settlement of Massachusetts, from whence they became settlers in different parts of the country. That the Gales of this country were from England there is no doubt at the present day, and that the tradition is further corroborated by the appearance of · John Gale at Boston in 1634, Richard at Watertown in 1640, Edmund at Cambridge in 1642 and Hugh at Kittory or York in 1652 is also settled beyond a doubt by the records of Massachusetts; but that the Gales of this country descended from those four is, as yet only established so far as relates to the descendants of Richard, and the further fact that John died young and probably unmarried.

Whether either Edmund or Hugh had families we have no records, but on tracing the family of Richard, the writer soon found Gales that he was satisfied did not belong to his descendants and must be accounted for on some other hypothesis. If the tradition is true, then these persons were evidently the children of Edmond and Hugh or one of them, but as we do not find any of them as far north as York, or bearing the name of Hugh, the writer is forced to assume the probability that they were the children of Edmond of Cambridge, but were born in England, as no record of their birth has yet been found in this country.

But if we are totally in error, either in the tradition or the assumed probabilities, we nevertheless accomplish the purpose of this work, of giving historically all the facts we can gather relating to the persons named. If they were not relatives as assumed, they nevertheless had an existence, and filled their appropriate niches in the great temple of the world.

1   EDMOND GALE, of Cambridge, died in Boston, in 1642. Supposed children:

2   1   *Thomas* b. and m. probably in England and settled in New Haven, Ct., where he had *Martha* bapt. March 18, 1660, and *Abigail*, bapt. June 22, 1660. Their births are mentioned as follows: Martha, b. May 6, 1655 and Abigail, b. May 5, 1660. We have no further mention of Thomas or his children:

3   2   *Robert*, b.—. The only mention of him were the facts that May 14, 1659, he receipted sugar of William Hollisworth at Salem, and again in 1666, receipted 3700 lbs. of Muscovado Sugar at Salem.

4   3   *Ambrose*, b.—; m. Deborrah—.

5   4   *Bartholomew*, b.—; m. Mary.

6   5   *Edmond*, b—; m. Sarah Dixey.

7   6   *Abell*, b.—; m. Dinah—.

8   7   *Eliezer*, b.—; m. Elizabeth Bishop.

SECOND GENERATION.

(4)   II   AMBROSE GALE, of Marblehead, m. pro-

bably in England. In a deed, in 1698, his wife was called Deborrah and Deborrah Gale was admitted to the church 1695, which is the only mention of her name that we have. His first three children were baptized at Salem. He first purchases land at Marblehead, Dec. 4, 1663, at which time he was called a Fisherman. His next purchase was June 28, 1666 when he was called a Planter. He became a frequent dealer in real estate, in the deeds of which he was called a Fisherman, Planter, Cooper and Merchant, and it is very evident that his business was to buy fish, pack them and send them to market.— Indeed, at that early day, fishing, agriculture and shipbuilding was the business of most of the people of Mass.

Ambrose was appointed by the general Court of Mass., "a commissioner to end small causes" at Marblehead, June 1, 1677 ; and Oct. 11, 1682, he was appointed "surveyor of damaged goods" for the same port. He was also the founder of the church at Marblehead and its leading member. He d. in August 1708, at Marblehead.

Children :

10 . 1 *Benjamin*, bap. at Salem, May 17, 1663.
11   2 *Elizabeth*, bap. the same time and place as Benjamin, m. Thomas Roots of Boston, and had dau. Mary, who m. Azor Gale.
12   3 *Charity*, bap. June 17, 1664 ; m. Mark Haskoll.
13   4 *Ambrose*, bap. 1665 ; m. Jemima—.
14   5 *Deliverence*, b—; m. Benjamin James.

(5) II BARTHOLMEW GALE, of Salem, m. in 1662, Mary—.

He was a shipwright by trade and resided in Salem.

Children :

15 1 *Samuel*, (?) b.— ; m. Mary—.

16 2 *Abraham*, b. Sept. 18, 1666 ; m. Lydia Ropes.

17 3 *Isaac*, b. May 2, 1669.

18 4 *Jacob*, b. Aug. 15, 1671. He was a shipwright and died in Boston, Aug. 6, 1727. No account of any wife or family.

19 5 *Bartholomew*, b. April 26, 1674.

20 6 *Daniel*, b. Aug. 17, 1676 ; m. Rebecka Sweatt.

21 7 *Mary*, b. twin with Daniel.

22 8 *Rachel*, b. March 17, 1678.

(6) II EDMOND GALE, of Beverly, m. SARAH, dau. of Capt. William Dixey, a yeoman, late of Beverly.

Edmond first appears as made freeman at Salem, in 1660, said to be of Salisbury ; then, Feb. 18, 1663, purchases land at Marblehead ; he sells his land, June 8, 16-69, and is called a "fisherman." In April, 1672, he appears at Beverly, where he is called a "seaman." Here he often buys and sells land until March 10, 1717—18, when "Sarah, of Beverly, widow of Edmond Gale," sells land to Azor Gale. Azor, the same year gives land to James Chapman, in consideration of money furnished by Chapman to Edmond and said Chapman and Mary taking care of Edmond Azor's "honored father" during his last sickness. Children :

23 1 *Azor*, b. 1668; m. Mary Roots, of Boston.

24 2 *Mary*, b—; m. James Chapman.

(7) II ABELL GALLE, of Jamaica, Long Island, N. Y., m. probably in England DINAH—. Abell first appears as having granted to him "a lot to set his house on," in Jamaica, Oct. 18, 1665. He was called "husband-

man" and in 1683, his rate list contained 2 horses; 2 oxen; 4 "cowse"; 2, 3 year olds; 3, 2 year olds; 6 swine; 21 acres of land; and "1 head," total value £98 10s.— Subsequent to this date he occasionally bought and sold land as shown by deeds still an record. The history of Jamaica shows that the first settlers were from Mass., and that Abell was a member of the first Presbyterian Church We cannot give the children in the order they were born:

25 1 *John*, b.—; a miller; had wife Mary
26 2 *Jacob*, b.—; a house carpenter d. 1720.
27 3 *Nehemiah*, b.—; a weaver.
28 4 *Thomas*, b.—; a weaver.
29 5 *Sarah*, b.—; m. Benjamin Smith.
30 6 *Andrew*, b.—. He made his will and dated it Dec. 24, 1742, which will was probated in court, July 26, 1743. He gave his son-in-law, Anthony Yarinton of "Pekepsee," £1, as he said in the will, "for I think he has had sufficient already." He also gave grandson Gale Yarinton a "gun, sword and baldfaced mare," and to Andrew Yarington a gun, and all the balance of the estate to his wife Mary. He evidently had only one dau. and no sons.

(8) II ELIEZER GALE, of Salem, m. Sept. 25, 1679, ELIZABETH BISHOP, of Salem. Children:

31 1 *James*, b. Nov. 15, 1679; d. May 20, 1689.
32 2 *John*, b. Aug. 31, 1681.
33 3 *Abigail*, b. Dec. 7, 1684.
34 4 *Ruth*, b. July 12, 1687.
35 5 *Edward*, b. April 28, 1689.
36 6 *James*, b. May 25, 1691.
37 7 *Samuel*, b. Sept. 17, 1698.

38 8 *Eliezer*, b. July 8, 1699.
39 9 *Mehitable*, b. April 11, 1701.

THIRD GENERATION.

(10) III BENJAMIN GALE, of Marblehead, m.
1st, LYDIA—, and second, after 1699, DELIVERANCE—.
He was called a "cordwainer" in a deed in 1710. He d.
August 13, 1714 and his wife, Deliverance, survived him.
Children :
40 1 *Mary*, b. April 6, 1677.
41 2 *Jo.eph*, b. Sept. 13, 1679 ; d. young.
42 3 *John*, b. about 1681 ; m. Marian—.
43 4 *Ambrose*, b. January 1, 1683.
44 5 *Elizabeth*, b. Feb. 1, 1685.
45 6 *Daly*, b. Feb. 29, 1690.
46 7 *Benjamin*, b. Nov. 5, 1694 ; m. Eleaner—.
47 8 *Joseph*, bap. Feb. 9, 1596 ; m. Hannah Charter.
48 9 *Samuel*, b, Oct. 3, 1699 ; m. Mary Hadden.

(13) III AMBROSE GALE, of Marblehead, m.
and lived at Marblehead. Had wife JEMIMA. He d. in
1717, and was called Ambrose Jr. Children :
49 1 *Elizabeth*, bap. March 22, 1690.
50 2 *Mary*, bap. Nov. 12, 1693.
51 3 *Sarah*,, bap. Jan. 12, 1696.
52 4 *Deborah*, bap. Nov. 26, 1697.
53 5 *Ambrose*, bap. June 30, 1700.
54 6 *Thomas*, b. 1712.
55 7 *Benjamin*, bap. Aug. 8, 1714.

(15) III SAMUEL GALE. of Salem, m. MARY—.
Children :
56 1 *Mary*, b. Jan. 17, 1690.

M1

57 2 *Samuel*, b. Jan. 25, 1693.
58 3 *Sarah*, b. Nov. 19, 1699.
59 4 *Abraham*, b. Sept. 6.

(16) III ABRAHAM GALE, of Salem, m. March
31, 1696, Lydia Ropes. Children :
60 1 *Edmond*, b. June 22, 1696 ; m. Anna—.
61 2 *William*, b. Aug. 13, 1699 ; m. Elizabeth
       Grant.
62 3 *Abraham*, b. Sept.

(20) III DANIEL GALE, of Bradford, m. Nov.
1700, REBECKAH SWEAT, dau. of Stephen Sweat of Newbury, and settled in that town. He was a shipwright,but
in the latter part of his life speculated some in real estate,
in Newbury, Haverhill, Amesbury and Bradford. He
finally removed to Bradford about 1740, and was there in
1742.
    Jacob is the only child we can find a record of, but we
give him Benjamin and Stephen on circumstantial evidence, which may prove an error. Children :
63 1 *Benjamin*, (?) b.—; m. Hannah Clement.
64 2 *Jacob*, b. Nov. 30, 1708 ; m. Susannah—.
65 3 *Stephen*, (?) b.—; m. Ednah Little.

(23) III CAPT. AZOR GALE, of Marblehead, m.
MARY ROOTS,of Boston granddaughter of Ambrose Gale,of
Marblehead,where he lived from about 1699 to 1710 when
he removed to Marblehead. He followed the sea for several years, became Captain of a vessel and after his settlement at Marblehead, a merchant. He d. January 28,17-
27 ; his will was proved Feb. 9, of the same year and his
estate valued in the inventory at £2943 8s. 9d.. He
dealt considerably in real estate. Mary, his widow, was

executrix. His monument still stands on 'Burying Hill,' at Marblehead. Children :

66 1 *Edmond*, b—; m. Anna—.
67 2 *Elizabeth*, b. March 25, 1701.
68 3 *Azor*, b. about 1702 : m. Anna Noyes, of Boston, niece of Gov. Belcher. He was a merchant in Boston, and d. in 1728, leaving dau. *Anna*, b. April 4, 1726. The widow m. Feb. 14, 1733, the celebrated Rev. Mather Byles, the Tory minister of Boston.
69 4 *Roots*, b. Aug. 7, 1704 ; d. Dec. 24, 1728.
70 5 *Sarah*, b—.
71 6 *Mary*, b.—.
72 7 *Joseph*, bap. Feb. 17, 1711, m. Mary—.
73 8 *Jemima*, bap. Sept. 28, 1712.
74 9 *Thomas*, bap. Aug. 30, 1713 ; m. Alice Bray.
75 10 *William*, bap. Oct. 10, 1714 ; d. young.
76 11 *Ambrose*, bap. Jan. 16, 1717.
77 12 *William*, bap. Aug. 24, 1718 ; m. Sarah—.

(25) III. JOHN GALE, of Goshen, N. Y. m. MARY —. He owned mills in Jamaica L. I. and was a miller until 1721, when he sold out for £1500—, and removed the same year to Goshen where he became one of the proprietors of the new town. The records of Jamaica say but little about the Gales. John, however, obtained leave of the town "to set up a grist mill" April 1, 1704 ; was a soldier in Capt. Peter Schuyler's company in 1692, probably to serve against the French ; Feb. 4, 1708-9 was rated 16s 8d on minister's salary and was vestry-man in 1717. In Goshen, John was appointed an *elizor* in a suit by the court in 1726. His will was dated May 3, 1746 and was proved up Oct. 24, 1750. He named in

his will the following children :

78 1 *John*, b—; m. Hannah—.
79 2 *Daniel*, b—.
80 3 *Thomas*, b—.
81 4 *Abraham*, b—.
82 5 *Hezekiah*, b—.
83 6 *Joseph*, b—; m. Rebecca —.
84 7 *Benjamin*, b. 1715.
85 8 *Catharine*, b—; m. — Ludlam.

(28) III. THOMAS GALE, of Jamaica of L. I., N. Y. m.—. He went to learn his trade of "weaver," of Richard Wright, but was dissatisfied and returned home in 1693, and Mr. Wright, to settle, gave Thomas the use of his "loom and privilege of weaving a piece of Dugget for himself." He was called a weaver in 1703, and in 1717 his father gave him his homestead for "natural love and affection" and probably received his support from Thomas the balance of his life. What became of Thomas and his brother Nehemiah we have no information, but like John, they probably removed from L. I. to some of the southern counties of New York. The writer has no records of their families.

FOURTH GENERATION.

(42) IV JOHN GALE, of Marblehead, m. MARI-AN—. He d. in 1724. Children :

88 1 *John*, bap. May 14, 1704 ; m. Susanna Dennis.
89 2 *Annis*, bap. Oct. 14, 1705.
90 3 *Joseph*, bap. Nov. 24, 1706 ; m—.
91 4 *Benjamin*, bap. Nov. 24, 1706 ; d. young.
92 5 *Ambrose*, bap. Oct. 8, 1710.
93 6 *Benjamin*, bap. Feb. 22, 1713.

94   7   *Edward*, bap. May 31, 1713.

(46)   IV   BENJAMIN GALE, of Marblehead ; m.
ELEANOR—.   Children :
95   1   *Deliverance*, bap. April 20, 1718;   m. William
          Smith.
96   2   *Mary*, bap. Feb. 14, 1719.
97   3   *Eliza*, bap. Nov. 5, 1721.

(47)   IV   JOSEPH GALE, of Marblehead, m. Oct.
21, 1729, HANNAH CHARTER, of the same town.   Children :
98   1   *Joseph*, b. March 21, 1730.
99   2   *Ambrose*, b. Jan. 1, 1732.
100   3   *John*, bap. May 4, 1735.
101   4   *Hannah*, bap. April 17, 1737.
102   5   *Samuel*, bap. Nov. 25, 1739.

(48)   IV   SAMUEL GALE.of Marblehead,m. Dec,7,
1718. MARY HADDEN.   Children :
103   1   *Mary*, bap. Oct. 21, 1722; m. Moses Phillips,
          Junior.
104   2   *Samuel* bap. Feb. 28, 1724 ; d. young.
105   3   *Eliza*, bap. Sept. 17. 1727.
106   4   *Deliverance*, bap. June 21, 1730.
107   5   *Hannah*, bap. May 20, 1733. '
108   6   *Samuel*, bap. Oct. 26, 1735 ; m. Hannah Vick-
          ary.

(60)   IV   EDMOND GALE, of Salem, m. ANNA—.
Children :
109   1   *Edmond*, b. July 7, 1723.
110   2   *Lydia*, b. Aug. 12, 1725.

(61)   IV   WILLIAM GALE, of Salem, m. Dec. 15
1721, ELIZABETH GRANT, of the same place.   Children:

111	1	*William*, b. Oct. 5, 1722.	
112	2	*Elizabeth*, b. July 26, 1724.	
113	3	*Samuel*, b. June 25, 1726.	
114	4	*Mary*, b. Oct. 3, 1728.	
115	5	*Ann*, b. March 8, 1730.	
116	6	*Abigail*, b. Oct. 3, 1735.	
117	7	*Sarah*, b. April 3, 1738.	
118	8	*Lydia*, b. Sept. 9, 1740.	
119	9	*Abraham*, b. Aug. 2, 1742.	

(63)   IV   CAPT. BENJAMIN GALE, of Haverhill, m.
Nov. 2, 1729, HANNAH CLEMENT, of the same place.

Capt. Gale was constable of the town, in 1741, Lieut.
and acting Capt. of the first company of militia, in 1757,
and afterwards Captain, and was prominent in town.
Children :

120	1	*Ruth*, b. March 31, 1731 ; d. Aug. 10, 1736.
121	2	*Samuel*, b. March 15, 1734 ; d. April 17, 1736.
122	3	*Samuel*, b. Oct. 11, 1736; m. Deliverance Wakefield.
123	4	*Daniel*, b. April 5, 1739 ; m. Ruth Carter.
124	5	*Benjamin*, b. April 1, 1741 ; d. July 19, 1746.
125	6	*Ruth*, b. Feb. 2, 1743.
126	7	*Moses*, b. March 21, 1745 ; m. Mary Appleton.
127	8	*Benjamin*, b. March 19, 1748.
128	9	*Hannah*, b. June 1751.

(64)   IV   JACOB GALE, of East Kingston, N. H.
m. SUSANNAH—.

In 1742, he was married and living in Kingston, N.H.
and that year, he and his wife, deeded a house and lot in
Newbury, Mass., in which deed he was called a "Joiner."
He removed and settled in East Kingston after 1756 and

previous to 1770. In 1774, he was a delegate to a convention at Exeter, N. H., held for the purpose of appointing members of Congress to Philadelphia. Children :

129 1 *Jacob* [?] b.—; m.—. Had a family in East Kingston, N. H.

130 2 *Susanna,* b. Nov. 28, 1737.

131 3 *Daniel,* b. Sept. 2, 1739 ; m. and removed to Gilmington, N. H. in 1780.

132 4 *Eliphalet,* b. Sept. 5, 1741.

133 5 *Amos,* b. April 9, 1744 ; m. Hannah Gilman.

134 6 *Eli,* b. Feb. 23, 1745 ; m Dorithy—.

135 7 *Mary,* b. Nov. 22, 1747.

136 8 *Benjamin,* b. March 6, 1749 ; d. Sept. 22, 1771.

137 9 *John Collins,* b. Nov. 26, 1750.

138 10 *Stephen,* b. Oct. 12, 1752 ; d. Oct. 23, 1754.

139 11 *Henry,* b. Oct. 2, 1754 ; d. Oct. 19, 1754.

140 12 *Stephen,* b. Jan. 5, 1756 ; d. Jan. 22, 1770.

(65) IV STEPHEN GALE, of Haverhill, m. Dec. 17, 1734, EDNAH LITTLE, of the same town. He d. early in 1736 and his wife was appointed administratrix, in Mar. 1736. Child :

141 1 *Stephen,* b. June 8, 1736. He belonged to the third company of militia in Haverhill, in 1757. He was a Joiner and removed to Epping, N. H., previous to 1760.

(72) IV JOSEPH GALE, of Boston, m. MARY—, probably of the same city. He was called an "Upholsterer" in Boston, and d, previous to 1785. His widow survived him. Children :

142 1 *Joseph,* b. March 1, 1736 ; m. Sarah Huntington.

143 2 *Mary,* b. July 30, 1738.

144   3   *Elizabeth*, b. May 18, 1740; d. in 1817 unm.; willed her property to her neices and nephew, valued at $1,200, and tomb at $150,00, in chapel burying ground.

145   4   *Lydia*, b. Jan. 2, 1743–4 ; m. —Symmes.

146   5   *William*, b. April 26, 1746 ; m. and had dau. *Elizabeth*, and *Lydia Symmes*, and son *William. Alden*. He was a merchant in Boston and d. previous to 1817.

(74)   IV   THOMAS GALE, of Marblehead, m. Dec. 25, 1735, ALICE BRAY. She d. Oct. 24, 1736 "aged 20 years" and her grave stone still stands on "Burying Hill." He m. second, ELIZA—; previous to 1739, and d. 1770 and his will was proved, April 2, 1770, by his son Ambrose.— Children :

147   1   *Ambrose*, bap. Oct. 31, 1736.

148   2   *Eliza*, bap. Oct. 14, 1739 ; m. Stephen Chipman, July 15, 1758.

(77)   IV   CAPT. WILLIAM GALE, of Marblehead, m. SARAH—,and d. Jan. 30,1762. His monument stands on the "Burying Hill" in Marblehead. In 1756, he was Captain of the militia, and twelve men were drafted from his company to serve in the French War. His will was proved, July 25, 1762 and property inventoried at £966 13s 0½d. Having no children he willed his estate to his wife.

(78)   IV   JOHN GALE, of Goshen, N. Y.,m. HANNAH—. He made his will, Oct. 10, 1760, which was proved up Jan. 27, 1761. It is supposed that he lived at Stamford, Ct., from 1732 to 1736 and was a Surveyor the latter year. Children :

149 1 *Daniel*, b.—; m. Dixan—; made his will, July
3, 1757, which was proved up, Oct. 14, of the
same year. He left sons, Daniel and Moses.—
Moses was a Physician, m. about 1750, Temperance—and d. in 1757. His widow then m. Rev.
Cotton Mather Smith, of Sharon, Ct.

150 2 *Samuel*, b.—; m. Elizabeth—.

151 3 *Coe*, b.—; m.—Carpenter.

152 4 *John*, b.—; m. Ann Jones.

153 5 *Benjamin*, b.—; m. Eleanor Carpenter.

154 6 *Sarah*, b.—.

155 7 *Cuzziah*, b.—; m. Roger Townsand, who was
killed ot the battle of Minisink ; his name is on
the monument at Goshen. She had, at least, one
daughter, *Sarah*.

(80) IV Hon.THOMAS GALE, of Goshen N.Y., was
a member of the New York General Assembly, from
Oct. 9, 1739 to 1750, and Judge of the Common Pleas
Court, of Orange Co., from 1740 to 1749. Judge Gale
and his brother Abraham, were petitioners for a grant
and patent of "Minissink" in 1770, but Judge Gale having died in the spring of that year, and having previously sold his interest, the patent was issued in the name of
the purchaser and Abraham Gale. Tradition assigns to
Judge Gale the following children who were said to have
been familiarly known as Tom, Dick, and Harry : Children :

156 1 *Thomas*, b.—.

157 2 *Richard*, b.—.

158 3 *Henry*, b.—.

(82) IV HEZEKIAH GALE, of Wallkill, Ulster

Co., N. Y. m. MARTHA —. His will was dated Aug. 20,
1784, and proved Nov. 12, of the same year.   Children :
156   1   *Abel*, b.—; m. Phebe Denton, 1770.
157   2   *Moses*, b—.
158   3   *Samuel*, b.—.
159   4   *Hannah*, b.—; m.—Smith.
160   5   *Martha*, b.—; m.—Lewes.
161   6   *Mary*, b.—; m. John Denton, of Goshen.

(84)   IV   Dr. BENJAMIN GALE, of Killingworth,
Ct. ; graduated at Yale College in 1733 ; studied medicine and settled as a physician at Killingworth, where he
died, May 21, 1790.   He became distinguished as a writer on Agriculture and Medicine.   An article on the
Small Pox, of his, was published and complimented by a
London Medical Magazine.   We have no records of his
family, but it is said that he had a son who was distinguished as a Divine and D. D.

(83)   IV   JOSEPH GALE, of Stamford, Ct., m. RE-
BECKAH—.   He was in the possession of a Fulling Mill
and was very fond of mathematics and is even said to
have calculated eclipses and made almanacs.   The family
traditions are that Joseph came from Yorkshire, England,
and that he had two uncles who came over and settled in
Massachusetts some years previous.   The traditions are
so common, in the different families, that, the writer thinks,
that they are not entitled to much credit and has therefore placed Joseph as a grand son, of Abel of Long Island, and as Joseph, the son of John, who otherwise could
not have been accounted for.   In April, 1760, Joseph sold,
for £160, his mansion house, shop and mill to his son,
William.   Since which time we find no further record of
him.   His children were :

162 1 *John*, b. Oct. 9, 1732 ; m. Sarah Waterbury.
163 2 *William*, b. May 29, 1735 ; m. Rebeckah Jaggery.
164 3 *Rogger*, b. Nov. 11, 1739.
165 4 *Mary*, b. March 25, 1740 ; m.
166 5 *Josiah*, b. June 5, 1742 ; m. Rachel Mead.
167 6 *Rebeckah*, b. Oct. 22, 1744.
168 7 *Sarah*, b. June 20, 1747.
169 8 *Samuel*, b. Dec. 16, 1748 ; m. Lydia Skinner.
170 9 *Noah*, b. Oct. 31, 1751.

FIFTH GENERATION.

(88) V JOHN GALE, of Marblehead, m. Oct. 23, 1727, SUSANNA DENNIS, of the same place. Children :
171 1 *Susan*, bap. July 11, 1728.
172 2 *Marian*, bap. May 2, 1731.
173 3 *Hannah*, bap. June 17, 1733.
174 4 *Sarah*, bap. May 30, 1735.
175 5 *John*, bap. April 17, 1737.
176 6 *Jonas*, bap. Aug. 19, 1739.

(108) V SAMUEL GALE, of Marblehead, m. Dec. 19. 1758, HANNAH VICKARY. Samuel is said to have been lost at sea. Children :
177 1 *Hannah*, bap. Jan. 17, 1762.
178 2 *Samuel*, bap. June 19, 1763 ; m. Bertha Humphrey.

(122) V SAMUEL GALE, of Haverhill, m. April 2, 1761, DELIVERANCE WAKEFIELD, of the same town.— He was a Blacksmith by trade and d. 1778. Children :
179 1 *Benjamin*, b. Jan. 2, 1762 ; d. July 7, 1763.
180 2 *Sarah*, b. Aug. 9, 1763 ; d. June 2, 1801.

181 3 *Benjamin,* b. March 12, 1765.

• 182 4 *Samuel,* b. Dec. 20, 1766.

183 5 *Joseph,* b. Nov. 18, 1768 ; m. Susannah Frye.

(123) V DANIEL GALE. of Concord, N. H., m.
Ruth, dau. of Dr. Ezra Carter of the same town. He
came from Haverhill and settled in Concord, N. H.
about 1760. He was a Blacksmith until about 1765,
when he became a celebrated Hotel Keeper for 35 years.
In 1798, he was Commissary of troops raised in N. H.,
in the expected war with France.. [See Hist. Concord,
N. H., p. 662.] He died Aug. 16, 1800, and his wife
April 1, 1832, aged 89. He is noticed in the history of
Concord, N. H. Children :

184 1 *Hannah,* b. April 20, 1762.

185 2 *Ezra,* b. Dec. 20, 1763.

186 3 *Moses,* b Nov. 15, 1765.

187 4 *Daniel,* b. Oct. 10, 1767.

188 5 *Benjamin,* b. June 5, 1769 ; m. Prudence Var-
          num.

189 6 *Ruth,* b. Oct. 6, 1771.

190 7 *Molly,* b. July 19, 1773.

191 8 *William,* b. Aug. 2, 1775 ; d. 1776.

192 9 *William,* b. March 17, 1777 ; m. Jane McCoy.

193 10 *Judith,* b. Jan. 17, 1779.

194 11 *Hubbard Carter,* b. Dec. 11, 1780.

195 12 *Sarah,* b. May 3, 1783.

196 13 *Betsey,* b. Jan. 13, 1786.

197 14 *Susey,* b. March 27, 1788.

(126) V MOSES GALE, of Haverhill, m. Oct. 12,
1769, MARY APPLETON, of the same town. He was a prominent merchant and leather dealer and advertised that he

would "exchange hides for shoes." His name appears several time; in Chase's History of Haverhill. Children :

198 1 *Moses*, b. Jan. 3, 1771.
199 2 *Mary*, b. Dec. 23, 1772.
200 3 *Hannah*. b. Sept. 25, 1779 ; m.—Appleton.
2)1 4 *Samuel*, b. Oct. 11, 1781 ; d. June 30, 1829.
2)2 5 *Nathaniel*, b.—; d. Jan. 1800.

(129) V JACOB GALE, of E. Kingston, N.H. m. ABIGAIL—. We have put Jacob as the son of Jacob of Kingston on circumstantial evidence, but he may not have been a son. Children :

293 1 *Abigail*, b. Nov. 28, 1763.
204 2 *Jacob*, b. Sept. 28, 1764.
205 3 *Henry*, b. Dec. 28, 1767.
206 4 *James*, b. Oct. 23, 1769.
207 5 *Apphia*, b. July 29, 1771.
2)8 6 *Israel* b. March 12, 1775.
203 7 *Stephen*, b. July 24, 1777 ; d. Jan. 23, 1782.
210 8 *Susanna*. b. Aug. 6. 1781.

(133) V DR. AMOS GALE, of East Kingston N. H., m. Nov. 12, 1765, HANNAH, only daughter of Daniel and Hannah Gilman. He studied medicine with Dr. Josiah Bartlett who was afterwards one of the signers of the Declaration of Independence, and from 1790 to 1794, Governor of N. H. Dr. Gale had an extensive practice in his profession, was a highly esteemed citizen and an early member of the N. H. Medical Society. Several young men studied the medical profession with him. He died of paralysis, June 8, 1813. They had children :

211 1 *Gilman*, b. Sept. 13, 1766.
212 2 *Amos*, b. Oct. 15, 1768 ; m. Sally Bartlett.
213 3 *Benjamin*, b. Nov. 25, 1771.

214 4 *Jonathan*, b. Dec. 9, 1773.
215 5 *Hannah*, b. Jan. 30, 1777 ; m. Dr. Ezra Bartlett, of Haverhill, N. H.
216 6 *Nathaniel*, b. Jan. 18, 1780.
217 7 *Stephen*, b. Jan. 28, 1783.
218 8 *Susannah*, b. Nov. 17, 1785 ; m. M. Atwood.
219 9 *Polly*, b. Dec. 12, 1789 ; m. Dr. John French, of Bath, N.H.
220 10 *Sally*, b. Jan. 4, 1793 ; m. Josiah Calif. of Saco, Me.

(134) V Capt. ELI GALE, of Amesbury, m. Dorithy—. Capt. Gale was a soldier in the Revolutionary War and was a Captain in the Militia as early as July 1775. Children :
221 1 *Ephraim Blaisdell*, b. Sept. 12, 1766.
222 2 *Hannah*, b. April 8, 1768 ; m. Ichabod Titcomb of Amesbury, Feb. 18, 1794.
223 3 *John*, b. Dec. 14, 1769 ; m. Sally Bagley.
224 4 *Stephen*, b. Sept. 16, 1771.
225 5 *Besorleal*, b. June 19,1773 ; m. Mary Worthen.
226 6 *Dimend Frameu*, b. July 13, 1775.
227 7 *Eli*, b. Dec. 25, 1777.
228 8 *Daniel*, b. March 11, 1780 ; m. Sally Quimby.
229 9 *William*, b. Nov. 3, 1781 ; m. Lucy—.
230 10 *Dorothy*, b. April 14, 1786 ; m. Josiah Barns.
231 11 *Reuben*, b. March 7, 1788.

(142) V Capt. JOSEPH GALE, of Norwich, Conn. m. June 13, 1765, SARAH HUNTINGTON. He was called, in a deed in 1785, a "Tin plate worker" ; was captain of a company from Conn.,in Col. Parsons 6th, Reg.,in Gen. Putnam's Brigade at the siege of Boston, in 1775, and af-

ter the close of the war, President Washington appointed him Collector of Customs in Conn., which office he held for several years. Capt. Glover used to say of him, that Capt. Gale was the only honest officer he ever knew, as he was the only one he could not bribe.

Capt. Gale, d. in 1799 and his wife. Sarah, 1787, aged 44 years and 7 months. Children:

232   1   *Azor*, b. June 10, 1766 ; m. Eunice Lord.

233   2   *Sarah*, b. March 10, 1768 ; m. Josiah Boutell.

234   3   *Joseph*, b. Nov. 29, 1770 ; went south where he married and died.

235   4   *William*, b. Dec. 10, 1776 ; m. Elizabeth Barr.

236   5   *Mary*. b. Aug. 21, 1779 ; d. Jan. 27, 1780.

237   6   *John*, b. May 4, 1781. He went south, m. Joseph's widow, removed to Alabama and d. about 1833.

238   7   *Mary*, b. July 21, 1783; m. Augustus Lathrop.

239   8   *James*, b. Jan. 3, 1786 ; d. April 26,of the same year.

(150)   V   Hon. SAMUEL GALE, of Goshen, N.Y. m. ELIZABETH—. He made his will Feb. 14, 1756,which was proved up, Feb. 28, 1757. He represented Orange Co., N. Y., from Sept. 1750, to his death,probably in Jan. 1757, in the New York General Assembly. In 1755, he was appointed Col. in the military.

240   1   *Samuel*, b.—; m, Christiana De Key.

241   2   *Richard*, b.—. A New York paper mentions the fact that May 25, 1767, "The house of Richand Gale of Goshen was burnt by accident, with the barn and outhouses. Household goods were saved."

242   3   *Asey*, b—.

243   4   *Juliana*, b.—; m. Geo. Dekey.

244   5   *Dorothy*, b.—; m. Verdine Ellsworth.   Licence dated May 16, 1759.

245   6   *Benjamin*, b. 1756, but after the date of his father's will. His name, of course, was not mentioned in this will, but he was named in the will of his uncle Benjamin as the "son of his brother Samuel." Samuel's will mentioned the fact that his wife was "big with child."

(151)   V   COE GALE, of New York, m. 1st,—Carpenter by whom he had four sons and two daughters. She d. and he m. 2d, Elizabeth Wisner, a widow, whose maiden name was Waters. He was a prominent member of the Presbyterian Church, of Goshen, N. Y., and an extensive merchant. From Goshen he removed to New York City and there lost his property about 1803, and died in 1826. By his special request, he was taken to Goshen and buried by the side of his old Pastor of the church. His widow d. in N. Y., in 1831 and was buried by the side of her late husband in Goshen. Children :

246   1   *John*, b.—; m. —Dunning and had two daughters who lived in N. Y. in 1866. He was a merchant in N. Y.

247   2   *Moses*, b.—; m. Susan—.

248   3   *Benjamin*, b.—; d. young.

248   4   *Sally*, b.--; m. Morris Thompson.

243   5   *Hannah*, b.—; m. —Jones.

248   6   *Coe*, b. —; m. only daughter of Anthony Steinbec, the architect of the City Hall, N. Y. Coe was a prominent lawyer in New York City and d. previous to 1840, leaving two daughters who

M2

m. rich and in 1866, were in Europe.

248 7 *Thomas Waters*, b. Aug. 3, 1790. His father having lost his property he commenced for himself at 13 years of age, became a merchant in New York City and amassed a large fortune.— He was still unmarried in 1866 and boarded at the popular Gramancy Park Hotel, N.Y.

248 8 *Benjamin Carpenter*, was a twin brother with Thomas W. and like him has been a successful N. Y. merchant, secured a fortune, is still a Bachelor and boards at the same Hotel.

(152) V Dr. JOHN GALE, of Goshen, N. Y., m. May 1756, Ann, dau. of Hon. David Jones, of Queens Co. N. Y., Speaker of the Colonial Assembly of N. Y. and a Judge of the Supreme Court. Dr. Gale was a prominent physician in Goshen and in 1756, was a Surgeon in the American Army in the French War. He lived and died in Goshen but we have no records of the family except the following in a New York paper: "July 18, 1790 Sanford Clark married Miss Arabella Gale, dau. of Dr. John Gale, all of Goshen, N. Y." The nephew, Thomas W. Gale, thinks Dr. Gale had other daughters but no sons.

(153) V Dea. BENJAMIN GALE, of Goshen, N. Y, m. Eleaner Carpenter. Licence given for marriage, June 2, 1763. He was Deacon of the First Presbyterian Church in Goshen, in 1775. His will was made, Feb. 8, 1782 and was proved in court May 13, of the same year. He was one of the Inspectors of Election, that elected, Nov. 27, 1775, Deputies to the Provincial Convention. He named in his will, nephew, *Benjamin*, son of his

n1

brother Samuel ; niece *Sarah*, dau. of Roger Townsend·
deceased ; nephews, *John*, *Moses* and *Benjamin*, sons of
his brother, Coe Gale and his own daughter, *Kesiah*.   He
had "Grist Mills, a lot now in possession of Coe Gale"
and considerable other property.   His brothers Coe and
Dr. John Gale were named as executors.   Child :
248   1   *Kesiah,* b.—.

(156) V THOMAS GALE, of Wallkill, N. Y.—
Children :
248   1   *John,* b.—.
249   2   *Henry,* b.—.
249   3   *Rebecca,* b.—.
249   4   *Sarah,* b.—.
249   5   *Abigail,* b.—.

(162) V JOHN GALE, of Stamford, Conn. m.
Sept. 20, 1752, SARAH. the sister of Gen. Waterbury, of
Revolutionary memory in Conn.   John was a seafaring
man and finally d. at sea.   He had children :
250   1   *John,* b. May 28, 1753.
251   2   *Sarah,* b. July 8, 1755 ; m.—Olmsted.   One
          of her descendants m. W. Sheldon Gale, of Gales·
          burg, Ill.
252   3   *Silvanus,* b. March 25, 1758.

(163) V WILLIAM GALE, of Stamford, Conn. m.
July 4, 1758, *Rebeckah Jagger*.   He purchased his father's mill and dwelling in 1760 and probably supported his
father the balance of his life.   He was surveyor in 1760
and renewed his allegiance to this government in 1777.
His children were :
253   1   *William,* b. Feb. 1, 1759.
254   2   *Isaac,* b. Nov. 17, 1760 ; m. Anne Lockwood.

255 3 *Reuben*, b. Jan. 30,1763 ; m. Martha Reynolds.
256 4 *Joseph*, b. Dec. 14, 1764.
257 5 *Nat*, b. Oct. 20, 1766.
258 6 *Isaac*, b. Sept. 27, 1768 ; probably an error in
        name.
259 7 *Betsey*, b. Dec. 19, 1770.
260 8 *Rufus*, b. July 14, 1774.
261 9 *Jeremiah*, b. Jan. 21, 1780.

(164) V ROGER GALE, of Stanford, N. Y., removed with his brothers from Stamford, Conn.,and according to Rev. Dr. Gale, had a large family, but we have
failed to get any record of them. However, Anson Gale
of Washington, D. C., says his ancestor, Jacob Gale, was
b. on the "Nine Partner's Patent," and if so, we think he
must be the son of Roger, as we do not find Jacob named
among the children of the other Gale families on that
Patent. Child :
262 1 *Jacob*,(?) b.—.

(166) V JOSIAH GALE, of Amenia,Dutchess Co.
N. Y., m. RACHEL MEAD. Josiah, with several of his
brothers, removed from Stamford, Conn, to a place called
Stanford, Dutchess Co. N. Y.,where they were afterwards
married. The writer cannot now locate any town of that
name in the same County, as Josiah died at Amenia, in
1797, he presumes that the name of Stanford was at an
early day changed to Amenia,which is located in the eastern part of the County on what was anciently called- "The
Great Nine Partner's Patent." Children :
263 1 *Sarah*, b.—; m. Henry Kinney.
264 2 *Rachael*, b.—; m. m. Dr. Barton of Amenia.
265 3 *Phœbe*, b.—; m. Andrew Finch.

266 4 *Rebecca*, b.—; m.—Goodrich.

267 5 *Roba*, b. —; m.—Curtis.

268 6 *Elizabeth*, b.—; m. Nathan Beckwith.

269 7 *Nancy*, b.—; m. Henry Griffin.

270 8 *Clarinda*, b.—; m. Eber Leete.

271 9 *Josiah*, b. 1787 ; d. 1809.

272 10 *George Washington*, b. Dec. 3, 1789 ; m. Harriet Selden.

(169) V SAMUEL GALE, of Stephentown. Rensselaer Co., N. Y. m. 1st, LYDIA SKINNER. She d. and he m. 2d, JERUSHA HIBBARD. By his first wife he had two children and the balance by his second wife. Samuel first settled at Stanford or Amenia, N. Y., on the "Great Nine Partner's Patent," but subsequently removed to Rensselaer County where he died. Children :

273 1 *Joseph*, b.—. Was a prominent Physician.

274 2 *Hulda*, b.—.

275 3 *Nathan*, b.—; m. Eleanor Miller.

276 4 *Samuel*, b.—. Removed to Michigan 1815.

277 5 *William*, b.—. Removed to Michigan 1815.

278 6 *Lydia*, b.—.

279 7 *Jerusha*, b.—.

280 8 *Prinia*, b.—.

(170) V NOAH GALE, of Amenia, N. Y. m. and had :

281 1 *Platt*, b—.

282 2 *Augustus*, b.—.

283 3 *Walter*, b.—.

SIXTH GENERATION:.

(178) VI SAMUEL GALE, of Marblehead, m..

BERTHA HUMPHREY, Nov. 20, 1783. by whom he had his first three children when she died and he m. 2d, Feb. 5, 1795, ELIZABETH PROCTOR and had Elizabeth. He was lost at sea in 1802. Children :

284 1 *Samuel*, b. Sept. 1, 1784.

285 2 *Hannah*, b.—. Still living in 1865.

286 3 *William*, b.—. Lost at sea with his father 1802.

287 4 *Benjamin*, b.—. Still living in 1865.

288 5 *Elizabeth*, b.— ; d. 1821.

(183) VI JOSEPH GALE, of Pembroke, N. H., m. Nov. 4, 1794, SUSANNAH FRYE. Children :

289 1 *Sally*, b. Aug. 12, 1795 ; d. Oct. 25, 1804.

290 2 *Wakefield*, b. Jan. 18, 1797 ; m. Mary Louisa Bigelow.

291 3 *John*, b. April 13, 1798 ; d. May 2, 1798.

292 4 *Susan*, b. June 27, 1799 ; m. Rev. Calvin N. Ransum, Sept. 28, 1828, who resided at Springfield, Ohio, in 1865. She d. at Jacksontown, O., July 29, 1845.

293 5 *Lucinda*, b. April 17, 1803 ; m. Rev. Solomon Kittridge, who settled at Bedford, Ia., where he died. She d. at New Albany, Dec. 26, 1859, without issue.

294 6 *John Adams*, b. May 19 1807. He was a merchant at Cincinnati, Ohio, and connected with the Commissary Department of the U. S. service in 1864, and has a wife and two sons.

295 7 *Joseph Worcester*, b. Feb. 8, 1809. He was a teacher, then Sabbath School Missionary, and agent for several years. Resided in 1864 at New Albany, Ia., and had wife but no children.

296 8 *Sally White*, b. Dec. 8, 1812 ; d, July 18, 1814.

297 9 *Mary White*, b. Dec. 6, 1815 ; d. Sept. 20,1817.

298 10 *Abraham Burnham*, b. Oct. 17, 1817 ; d. Aug. 27, 1825.

299 11 *Samuel Mills*, b. April 16. 1822 ; d. Aug. 28, 1825.

(188) VI BENJAMIN GALE, of Concord, N. H., m. Nov. 28, 1801. PRUDENCE, daughter of Col. James Varnum of Dracut, Mass. Benjamin succeeded his father, Daniel, in the Hotel business at Concord, N. H.

Children :

300 1 *James Varnum*, b. Aug. 18, 1804 ; d. young.

301 2 *James Varnum*, b. Nov. 2, 1806.

302 3 *Ruth*, b. Sept. 23, 1808 ; d. Oct. 3, 1809.

303 4 *Ruth C.* b. Aug. 23, 1810.

304 5 *Elenor V.* b. Sept. 16, 1812.

305 6 *John V.* b. April 5, 1814.

306 7 *Benjamin*, b. April 13, 1819.

307 8 *Levi B.* b. May 17, 1821.

(192) VI WILLIAM GALE, of Hebron, N. H., m. JANE McCoy, of Dracut. Mass. Children :

308 1 *Adams Hugh*, b. 1806 ; m. Louisa Slack.

309 2 *Sarah*, b.—; m. Thompson Patter, of Cornwall, Vt.

310 3 *Hubbard C.* b.—; m—; no children. Lives in Wrenthan, Mass.

311 4 *Jane*, b.—; d. at 23 years of age.

312 5 *Page T.* b.—; m. Laura Chamberlain.

(212) VI DR. AMOS GALE, of Kingston, N. H., m. 1796, SALLY, youngest daughter of Gov. Josiah Bartlett. He studied medicine with his father and Dr. Levi Bartlett, and attended medical lectures in Boston. **He**

was an athletic and energetic man and characterized for his great assiduity and self-denial in the discharge of his profession. He had various town offices, was elected a member of the N. H. Medical Society, in 1800, and a member of the State Legislature in 1808. About twenty young men received their medical education under his instruction. Children :

313 1 *Ezra Bartlett*, b. Oct. 13,1797 ; m.Ruth White.

314 2 *Levi Bartlett*, b. Aug. 29, 1800 ; m. Sarah B. Keygan.

315 3 *Josiah Bartlett*, b. Jan. 11, 1803 ; m. Hannah F. Merrill.

316 4 *Amos Gilman*, b. Feb. 17, 1807 ; m. Mary G. Ayer.

317 5 *Stephen Madison*, b. Oct. 20, 1809 ; m. Hannah W. Johnson.

318 6 *Sarah Bartlett*, b. Sep^t. 5, 1811 ; m. R. White Esq. of South-Hampton, N. H., in 1835.

319 7 *Mary Bartlett*, b. Aug. 20, 1815; m. John Brown, of Haverhill, Mass.

(232) VI AZOR GALE, of Norwich, Conn., m. at same place, Feb. 3, 1793, EUNICE LORD, who d. July 26, 1819. Children :

320 1 *Sarah Edgerton*, b. Nov. 9, 1793 ; d. in 1808.

321 2 *Charles*, b. March 18, 1796.; m. Annie M. Marshall.

322 3 *Lydia Lord*, b. July 21, 1800; d. in infancy.

(233) VI JEDEDIAH BOUTELL, of Norwich, Conn., m. Oct. 1, 1794 SARAH, dau. of Capt. Joseph Gale of the same place. They removed to Troy, N. Y, where their children were born. She d. 1849. Children :

· **323** 1 *Sarah*, b. July 18, 1795 ; m. Elisha Corning,
in New Canaan, N. Y., March 16, 1814, and re-
moved to Otsego, N. Y. where they had *Harriet
E.*, b. April 5, 1815 ; m. Amos Dean, March 16,
1838 ; *Louisa F.*, b. March 2, 1817 ; m. Abner
Howe, of Cleveland, Ohio, May 12, 1850 ; *Mary
Fitch*, b, Feb. 22, 1819 ; m. James White, of N.
Y. City and d. at Oswego, N. Y., 1854.

324 2 *Harriet*, b. June 6,1798 ; d. 1799.

(235) VI WILLIAM GALE, of New London,
Conn. m. May 23, 1801, ELIZABETH BARR. Children :

325 1 *Betsey*, b. Feb. 13, 1802 ; m. May 12, 1825,
Nathaniel Richards and had dau, *Elizabeth*, b.
March 30, 1833.

326 2 *Mary Ann*, b. June 15, 1805 ; m. Charles
Bolbes, Nov. 18, 1822 ; had *Charles*, b. Feb. 3,
1824 ; *Elizabeth Richards*, b. Dec. 6, 1825 ;
William Gale, b. Nov. 19, 1827 ; *Nathaniel
Richards*, b. Nov. 11, 1829.

327 3 · *Sarah Edgerton*, b. Sept. 21,1810 ; m. Aug. 15,
1832, Samuel Lloyd, and had *Ann Huntington*,
b. May 26, 1833 ; d. 1837 ; *Samuel Hubbard*, b.
April 8, 1841

(238) VI AUGUSTUS LATHROP, of Norwich,
Conn., m. Nov. 15. 1808, Mary, dau. of Capt. Joseph
Gale, of the same town. She d. July 4,1839. Children :

328 1 *Azariah*, b. May 7, 1810 ; m. Sept. 11, 1836, at
Williamantic, Conn., Jane Fish. He d. 1862.

329 2 *Augustus Fredrick,*, b. Oct. 15. 1811; d. Nov.
7, 1818.

330 3 *John*, b. June 3, 1813 ; m. July 27, 1846, Laura

Tilton. Had no children.

331 4 *Mary Edgerton,* b. Dec. 19, 1814; m. May 1855, Lyman Baker. No children.

332 5 *Abby Whiting,* b. —twin with Mary; d. 1861.

333 6 *James Steadman,* b. July 2, 1816; m. Juliet A. Stanley, of Meriden, Conn.; had *Henry Augustus,* b. April 1, 1845; d. in the Union Army, Sept. 1864.

334 7 *Sarah Gale,* b. April 2, 1818; m. June 26,1845, Charles T. Champlain, of New London. Conn. and had *Sarah Bliss,* b. Oct. 13, 1848,

335 8 *Charlotte Augusta,* b. Feb. 23, 1820; m. Dec. 31, 1843, Henry W. Morgan, of Norwich, Conn. and had *Mary Augusta,* b. April 15, 1845, and *Sarah Lathrop,* b. Dec. 15, 1850

(240) VI Hon. SAMUEL GALE, of Goshen, N. Y. m. CHRISTIAN DeKEY license granted June 3, 1757.— He was a merchant in Goshen and furnished supplies to the army on the frontier in the French war of 1755 to 1760; was one of the Commissioners to run the boundary line between N. Y. and N. J. and member of the N. Y· Assembly from April 1769, until it was dissolved,Dec. 1775.

On the breaking out of the Revolution, Samuel was arrested by the Continental authorities for holding a treasonable correspondence with the British, and his name occurs among the published lists of Loyalists. We have no further record of him or his family,

(245) VI Dea. BENJAMIN GALE, of Goshen, N. Y., m. Nov. 8, 1781, MARY BRADNER, who was b. Feb. 20, 1764 and d. March 15, 1807. Dea. Gale d. March 8, 1813. Children:

1   *James*, b. Dec. 29, 1785 ; m. Elsa—who d. Nov. 5, 1844, aged 64 years.

335½ 2   *Gilbert Bradner*, b. April 14, 1797 ; m. **Dolly** Maria Gale.

(247)   VI   MOSES GALE, of New York, m.—Su- sAN—. He was a merchant in New York and made his will, Sept. 17, 1824, which was proved in court, June **24,** 1825. The children were minors at the father's death.— Children :

    1   *Edward B.* b.—; was living at Mobile, Alaba- ma, in 1866.

    2   *John C.*, b.—.

    3   *Coe*, b.—.

    4   *Eliza*, b.—.

The last three children are said to have d. unmarried.

(249)   VI   HENRY GALE, of Wallkill, N. Y. Children :

    1   *Cornelia M.* b. Sept. 17, 1817 ; m. William Ful- lerton Esq. a prominent lawyer at 11 Pine St., N. Y.. in 1866.

335¾ 2   *Benjamin Carpenter*, b. Sept. 15, 1819 ; m. Elizabeth C. King.

(250)   VI   JOHN GALE. We have no records of what became of him nor as to his family, and he **may** have followed the sea as did his father ; but solely on **the** ground of the similiarity of family names and location, we have taken the liberty to assign to him as a son, Griffin, who was known to have lived at Mamaroneck, N. Y.— Griffin, might, however, have been a brother of **John,** born after the family left Stamford, Conn. Child :

336   1   *Griffin*, b—.

(254) VI ISAAC GALE, of Stamford. Conn., m. July 4. 1779, ANNE LOCKWOOD. Has children :
337 1 *Josiah*, b. March 18, 1780.
338 2 *R.becra*, b. April 6, 1782.
339 3 *Amy*, b. Aug. 13, 1784.
340 4 *Seymour*, b. July 1, 1787.

(255) VI REUBEN GALE, of Stamford, Conn., m. June 1782, MARTHA REYNOLDS. Had children :
341 1 *Sally*, b. Sept. 13, 1782.
342 2 *William*, b. Oct. 3, 1784.
343 3 *Polly* b. April 5, 1787.
344 4 *Nathaniel,* b. Jan. 1, 1790.

(262) VI JACOB GALE, of Stauford, N. Y., m and had sons. Children :
345 1 *Jeremiah*, b.—; m. Elizabeth Armstrong.
346 2 *Ira,* b—.
347 3 *Joseph*, b.—.

(272) VI REV.GEORGE WASHINGTON GALE, D.D., of Galesburg, Ill., m. 1st, in 1820, HARRIET, dau. of Hon. Charles Selden, of Troy, N. Y., who was an officer in the Revolutionary War. She d. in 1840 and he m. 2d, in 1841, ESTHER, dau. of Daniel Williams, of Galesburgh, Ill. She d. the following year, and he m. 3d, in 1844, Lucy Merriman, of New Haven, Conn., who survived him. He d. Sept. 13, 1862. Had children :
348 1 *William Selden*. b. Feb. 1, 1822 ; m. Caroline Ferris.
349 2 *Harriet Y.* b Oct. 1823.
350 3 *George*, b. Jan. 1826 ; m. in 1857, Elizabeth Kennedy. Has no children ; lives in California.
351 4 *Josiah*, b. Nov. 1827 ; m. Dec. 1862, Louisa,

dau. of Samuel Clinton Jackson, of Galesburg.
He d. in June 1863.

352 5 *Mary Elizabeth*, b. Nov. 1829 ; m. 1856, Rev.
Edwin L. Hunt, of Augusta, Hancock Co., Ill.

353 6 *Margaret*, b. Dec. 1831; m. 1851, Prof. Henry
E. Hitchcock, of Galesburg.

354 7 *Charles Selden*, b. 1835 ; d. 1836.

355 8 *Joseph Dudley*, b· 1837 ; d. 1856.

356 9 *Roger*, b. and d. in March 1840.

357 10 *Henry Williams*, b. and d. in 1842.

We present an engraved likeness of Dr. Gale with a
biographical sketch written by Dr. Brainard of Philadelphia, taken from Wilson's Presbyterian Almanac for
1863

"George W. Gale, son of Josiah and Rachael Gale, of
Amenia, N. Y., was born at North East, Dutchess county,
New York, December 3, 1789. He graduated at Union
College, N. Y., studied Theology at Princeton, N. J., and
was licensed to preach the gospel by the Presbytery of
Hudson, in Sept. 1816. His first charge was at Adams,
Jefferson County, N. Y., where he was ordained by the
Presbytery of St. Lawrence, Oct. 29, 1819. Here he en-
joyed a great revival of religion; among the converts of
which he reckoned Rev. Charles G. Finney and many
other eminent men.

His health failing about 1826, he gave up his pastoral
charge, hired a farm in Western, Oneida Co., N. Y., and
took a class of students whom he instructed, allowing
them to pay for their board and tuition by laboring three
or four hours a day on his farm. Succeeding in this enterprise, he founded the Oneida *Manual Labor Institute*,
at Whitesboro', N.Y. For a time the Institution had a
great popularity and usefulness, educating probably some

... at Senior Christian Packard, of Galesburg.
... in some ...

352 ... *Mary Elizabeth* ... N. 1829; m. 1856 Rev.
... ... the ... name ... Horack Gale ...
... of ... ... Prof. H ...
... ...

354 7 ... S ... in ... 1838.

355 8 ... *pe ...* ... in 18 ... 1856.

356 9 ... *Josepe ...* ... b. in May ... 1840.

357 ... *Paro ...* ... b. ... d. in 1842.

... ... was ... of Dr. Gale with a
... ... Dr. Bushnell of Philadel-
... ... taken ... m ... Presbyterian Almanac for
1 ...

... ... Josiah and Rachael Gale, of
... South East, Dutchess county,
... He graduated at Union
... ... at Princeton, N. J., and
... ... by the Presbytery of
... ... His first charge was at Adams,
Jefferson ... N. Y., and he was ordained by th.
Presbytery of ... Lawrence, Oct. 20, 1819. Here he en
... ... revival ... ... among the converts of
... ... Rev. Charles G. Finney and many
... ...

... ... of ... Leaving ... his pastoral
cha ... ... in Western, Oneida Co. N. Y., an
in ... ... where he instructed, allowing
... ... to aid in it him by advice, those
for b ... ... at time. So wishing to educate
aga ... ... John *Howard* ... the ... far
... N. ... ... he ... the Institution had a
... perpendicularly ... in defures, educating probably some

Engraved by Samuel Sartain

Geo. W. Gale

hundreds of ministers and influential layman, and prompting to the establishment of similar institutions elsewhere over the country. We believe that this prosperity continued so only as Mr. Gale managed its affairs; but after he left, a spirit of ultraism and division arose, so that finally the Institution passed into other hands and lost its distinctive character. Nearly all Manual Labor Schools have failed, showing that the Oneida Institute owed its long success more to the wisdom, energy and benevolence of its founder than to the complex principle on which it was established.

But the great life-work of Mr. Gale was the founding of Knox College, at Galesburg, Illinois, in the year 1835. With herculean labor he first procured among Eastern churches funds for the purchase of a township of land and induced a large number of intelligent and influential families to migrate West, as the nucleus of a Christian community, in the midst of which the new College was to rise. He headed this migration, spent his first season in a log shanty, and shared the general hardships and perils of the undertaking. As our readers know, the enterprise was a complete and glorious success. The city of Galesburg with its ten thousand inhabitants, moral, healthy and prosperous; and Knox College, with an endowment of near a hundred thousand dollars, attest the wisdom, energy and benevolence of Mr. Gale. Visiting Galesburg, *si ejus monumentum quaeris—circumspice !*

In the College which he had founded, Dr. Gale officiated many years as a Professor, and held the office of Trustee at the time of his death. He was, from intellectual conviction, a sound Presbyterian; and therefore he resisted, with great earnestness and final success, all efforts from any quarter to unsettle the principles on which Knox College was founded. He was also much interested and engaged in protecting the Presbyterian churches of his vicinity from sectarian Proselytism, which has been attempted with plausible motives and on a grand scale.— Hence'he urged and advocated those Presbyterian organizations for Home Missions, which should secure the fair and natural development of Christianity under the church forms which he loved and regarded as most wise, orderly and scriptural. For this faithfulness to his ordination vows and his honest convictions, he received from influential sources a great storm of opposition and abuse, which burdened his last days, but which he bore with unflinching fortitude, and as great a measure of meekness as ordinarly pertains to the best of men.

In person, Dr. Gale was rather slightly formed, but his air was graceful, dignified and commanding. His features were regular and his countenance habitually expressed pensive thoughtfulness, firm resolution, and Christian benevolence. His mental constitution fitted him for bold enterprises ; and in the early part of his ministry, especially, he moved in the front rank with those who ventured upon strong measures for the advancement of Revivals, Sabbath-keeping and Temperance. He hated slavery always, but never allowed himself to run into a ruinous fanaticism "making havoc of the church."

He was thrice married. His first wife was Harriet, dau. of Charles Selden, of Troy, N. Y. ; his second, Esther, daughter of Daniel Williams, of Galesburgh, Illinois ; the third, Lucy, daughter of James Merriman, of New Haven, Connecticut. The last survives him. He left six children, all of them, it is believed by his first marriage.

As a husband and a father he was without reproach.— So far as we know, his children not only inherit the hon-

ored name, but many of the virtues of their excellent
father. His health was always feeble, especially in his
latter years. Probably his active mind, acute sensibility,
and laborious habits, wrought too powerfully for his physical strength. His trembling hand gave long premoni-
tion of that sudden paralysis, which closed his life at
Galesburgh, September 13, 1862, at the age of seventy-
two. At a good age, in the bosom of his family, of a gen-
tle disease, with the hopes of the gospel, surrounded by
the rich and enduring monuments of his piety, energy,
and benevolence, he passed quietly from earth to heaven.
So far as he is concerned such a life needs no eulogy, such
a death no regret. But we may remind ourselves of his
virtues for our imitation, and we may lament a death
which bereaves us of his friendship, his example, and his
prayers ; and the church of his presence and his influence.

His intellect was strong, clear, logical, acute, penetrat-
ing, active, well furnished, and well disciplined. In imag-
ination, style, and pulpit power he was respectable, but
not eminent. His judgment of men and things was
sound ; his hopefulness was large, his faith confiding, his
will resolute, his fortitude unshrinking, and his courage
unfaltering. A man governed by reason and conscience,
rather than by impulse and passion, you knew where to
find him. His prejudices, founded in conviction, were
strong, and his antipathies liable to be shaded with sever-
ity. His friendships were affectionate, trustful and enduring ; justifying the adhesion and confidence of his true
friends. His piety was a governing principle organized
into his whole being, and controlling his plans, his labors,
his comforts and his purse. Before those who deserved
rebuke he stood up sternly, but before his Maker he lay
in the dust. His works praise him, and his memory will

long be fresh and fragrant in the church."

(275) VI NATHAN GALE, of Nassau, Rensselaer Co., N.Y. m. Eleanor Miller. He d. in 1814, but his widow was alive in 1865. They had Children:

358 1 *Harriet*, b. 1807 ; m. Henry Young and has *Henry*, *Martin VanBuren* and *Elenor Frances*.

359 2 *Alanzo H.* b. 1809 ; m. Harriet Amanda L'amoreaux.

360 3 *Calvin S.* b. 1811; m. Harriet N. Blair..

361 4 *Fanny*, b. 1814 ; m. Royal B. Wright and had children : *Louisa Amanda*, *Cordelia Frances*, *Fredrick Nathan*, *Harriet Jane*, *Mary Melvina*, *Emma Adelia* and *Albert*.

SEVENTH GENERATION.

(284) VII SAMUEL GALE, of Marblehead, m.—Children :

362 1 *Samuel*, b. Nov. 8, 1808 ; m. Eliza—.

363 2 *Anna*, b. May 27, 1810.

364 3 *William*, b. Oct. 17, 1814.

365 4 *Charles*, b. Feb. 15, 1819.

(290) VII Rev. WAKEFIELD GALE, of Rockport, m. Sept. 18, 1828, Mary Louisa Bigelow, of Colchester, Conn. She d. April 12, 1861.

Wakefield fitted for college at Phillips' Academy, Andover, and entered Dartmouth College, in 1818 and graduated in 1822 ; entered the Theological Seminary at Andover, the same year, and graduated there in 1825. He commenced his ministerial labors at Eastport, Me., Oct. 30, of the same year, ordained an evangelist at Salem, May 17, 1826, but continued at Eastport, where he was installed pastor in 1829. He was dismissed from this church, Nov. 24, 1835 and May 4, 1836, installed pastor of the first Congregational Church at Rockport, where he continued until his dismissal, Feb. 10, 1864.

Mr. Gale is a sound theologian, an eloquent preacher and has proved a successful one, having, during his pastoral services of about 37 years, baptized about 576, admitted to the church 450, attended 842 funerals, married 856 persons, and written and preached over 3000 sermons. His health, in 1864 was remarkably good, and his eyes never had required glasses. His wife was an active, pious woman, and had been a great help to him in his ministerial labor. Children:

366 1 *William Wakefield*, b. and d. March 5, 1832.

367 2 *William Turner*, b. and d. Aug. 18, 1833,

368 3 *Ann Eliza Safford*, b. Oct. 19, 1835 ; m. Aug. 5, 1857, Lyman R. Williston, a teacher of a young ladies school at Cambridge.

369 4 *William Turner*, b. Dec. 31, 1837 ; is a merchant in Boston.

370 5 *Joseph Wakefield*, b. Sept. 18, 1839 ; m. Nov. 26, 1863, Hattie L. Jewell ; is a merchant in Rockport.

371 6 *Edwards*, b. Aug. 31, 1841 ; d. Sept. 22, 1842.

372 7 *Justin Edwards*, b. Nov. 10, 1844 ; is in the Junior Class of Harvard University in 1865.

373 8 *Jeremiah Evarts*, b. a twin brother with above ; and d. Nov. 10, 1844.

374 9 *Mary Louisa*, b. May 22, 1846 ; a pupil. in 1864, in Mr. Williston's school.

375 10 *John Newton*, b. Feb. 4, 1848 ; d. Jan. 27, 1849.

376 11 *Newton Bigelow*, b. Dec. 2, 1850 ; d. Jan. 4, 1851.

(308) VII ADAMS HUGH GALE, of New York
City, m. in 1829, Louisa Slack. She d. about 1844 and
he m. 2d, Margaret Harrison, N. Y. Adams H. is
the principal ot the firm of A. H. Gale & Co., No. 107, E.
12th St. N. Y. Piano Forte manufacturers. The firm is
composed of Adams H., Page T., his brother and Edward
G. Moran. The firm have a large capital invested in the
business which was established many years since. They
manufacture very superior toned instruments, which are
celebrated throughout the U. S., and have a very extensive sale. The firm are also distinguished for their benevolence in aiding in the establishment of educational institutions. They donated to Galesville University, in 1864
one of their best $450 pianos. In speaking of this dona-
tion the committee on education of the N. W. Wisconsin
Annual Conference of the Methodist Episcopal Church,
(having charge of the University) say : "The visitors (of
the Conference) also report the donation to the Musical
Department, of the University of a large, fine toned and
valuable piano forte, manufactured by A. H. Gale & Co.
of New York city. This munificence of strangers in a
distant city, not only challenges emulation, but evinces a
pure benevolence and an ardent love ot the science
of music, which are superior qualifications for manufacturers of those instruments. The friends ot the University
will long remember those lovers of good music by this act
of kindness."   Child :
377 1 *William Adams*, b. Sept. 12, 1854.

(312) VII. PAGE T. GALE, of New York City,
m. Laura Chamberlain, of the same city.
He is an active member of the firm of A. H. Gale &
Co., N. Y. piano forte manufacturers.   Children :

378 1 *Jane*, b—.
379 2 *Laura*, b—.
380 3 *Joseph*, b—.

(313) VII DR. EZRA BARTLETT GALE, of Kings..
ton N. H. m. July 31st, 1823, RUTH daughter of Richard
White Esq., of South Hampton, N. H. She died July
6, 1841 and he m. 2d, Nov. 22, 1842, EMILY, daughter of
Moses Atwood Esq., of Atkinson, N. H. He studied
medicine with his father and uncle, Dr. Levi Bartlett, attended medical lectures in Boston and at Brown University and received his degree of M. D., at that University,
in 1823. He was elected member of the N. H. Medical
Society and was highly esteemed as a physician, citizen,
and christian; he died suddenly in church of heart disease
March 19, 1854. He had children :

381 1 *Ezra White*, b. May 9, 1824. Graduated at
        Dartmouth College in 1843.
382 2 *Richard White*, b. Feb. 21, 1826 ; removed to
        Charlestown, S. C. in 1849.
383 3 *Amos Levi*, b. Aug. 2, 1828 ; resides in Methu-
        en, Mass.
384 4 *Sarah Ruth*, b. Feb. 10, 1832.
385 5 *Mary Bartlett*, b. Jan. 20, 1835.
·386 6 *Josiah Bartlett*, July 2, 1838 ; killed at the bat-
        tle of Antietam, in 1862.
387 7 *Rebecca White*, b. Nov. 16, 1840.
388 8 *Emily F. H.*, b. Oct. 7, 1843.
389 9 *Harriet Newell*, b. July 17, 1845.
390 10 *Helen Susan*, b. March 9, 1848.
391 11 *Moses Atwood*, b. Aug. 23, 1850.
392 12 *James Atwood*, b. Aug. 19, 1853. .

(314) VII Dr. LEVI BARTLETT GALE, of Boston, Mass., m. May 1837, Sarah B. Keygan. He studied medicine with his father, Dr. E.B. Gale and attended medical lectures in Boston and Brown University and received his degree of M. D. at that University. He practiced his profession a short time at Kingston, N. H. and removed to New York, in 1828. In 1830, he removed to Boston and became distinguished as a surgeon and occulist. In 1832. he was admitted a fellow of the Mass. Med. Society and the Boston Medical Association. He died of dysentery Aug. 1859. Had children :

393 1 *Isabel Bartlett,,* b. 1840.

394 2 *Frances Josephine,* b. 1843.

(315) VII Dr. JOSIAH BARTLETT GALE, of Salisbury, Mass., m. 1829, Hannah F., daughter of Jacob Merrill Esq., of Salisbury, Mass. He studied medicine with his father, and his brother L. B. Gale, and attended lectures and received his degree of M. D., at Brown University. He practiced a short time at Brentwood, N. H. and in 1826, settled at Salisbury, Mass., where he still resides. He had children :-

395 1 *Josiah Bartlett,* b.—.

396 2 *Howard,* b.—; d. in infancy.

(316) VII Dr. AMOS GILMAN GALE, of Manchester, N. H., m. Mary Green, daughter of Hon. Richard H. Ayer. Amos studied medicine with his brother, L. B. Gale and attended medical lectures at Dartmouth College. He first practiced his profession at Hocksett, N. H. for several years, and then removed to Manchester, N. H., where he had an extensive practice as a physician and surgeon ; he died of typhoid fever, Jan. 24, 1861.

The Manchester Mirror remarked of him as follows : "It is a heavy loss to any place to have the king of terrors remove such a man as Dr. Gale. Wealthy, enterprising,liberal to the poor, particularly encouraging to all deserving young men, his loss will be sincerely mourned by this community." Children :

397 1 *Susan Rebecca*, b. 1833 ; d. July 5, 1855.

(317) VII DR. STEPHEN MADISON GALE, of Newburyport, Mass., m. 1st, March 28, 1843, HANNAH W. JOHNSON ; she died March 19, 1850. He married 2d, April 28, 1853, P. JANE How, of Haverhill, Mass. ; she died May 7, 1860 and he married 3d, April 3, 1861, Mary H. How. He studied medicine with his brothers, Dr. E. B. Gale, of Kingston, N.H. and Dr. L. B. Gale, of Boston,attended three courses of Medical Lectures at Boston for three successive years and received his degree of M. D. at Harvard University in 1837. He commenced the practice of medicine at Derry, N. H., but in 1839, removed and settled in Methuen, Mass. and was that year admitted Fellow of the Mass. Med. Society In 1850, he removed and settled at Newburyport, Mass. and in 1856, was admitted a Fellow of the Mass. Homoepathic Med. Society. He had children :

398 1 *Alice Bartlett*, b. May 22, 1844 ; d. Sept. 14, 1846.

399 2 *Anna Bartlett*, b. March 14, 1848.

400 3 *George How*, b. May 1, 1860.

(320) VII CHARLES GALE, of Norwich, Conn. m. April 4, 1822, ANNIE M. MARSHALL of the same place. Children :

401 1 *David Lord*, b. Feb. 22, 1823 ; m. Lydia M. Phillips.

402 2 *John Hamilton*, b, Jan. 12, 1825 ; m.Phebe A. Pendleton.

403 3 *Eunice Lord*, b. May 4, 1827 ; m. William N. Delanoy.

404 4 *Thomas Marshall*, b. Sept. 8, 1829 ; m. Lucy M. Nimocks.

405 5 *Horace Eugene*, b. May 14, 1832 ; d. Aug. 8, same year.

406 6 *George Horace*, b. Aug. 3, 1833 ; m. Ellen Green.

407 7 *Charles Eugene*, b. Feb. 21, 1836 ; resides in Warren, Jo Davis Co., Ill.

408 8 *William Lyman*, b. Jan. 26, 1840 ; resides in Warren, Jo Davis Co., Ill.

(335½) VII GILBERT BRADNER GALE, of Elizabeth Port, N. J., m. DOLLY MARIA GALE, Jan. 16, 1817. Dolly was of another family of Gales, and was b. Oct. 1, 1798. The most of Gilbert's family were born in Goshen before he removed to Elizabeth Port. He was by occupation a farmer and highly esteemed in the community where he lived and d. about 1860. His widow still survived in 1866. Children :

1 *Harriet*, b. Dec. 16, 1817 ; m. Nov. 5, 1850, John H. Rolston and resides at Elizabeth Port, N. J.

2 *James*, b. May 23, 1820 ; unmarried and resides at Caldwell, Warren Co., N. Y.

3 *Daniel*, b. Sept. 14, 1822 ; m. Elizabeth Goodman and has *Ida, Florence* and *Thomson* and reside at Caldwell, N. Y.

4 *John Baird*, b. Jan. 24, 1826 ; m. C. C. Clark and has daughters *Minne* and *Edith May*. He

is a druggist at 186 Greenwich St., N. Y. and is doing a successful business.

5   *William Frederick*, b. March 11, 1828 ; m. Miranda H. Harrison and resides at Elizabeth, N. J. He is agent of the Jersey Central R.R.

6   *Gabriel Norton Phillips*, b. Aug. 7, 1830 ; unmarried and salesman at 257 Pearl St. N.Y.

7   *Egbert Jansen*, b. Aug. 7, 1830 ; m. **Mary** Hinchman and has son *Herrick*, and dau. *Matilda*. He is salesman at 78 Murray St. N.Y.

8   *Charles Henry*, b. Feb. 5, 1834 ; d. Sept. 17, 1850.

9   *George Halstead*, b. Nov. 1839 ; m. Miss Tarbell. He was Book-keeper at 257 Pearl St. N. Y., in 1866.

10   *Thomas Alexander*, b. Dec. 5,1841 ; m. Miss L. Brown.

(235¾) VII BENJAMIN CARPENTER GALE, of New York, m. Dec. 14.1842, ELIZABETH C. KING, of Middletown, Orange Co. N.Y. In 1866, and for several years previous, Mr. Gale was a wholesale and retail carpet merchant at 413 Canal St., N. Y. and had evidently accumulated considerable wealth. Children :

1   *William Henry*, b. Sept. 16, 1843. He read law and was admitted to the bar of the Supreme Court of N. Y., in April 1866, and is a young lawyer of good talents and education. His office was at 11 Pine St. N. Y.

2   *Sidney K.*, b. Sept. 10, 1854.

(336) VII GRIFFIN GALE, of Mamaroneck, N.Y. Nothing is known of his wife and the usual tradition says he was from England or Wales. We have placed him

on probilities, as the son of John, of Stamford, Conn. If
we are in error in this, his proper *status* will probably be
found when the other families of Abel's children are
traced out.   He had children :

409 1   *Sarah*, b.—.
410 2   *Sylvanus*, b.—; m. Abigail Smith.
411 3   *Andrew*, b.—.
412 4   *Griffin*, b—.
413 5   *Samuel*, b. Jan. 17, 1779.
414 6   *Dorothy*, b.—; m. Stephen Carpenter.
415 7   *Abby*, b.—; m. Stephen Roe.
416 8   *Elizabeth*, b. —,and m. —Lewis.
417 9   *Mary*, b.—; m. Haviland Cornell.

(345) VII JEREMIAH GALE. of Pokepsie, N.Y.
m. ELIZABETH ARMSTRONG of the same place.   Children :
418 1   *Peggy*, b.—; m. Dr. Christopher Kinsted, of
         N. Y. City.
419 2   *Eilza*, b.—; m. Dr. Frieghley of N.Y. City.
420 3   *Anson*, b. March 20,1794 ; m. Polly Hornbeck.
421 4   *Sally*, b.—; d. about 20 years of age.
422 5   *Edwin*, b.—; m.—, dau. of Judge Thompson,
         of Sullivan Co., N. Y.   He was connected with
         the N. Y. Sun for several years and d. about 18-
         59.   Had no children.

(347) VII JOSEPH GALE, of Peakskill, N. Y.
He served in the Revolution, m. and had children :
423 1   *Joseph*, b.—; Lives in Michigan.
424 2   *Daniel*, b.—; m. and had a provision store at
         No. 109, First St., N. Y., in 1864.

(348) VII WILLIAM SELDEN GALE,of Gales-
burg, Ill. m. in 1845, CAROLINE FERRIS,a lineal descend-

ant of Sarah who m. Mr. Omstead. Children :

425 1 *William Selden*, b. 1846.
426 2 *George Washington*, b. 1848.
427 3 *Charles*, b. 1850 ; d. 1851.
428 4 *Calvin*, b. 1852.
429 5 *Harriet*, b. 1854.
430 6 *Joseph Dudley*, b. 1856 ; d. 1857.
431 7 *Josiah*, b. 1858.
432 8 *John*, b. 1860 ; d. 1863.

(359) VII ALONZO H. GALE, of Brooklyn N.Y.
m. HARRIET L'AMOREAUX, Mr. Gale is a clothier by trade
but never pursued it as a business.   From 1828 to 1836
he was engaged in transportation ; from 1836 to 1849 he
was a money broker in N. Y. city ; from 1849 to 1853 he
was engaged in the Revenue Dep't of Government ; from
1853 to 1858, he practiced law in N. Y. city ; from 1858
to 1861 he was Port Warden of the Port of N. Y., and
from 1861 to 1866 he was Master Laborer of the Navy
Yard. They had children all of which died young
without issue :

433 I *Orphilia A.* b.—.
434 2 *Nathan A.* b.—.
435 3 *Francis L.* b.—.
436 4 *Laura A.* b.—.

(360) VII CALVINE S. GALE, m. HARRIET
NEWELL BLAIR. Children :

437 1 *Alanzo*, b.—.
438 2 *Adelaid*, b.—.
439 3 *Charlotte Newell*, b.—.
440 4 *Albert Hibbard.* b.—.
441 5 *Amelia*, b.—.

EIGHTH GENERATION.

(362) VIII SAMUEL GALE, of Lynn, m. Eliza.
He is a shoe manufacturer. Children : ·
442 1 *Hannah,* b. Nov., 25, 1835.
443 2 *Samuel,* b. August 14 1833 ; m. May 30,1859,
Susan A. Churchell ; had son, *Samuel.* b. Nov.,
11, 1860. He is a shoe-cutter, and resides in
Lynn.
444 3 *Mary,* b. Nov. 80, 1841.
445 4 *Sarah Jane,* b. May 29, 1848.
446 5 *Charles,* b. Sept. 12, 1852 : d. 1861.

(401) VIII DAVID LORD GALE, of Norwich
Conn., m. Jan. 14, 1844, LYDIA M. PHILLIPS of the same
place. Children :
447 1 *Charles William,* b. July 1, 1846.
448 2 *Ella Lucy,* July 1, 1849.

(402) VIII JOHN HAMILTON GALE, of Chi-
cago Ill., m. Oct. 8, 1849, PHEBE A. PENDLETON, of Nor-
witch Con. He is a merchant in Chicago in company
with a brother, George H. Children :
449 1 *Mary Emma,* b, Nov. 8, 1855.
450 2 *Annie Pendleton,* b. Aug. 4, 1859 : d. in Sept.
of same year.
451 3 *Clara,* b. March 1861 ; d. July 14, same year

(403) VIII WILLIAM NELSON DELANOY,
of Norwich, Con. m. Jan. 24, 1848, EUNICE LORD GALE,
of the same town. He d. at Havana, Cuba, Nov. 19,
1850, aged 34 years, and was brought home for inter-
ment. Children :

452   1   *Fred Nelson*, b. June 16, 1849.

453   2   *Elwood Marshall*, b. April 25, 1854, d. April 27, 1864.

(404) VIII THOMAS MARSHALL GALE, of San Francisco, Cal., m. Sept. 2, 1857, LUCY E. NIMOCKS at Carthage, N.Y. and removed to California. Children:

454   1   *Frank Walter*, b. at Folsom, Cal., Feb. 2, 1862.

455   2   *Charles Piercy*, b.—. twin brother with **Frank W.**; d, May 1862.

(406) VIII GEORGE HORACE GALE, of Chicago Ill., m. in Chicago, May 1, 1861, ELLEN GREEN, of the same place.

He is a Commission Merchant with his brother under the head of J.H.Gale & Co.,No.3,Hillard's Block,corner of Clark and S. Water St. The firm is doing a prosperous business. Child :

456   1   *Edward Russell*, b. Feb. 16, 1852.

(410) VIII COL. SYLVANUS GALE, of Galesville Ulster Co., N. Y., m. 1792, ABIGAIL SMITH. Col. Gale in the early part of his married life lived in Westchester Co., N. Y., then removed to the central part of the state and finally started the small village of Galesville in Ulster Co. He was a Colonel in the war of 1812.

457   1   *Walter C.* b.—. m. Ann Terpenning and had dau. *Maria*. He d. 1855.

458   2   *Sarah S.* b.—. , m. Gilbert Mulford : Had *James G. Abigail, Catharine, Green R.* She d. 1858.

459   3   *Ann*, b.—. ; m. Sepharine Masten ; Had *Sylvanus, Sepharine, Abba Jane, George, Emily* and *Seelah.*

460   4   *Elizabeth*, b.—. ; m. Issac Scudder. Had *Abba Jane*, *Mary* and *Emery Gale*.

461   5 · *Abel S.* b.—. ; m. Jennette Ray.

462   6   *Deborah*, b.—. ; m. A. Lane, and had five children.

463   7   *Freelove*, b.—. ; m. Joshua Reynolds. Had *Abba Jane* and *Sylvanus*.

464   8   *John*, b.—. ; m. Eliza Seymour. ·

465   9   *Maria*, b.—. ; m. Daniel Termilliger.

466 10   *Abba*, b.—. ; m. Marcus Henston. Had child *Matilda*.

467 11   *Dewitt Clinton*, b. April 9, 1813 ; m. Mary Jane Smith

468 12   *Peter Jay Monroe*, b. Sept. 5, 1815 ; m. Catharine Garrison.

469 13   *Bathsheba*, b.—. ; m. Denton Gerow. Had children : *Green*, *James*, *Baily*, and *Mary Jane*.

(411)   VIII   ANDREW GALE, of Westchester Co. N. Y., m. HANNAH DEVEAU. He d. in 1825. Children:

470   1   *Benjamin*, b.—. ; m. ; Had son *Benjamin*.

471   2   *Nicholas*, b.—.

472   3   *John*, b.—. ; m. and had *Frederick*, *Cornelia*, *Angeline*, and *Amarillae*.

473   *Lorinzo Dow*, b. —; m. Had dau. *Lucy*.

474   5   *Andrew Deveau*, b. Aug. 22, 1808 ; m. 1st, Lilles Carpenter.

475   6   *Mary*, b.—.

476   7   *Phebe*, b.—.

477   8   *Anna*, b.—.

478   9   *Susan*, b.—.

(412) VIII GRIFFIN GALE, m. —. He had children :

479 1 *Hiram*, b.—.
480 2 *Stephen*, b—.
481 3 *William*, b.—.
482 4 *Abba Jane*, b.—; m. Henry Strong.
483 5 *Phebe*, b.—; m. Floyd Cox.
484 6 *Sands*, b.—.
485 7 *Matilda*, b.—.
486 8 *Elizabeth*, b.—.
487 9 *Leonard*, b.—.
488 10 *James*, b.—.
489 11 *Griffin*, b.—.
490 12 *Elisha*, b.—.
491 13 *John*, b.—; m. and had *Leander*, *Morgan* and *Arthur*.

(413) VIII SAMUEL GALE, m. and had children
492 1 *Freelove*, b. June 5, 1802.
493 2 *Clarissa*, b. Aug. 20, 1803 ; m. Timothy Conklin.
494 3 *Thurza*, b. May 10, 1805.
495 4 *Phebe*, b. Jan. 21, 1807 ; m. Josiah Travis.
496 5 *Susan*, b. April 20, 1808 ; m. James Travis.
497 6 *Jane*, b. Feb. 28, 1810.
498 7 *Edmond*, b. Oct. 4, 1811.
499 8 *Esther*, b. Aug. 8, 1813 ; m. Henry Griffin.
500 9 *Leonard*, b. Nov. 14, 1815.
501 10 *Stephen*, b. April 24, 1820 ; m. —Summerbell.
502 11 *Moses*, b. Jan. 1, 1822.
503 12 *Martha*, b. Dec. 7, 18—; m. James Letchell.

(420) VIII ANSON GALE, of Montecello, N. Y.

m. POLLY HORNBECK. Children :

504 1 *Anson,* b. 1814 ; m. Lucinda Johnson.

505 2 *Elizabeth,* b.——; m. Dr. Hiram Dale. She had dau. *Jane,* when Dr. Dale died and Elizabeth now lives with her father.

506 3 *Jane,* b.——; d. at 19 years of age.

507 4 *Hiram,* b.——; m. and resides in Wawasing, Ulster Co. N. Y. No children.

NINTH GENERATION.

(464) 1X JOHN GALE, m. ELIZA SEYMOUR.—— They had children :

508 1 *Charlotte,* m. Isaac Decker.

509 2 *Mary Susan.*

510 3 *William.*

511 4 *Electa.*

512 5 *Rebecca.*

513 6 *Isaiah.*

514 7 *Sylvanus.*

515 8 *Abel.*

(467) 1X DEWIT CLINTON GALE,——; m.1st, Sept. 1835, MARY JANE SMITH. She d. Dec. 5, 1844 and he m. 2d, RACHEL MILLER, Sept. 11, 1860. He was killed at Wilmington, Ill., July 10, 1863, at the time of an accident on a R. Road. Children :

516 1 *Abel S.* b. July 21, 1836. He was first Lieut. in Capt, Rogers Battery and was at the capture of Vicksburg. He resigned his commission and enlisted in the 6th, N. Y. Cavalry and served under Sheridan on the Shenandoah and at the capture of Gen. Lee's Army.

517 2 *Sylvanus G.* b. Aug. 22, 1838 ; m. Lettie M.

Brinton.

518 3 *Louisa S.*, b. Dec. 22, 1840. She was a teacher in the N. Y. Conference Seminary in 1864–5 and 6.

519 4 *Anna Maria*, b. Nov. 21, 1842; m. July 24, 1864, George B. Travis.

520 5 *Hannah Jane*, b. Dec. 5, 1844. She is teacher at Monticello, Ill.

(468) IX PETER JAY MONROE GALE, m. in 1841, CATHERINE GARRISON. Children :

521 1 *Dewett*, b. Jan. 13, 1842.

522 2 *Anna Eliza*, b. Sept. 16, 1843; m. David Davis, Oct. 1860.

523 3 *Catharine*, b. March 24. 1845.

524 4 *Abigail*, b. Aug. 5, 1847.

525 5 *Adelaide*, b. Nov. 20, 1849.

526 6 *Sarah Maria*, b. Nov. 27, 1850.

527 7 *Monroe*, b. May ?, 1852.

528 8 *Isaac*, b. Aug 13, 1853.

529 9 *Rachel Jane*, b. Oct. 16, 1855.

530 10 *Emeretta*, b. Oct. 26, 1857.

531 11 *Sylvanus*, b. Oct. 10, 1862.

(474) IX ANDREW DEVEAU GALE, of New York, m. 1st, LILLES CARPENTER, in 1831, who d. in 1855, when he, soon after, m. 2d, SUSAN DWIGHT, who was the widow of the late Rev. Vincent Shepherd. Mr. Gale, in 1866 and for some years previous was a prominent wholesale shoe merchant at 44 Dry St. New York and a very worthy member of the Methodist Church.— Children :

532 1 *Hannah Louisa*, b. Dec. 8, 1833.

533   2   *Francis Asbury*, b. June 28, 1835 ; m. Adalade
       L. Powell.

534   3   *Georgiana*, b. April 29, 1837 ; d. young.

535   4   *Charles Insley*, b. 1839.   He was drowned
       while young.

536   5   *John Griffin*, b. July 5, 1841 ; d. young.

537   6   *John Summerfield*, b. April 27, 1844 ; d.young·

538   7   *Caroline Hull*, b. Dec. 17, 1846.

(498)   IX   EDMOMD GALE, m. and had children:

539   1   *James C.*, b.—.

540   2   *Sarah*, b.—.

541   3   *Susan*, b.—.

542   4   *Charles Edmund*, b.

543   5   *Cornelia*, b—.

544   6   *Mary Frances*, b.—.

545   7   *George*, b—.

546   8   *Amelia*, b.—.

(500)   IX   LEONARD GALE, m. and had :

547   1   *Rosetta*, b.—; m. Aaron Underhill.

548   2   *Elizabeth*, b.—.

549   3   *Nathan*, b.—.

550   4   *Leonard*, b.—.

551   5   *Frankie*, b.—.

552   6   *Adelaide*, b.—.

553   7   *Georgiana*, b.—.

(502)   IX   MOSES GALE, m. and had :

554   1   *Ophilia*, b.—.

555   2   *Thurza*, b.—.

556   3   *Virginia L.* b.—.

557   4   *Lucy P.* b.—.

558   5   *Emma L.*, b.—.

(504) IX ANSON GALE, of Washington, D. C., m. 1st, in 1832, LUCINDA JOHNSON, dau. of the high Sheriff of Hunterdon Co., Pa. She d. in twelve weeks after marriage and he m. 2d, 1852, ELIZA BONNER, of N. J.—. Anson keeps a Hotel and Boarding house in the City of Washington, D. C. Child :

559 1 *Edwin*, b. March 1853 ; d. at 5 years of age.— After the death of Edwin, Anson adopted George whom he calls George Gale. He was b. 1852.

TENTH GENERATION

(517) X REV. SYLVANUS G. GALE, A. M., of Charlottville, N. Y., m. Sept. 11, 1861, 1st, LETTIE B. Brinton. She d. and he m. 2d, Sept 9, 1864, JENNIE E. Cloyd. Sylvanus pursued a classical course of study and graduated A. B. in 1860 at the Wesleyan University, at Middleton, Conn., and joined the N. Y. Conference of the M. E. Church the same year. In July 1861, he was appointed First Lieut. in the 48 Reg. N. Y. Vols. and was in the expedition to Port Royal, S. C., but resigned his commission, May 1, 1862. In 1864, he was appointed Principal of the N. Y. Conference Seminary, which post, we believe, he held in 1866.

(533) X FRANCES ASBURY GALE, of New York, m. in 1857, ADALAIDE L. POWELL. Mr. Gale, in 1866, was a prominent wholesale leather merchant, at No. ?, Ferry St. New York. Children :

566 1 *Lillis Adalaide*, b. 1858.

561 2 *Charles Irving*, b. 1864.

INDEX.

THE DESCENDANTS OF RICHARD GALE, AND THE GALES OF ENGLAND.

INDEX

TO THE DESCENDANTS OF EDMOND GALE,
THE SECOND FAMILY OF GALES, IN AMERICA.

INDEX